Grateful Press is proud to announce that
Conversations with Jerry and Other People I Thought Were Dead
has been honored with multiple awards. We are grateful
for these honors, which will allow the book's
timeless messages to reach so many more readers:

USA Book News, Best Book Award
Winner, Death & Dying

Independent Publisher Award (IPPY)
Silver Medal Winner, Death & Dying

Eric Hoffer First Horizon Award
Highest Scoring Book by a Debut Author

(2) National Indie Excellence Awards
Finalist, New Age Non-Fiction
Finalist, Death & Dying

International Book Awards
Winner, Death & Dying

Global eBook
Winner, Death

D0813703

In Praise of *Conversations with Jerry and Other People I Thought Were Dead*

"This remarkable book by Irene Kendig offers deep comfort and gentle peace to anyone grieving the death of a loved one."

—Neale Donald Walsch
NY *Times* Bestselling Author of *Conversations with God*

"I have communicated with the deceased, had messages from them through mediums, had a near death experience and a past life experience. This book speaks truth. Consciousness is immortal and distinct from the body."

—Bernie Siegel, M.D.
NY *Times* Bestselling Author of *365 Prescriptions for the Soul*

"Irene Kendig has written a very important book. Many of our beliefs about death are based on superstition and myth; the truth is so much more empowering."

—Mary Morrissey,
Founder of Life Mastery Institute

"If you would like to know where your deceased loved ones are and what they are doing, this wonderful book, filled with love and wisdom, provides many answers. Highly recommended."

—Robert Schwartz
Amazon Bestselling Author of *Your Soul's Plan*

"This amazing book of conversations with people from the 'other side' will be intriguing to skeptics, fascinating to the curious, and enthralling to believers in reincarnation and past life regression. Irene Kendig asks all the right questions, and gets answers that can help us all live better on 'this side.'"

—Jim Barnes, Editor
Independent Publisher Online

"This simply delightful book is chock full of wisdom and healing. Irene has a gift for presenting complex spiritual concepts in a very easy to understand, common sense, and fun way. This is one of those rare books that is hard to stop reading. Highly recommended!"

—David H. Paul, M.D., Ph.D.
Co-Director, Freedom to Choose Foundation

"I fully intend to use this life-affirming book to facilitate my grieving and dying clients in opening up to new ways of thinking. This is a delightful guide to our inner Spirit that diminishes death anxiety. Everything is in order and everything is for the greater good. This book will be a great contribution to so many!"

—Peg Armstrong, M.A., LPC Psychotherapist
How to Be with Someone Who is Dying (DVD)

"This 'Work of Love' is a fascinating and intriguing read full of surprises, infinite possibilities, and assurances that there is indeed life after death. Irene permeates the conversations with her insights and learnings, enabling readers to experience the dialogues from their own level of Consciousness and Light."

—Sister Judian Breitenbach, PHJC
(Poor Hand Maidens of Jesus Christ)
Namaste Center for Holistic Health and Education

"As I read *Conversations with Jerry and Other People I Thought Were Dead,* I began marking important passages. Then I began underlining passages of exceptional clarity. I soon realized I was marking nearly every page because nearly every page provided new and clear understandings. I have been studying near-death experiences (NDE) for fifteen years and gaining bits of information about life beyond the physical. Each NDE is like a thread. Then I read Jerry's descriptions of life beyond and I saw the tapestry. That's the real significance for me. I feel like a study of NDE is unnecessary any longer because I have the whole picture. This is the best book I've ever read."

—Chaplain Dick Dinges
Fellowship of the Inner Light, Virginia Beach, VA

"Powerful, courageous and enlightening, *Conversations with Jerry and Other People I Thought Were Dead* restores our conscious awareness to the continuity of life and our eternal nature as unconditional love. Irene opens our hearts and minds to a deeper understanding of the journey of our soul."

—Harold W. Becker
Founder of The Love Foundation, Inc.

"I was uplifted by the wisdom and compassion of these dialogues. The perspective offered from the 'other side' does much more than clarify what dying and the afterlife are about. These dialogues address the fundamental philosophical questions of life in a very clear and loving way. Irene Kendig gently but consistently shows the reader how life always invites us to take responsibility and let go of judgment. I am grateful for this book."

—Pamela Kribbe
Author of *The Jeshua Channelings*

REVIEWS

"Author Irene Kendig strikes gold while digging for answers about life from those who have lived, died, and are now 'living on.' It is impossible not to learn something about life from this book. Some of the revelations are startling, some are simple, some are complex, some are transforming, and some are comforting, while others are controversial and difficult to fathom. Almost every page of this book has decidedly profound insights to offer. Kendig's interviewing skills are incredible. Her questions are direct and weighty. Her writing is concise and cohesive. The book not only presents the reader with specific details about our transformation in death, it is also brimming with suggestions that can transform us into happier, more loving and forgiving people in life."

—Claudia Pemberton, *US Review of Books*

"'*Conversations . . .*' affirms the most ancient and elemental of spiritual truths that anyone can benefit from now, regardless of what beliefs they may hold dear about life after death. It is an inspiring reminder to live life joyfully. This page-turner will warm your heart and stimulate your mind; both personal and metaphysical, each conversation will turn your thoughts simultaneously outward and inward. Fair warning: you may have a hard time putting it down!"

—Julie Clayton, *New Consciousness Review*

"This is a book rich in thought and wisdom that makes the concept of dying not only a process to not fear, but one to anticipate." (5/5 star Amazon rating)

—**Grady Harp, Top 10 Amazon Reviewer**

"What does it feel like to take one's last breath as a living person and one's first in the world of spirit? Author Irene Kendig asks the 'deceased' this and other thought-provoking questions in her book, *Conversations with Jerry and Other People I Thought Were Dead.* The answers she receives through gifted medium Jana Anna will surprise, delight, and comfort readers."

—**Kristine Morris, *ForeWord Reviews***

"A 256-page compendium that includes an informative introduction, a 'Notes to the Reader' section, and an Epilogue, *Conversations with Jerry and Other People I Thought Were Dead* features extended 'conversations' that touch upon a wide range of issues and questions. Of special note for students of metaphysics is what happens to human beings when transitioning from a physical to a non-physical life. Offering a wealth of spiritual wisdom, insights, and perspectives, *Conversations With Jerry And Other People I Thought Were Dead* is a fascinating and informative read which is strongly recommended for both personal and community library collections." (5/5 star rating)

—**Jim Cox, *Midwest Book Review***

"By turns intensely personal and grandly philosophical, Kendig's renderings of her sessions with Anna are a joy to read."

—**J. Blackmore, *Allbooks Reviews***

What Readers are Saying

"I love these conversations. They have taken away my fear of death and inspire me to live my life with more love and joy. What a gift!"   **—Janine Sagert, Ph.D.**

"This is the first book I've been able to read cover-to-cover since the death of my husband almost a decade ago, and it's got me thinking again . . . in a big way. It's got my mind really working! Daily activities now have an entirely different meaning, as I see them in a whole new light. Fantastic book!"

—Marcia Strommer

"This is a book to be read slowly and digested, like a meal at a five star restaurant. There are delicious kernels in every paragraph . . . truth on every page . . . wise angels waiting to serve in every chapter. This is a book that speaks to the soul."

—Glen Schiffman

"I lost my only brother Dean to suicide just over ten years ago so I was particularly interested to read what your friend Bill had to say about his own suicide. I have done a great deal of healing, much of it through reading and trying to put together all of the many complicated pieces I was left with as a result of Dean's passing. Losing my brother has been the most painful experience of my life. I thank you very much for your book. It has touched me in many ways."   **–Greg N.**

"Today is the 6th anniversary of our son's death. After reading your book, I felt so consoled. As I placed flowers on James' bridge today, it was the first time I haven't cried my heart out."

—**Cheryl Z.**

"I keep this book by my bed and refer to it all the time. It is full of post-its, underlines, highlights and tearstains of love and understanding. I will be ordering a lot of these for friends. I can't stop talking about it!"

—**Lorelei Shellist**

"This wonderful book is as much about living more fully as it about death and the afterlife. Very inspiring and positive. Soothes and nurtures my heart."

—**Janet Spitze**

"'*Conversations with Jerry and Other People I Thought Were Dead* is one of the most enlightening books I've ever read. I'm now able to embrace the thought of death in a whole new light. Not only did I learn more about the 'hereafter' than I ever thought possible, I now know how to create Heaven on earth. This book has 'bestseller' written all over it!"

—**Miguel Gabriel Vazquez**

"Your book has really impacted me and helped me to understand so much. I seriously think it has given me more insight than any other book of its kind."

—**Anne Logue**

"Fascinating and eloquently written, this book is a lovely contribution to remembering Who We Are."

-**Jeroen de Wit**

"This book brought a level of comfort that I didn't even know I needed."

—**Deeana Joseph**

"Peace. That's what I felt every time I read this book. I felt as though I had taken a deep, relaxing breath. Thank you for this gift, Irene."   **—Stephen Witmer**

"Irene Kendig is a wise translator and guide, and her 'characters' teach valuable life lessons that inspire and uplift the human heart. I've purchased six copies and keep thinking of more people I'd like to share this gift with. It's one of those books you'll want to read more than once—not because it's hard to understand (the writing is graceful and accessible) but because it'll make you feel good!"   **—Bella Mahaya Carter**

"I have had a death obsession and deeply-held fear of dying since childhood. My intuitive guidance to read this book has been a godsend. I feel uplifted, hopeful and almost excited about the 'transition' and 'life-review' process to come."   **—Pie Dumas**

"These eye-opening dialogues are full of detail and inspiration. As I was reading it, one of my relatives faced a terminal diagnosis. The book provided a level of comfort that allowed me to view this universal experience with peace of mind. I recommend it to anyone facing such a diagnosis or to those who have recently lost a loved one."   **—Mary Good**

"Thank you so much for sharing this information. It holds such a resonant truth for me, and leaves me feeling that it's all one life—here and there—no separation . . . and that is a deep blessing for me."   **—Howard Woodman**

"It was a 'can't put it down' kind of book."   **—Patricia Gomez**

"Irene Kendig has written a book that will appeal to a wide range of readers, regardless of differing backgrounds. I have gifted it to those who are struggling with the death of a loved one, and they have found comfort and practical wisdom in its pages."
—**Sarah Aschenbach**

"I thoroughly enjoyed reading this book and had a hard time putting it down. Everyday I reflect on what I've read/learned and I'm tasked with, *how can I love more?* It just confirms the most important teaching from my religion . . . God is love and this book perpetuates His message."
—**Gloria Lammers**

"There is something for everyone in this book! It addresses the core of what it is to live a more loving, forgiving and harmonious life on this Earth. It is not only a powerful resource for those who question their purpose or what is missing in life; it will nurture the spirit and soul of anyone who wraps their hands around it." *(5/5 stars on Amazon)*
—**J. Roseberry**

"These transformative and heartwarming dialogues definitely lend peaceful insight to the healing process after the loss of a loved one."
—**Marsha Victor**

"This book answered questions I'd always had and gave me insight into things I never thought I would understand."
—**Maharshi Roy**

"This book has so much information in it, I think I will reread it continuously for the next decade."
—**B. Doggrell**

"There is nothing more important in the human condition than having insights into where we come from, what we are to do here, and where we go. Your gift will encourage, soothe, and expand those studying Christian, Jewish, Islamic, Buddhist, and Hindi scriptures and traditions." **—Peg Armstrong**

"This book could potentially raise the consciousness of the planet! So eye-opening and uplifting! Who could ever be the slightest bit fearful or lonely after reading about our eternal connection to each other?" **—Trisha McCracken**

"We all learn by association in our early developmental years. As such, the experience we call death becomes misperceived as negative once we have unconsciously associated it with fear, pain and/or suffering. As I opened my mind and sincerely contemplated the possibilities that Irene has so lucidly communicated in this book, my heart expanded, my fears ceased to exist, and I appropriately re-associated hope with the birth we've named death." **—Rhonda Christensen**

"What you take away from this book isn't so much the great and grand knowledge of what the afterlife will be like, but the great and grand knowledge of what our lives can be like while we are still living them." **—Michelle Taylor**

"Excellent book! The conversation with Bill, who committed suicide, is life changing!" **—Debbie Brown**

"If you are looking for guidance, for insight, for a connection with someone who understands . . . *this is the book.*"

—Essa Adams

Conversations
with Jerry
and Other People
I Thought
Were Dead

Conversations
with Jerry
and Other
People
I Thought
Were
Dead

Seven compelling dialogues
that will transform the way
you think about dying...and living

IRENE KENDIG

GRATEFUL PRESS

GRATEFUL PRESS

Charlottesville, VA 22903
info@gratefulpress.com
(571) 271-7989

Conversations with Jerry and Other People I Thought Were Dead
Copyright © 2010, 2016 by Irene Kendig
www.conversationswithjerry.com
irene@conversationswithjerry.com

Cover Design by George Foster – Interior Layout by William Groetzinger

Quote on page 134 from *Man's Search for Meaning* by Viktor E. Frankl
Copyright © 1959, 1962, 1984, 1992 by Viktor E. Frankl
Reprinted by permission of Beacon Press, Boston

ISBN-13: 978-0-9824567-0-5
Library of Congress Control Number: 2009904329

Printed in the United States of America

To my beloved husband,
Charles Kendig,
whose love and devotion
made this book possible.
Thank you,
Sweet Hershey Boy.

CONTENTS

This lifetime is a thread in the fabric of your soul.

Acknowledgements

First and foremost, I am grateful to the Infinite Beneficence for the miracle of my joyful existence.

My deepest gratitude to Jana Anna, whose ability to connect with the non-physical world amazes and inspires me. This book would not have been possible without her.

Special thanks to my friends and family in non-physical form who lovingly came forward in service to this project.

I am deeply grateful to my son, Joshua Merrill, who was an integral part of this project, and who generously contributed a wealth of skills and talents on a daily basis.

Heartfelt thanks to my two editors, Sarah Aschenbach and Bella Carter, for making me a better writer. What a privilege to work with such gifted professionals.

I was blessed with two exceptionally talented designers who also demonstrated patience, generosity and kindness on a regular basis. George Foster did the cover and Bill Groetzinger did the interior layout. Thank you for making my book look so beautiful.

Thank you to Drs. Ron and Mary Hulnick, President, and Chief Academic Officer, respectively, of The University of Santa Monica (USM), for providing me with a soul-centered education par excellence. Special thanks to three extraordinary USM class-mates for their unwavering support: Rhonda Christensen, Stephen Witmer, and Jennifer King.

My thanks to Shannon Dayan, Eddie Oliver, Peg Armstrong, Jasa Johnson, David Dayan, David Cordova, and Carol Augustus for initial readings and feedback at various stages.

To my family and friends, your loving presence in my life is a gift beyond measure.

Conversations
with Jerry
and Other People
I Thought
Were Dead

INTRODUCTION

Two years ago, on a cool October afternoon, a friend called to tell me about an extraordinary woman.

"Jana has the most amazing gift," she said. "She can communicate with people who've passed on. She wants to make this her life's work. Would you be willing to do a phone session with her?"

I hesitated. A lot was going on in my life, and even if she *did* have this remarkable gift, I didn't feel compelled to speak to anyone who'd passed on. Still, I was curious.

"She wouldn't charge anything," my friend added, sensing my hesitation. "She'd just want you to tell other people if you thought she was the real deal."

I figured I had nothing to lose, so I scheduled an appointment for later that week.

I phoned Jana on a Thursday. I was in my home office, sitting on the futon with my dog, Scooter. I placed a pen and a pad of paper by my side in case I wanted to take notes.

"Hello?" she asked, picking up after only one ring.

"Hi. This is Irene Kendig, Cindy's friend."

"Hi. I've been waiting for your call."

"Is this still a good time?"

"Perfect. Thanks for agreeing to the session."

"No problem. Your work sounds fascinating."

"I love it. I share what I hear from those who've crossed over. Why don't you give me the first name of someone with whom you'd like to connect?"

Crossed over. I've always liked those words. It's as if people who've died aren't dead at all, as if they've paid their toll and crossed a bridge, as if they've gone from Manhattan to Staten Island, and not from life to death.

"Beba," I answered. "I'd like to connect with Beba." I didn't tell Jana that Beba was my mother or that it had been three years since her death.

Jana repeated the name, mispronouncing it. "Beebee," she said. "Let's see if she's here." An awkward silence followed.

"That's Bee-*buh*..."

"She's here... Beba? She has a big personality; she's not someone you could easily ignore. She's wearing a hat. She's in her late fifties or early sixties and has dark hair and pale skin."

That sounded like my mother. Although she had died at the age of seventy-four, she prided herself on her youthful appearance. Her face had almost no wrinkles. She spent a fortune on facial creams.

"Does she like to play cards?" Jana asked. "Because she's playing cards. She's laughing; she says she's winning."

I gasped. Some of our most intimate conversations had taken place over games of gin rummy.

"Does this sound like Beba?" Jana asked. "I want to make sure I've got the right person."

Astonished, I nodded my head, and she must have felt it because she continued speaking.

"She has a daughter?"

"Uh-huh," I mumbled.

"Does her daughter have children?"

"Uh-huh."

"She says her daughter doesn't consider herself a good mother. She says that's nonsense. Do you have any questions you'd like to ask Beba?"

My thoughts flashed on my eldest son, David. I'd given birth to him when I was nineteen, and I still hadn't gotten over feeling guilty and inadequate as a mother.

"Do you have any questions you'd like to ask Beba?" Jana repeated.

I didn't know what to say, since I hadn't expected to connect with anyone. "So how *are* you?" I blurted. I had no idea it would be the first of many questions, nor could I have known how the answers would change my life.

During that first hour-long session, I connected briefly with four loved ones. Each of them came through in a way that was unmistakable, unequivocal, and irrefutable. It was mind-boggling.

The experience came full circle a couple of days later. I was reading an excerpt in *Time* magazine from Barack Obama's book, *The Audacity of Hope.* Obama writes about an exchange with Sasha, his youngest daughter.

"What happens when we die?" Sasha asked her father. "I don't want to die, Daddy."

Barack hugged Sasha and said, "You've got a long, long way before you have to worry about that."

Although his answer had seemed to satisfy Sasha, Obama wasn't sure he'd said the right thing. "I wondered," he wrote, "whether I should have told her the truth, that I wasn't sure what happens when we die, any more than I was sure of where the soul resides or what existed before the Big Bang."

Reading this, I couldn't help but think of my youngest son, Josh, who'd asked me the same question twenty years earlier when he was three.

"I don't know what happens when we die," I'd told him. "And I don't know if anyone knows."

He didn't like my answer, and frankly, it wasn't reassuring; yet we have a relationship built on trust and I've never regretted my response.

I phoned Josh after my session with Jana to share what I'd heard from his grandmother, Beba. I reminded him of the question he'd asked me twenty years earlier and asked if he remembered. He did.

"Well," I said, "today I have a different answer to your question. I know with certainty that we go on."

Before meeting Jana, I'd had my share of spiritual experiences that pointed toward life after life, but I'd always had my doubts. Unless I could actually connect with someone who'd made the transition—and lived to tell about it—how could I know for sure? Well, now I *do* know. My reality has shifted to accommodate this truth.

Three days after the first session, I phoned to schedule another. I was so inspired by the end of *that* session that I spoke with Jana about collaborating on a book. We agreed to meet by phone—one hour a day, five days a week—and we did this for eighteen months. The result: a series of conversations with seven loved ones, each sharing their unique, first-hand experience of transitioning from physical to non-physical reality.

Jerry, for example, was a deeply spiritual man whose desire to be of service to God began in childhood after a transcendent experience. Jerry was confident he was moving toward loving expansion. Jared, the second person you'll meet, had been in chronic pain for a number of years before transitioning at age thirty. Beba, my mother, was fearful that there would be nothing after physical life. My friend Bill committed suicide in his mid-thirties. Vince was a seventy-something artist and freethinker, curious and open about what was to come. Zaydeh, my grandfather, transitioned suddenly from a heart attack in his sixties; and my Aunt Paula, a strong-willed, adored-by-her-family octogenarian, died in her sleep.

Each conversation begins with the same question: "What did you experience when you released your last breath on earth?"

Prior to these sessions, I was ninety-five percent sure we continued on after transitioning. Now, I'm one hundred percent sure. While five percent may not seem like much, experientially the difference is monumental. Knowing with certainty that I'll continue to evolve after transitioning from my physical body inspires me to live my most loving life—*now.* Knowing I'll review my life and experience how I've affected sentient life around me with every breath I've taken and every word I've spoken, makes me want to live more consciously, graciously, and respectfully—*now.* Knowing I won't cease to exist, I am empowered to live courageously—listening to and acting on my heart's desires—*now.* Knowing I am an eternal being living in a beneficent universe, I am open and available to the miracle of each moment, and my moments are filled with peace, trust, and joy—*now, now, now*...

When people ask me what my book is about and I tell them it's a series of conversations with seven people who've died, they sometimes ask, "Aren't you *afraid?*"

The question always comes as a surprise, since my sessions with Jana have been inspiring, uplifting, and have always connected me more deeply with my own loving nature. Afraid of *what?*" I ask.

Their answer is usually based on a biblical idea that it's verboten to speak to the dead because it creates a distraction from the work they're doing.

This fascinated me, so I decided to ask my Aunt Paula about it during a session.

"Aunt Paula, a religious person recently shared a concern with me. He said it's written in the Bible that we should not contact those who've transitioned because it's a distraction from the work you're doing. Do you agree?"

"It's impossible *not* to communicate with those we love, for it's the love that draws us together."

"Why would it be written in the Bible?"

"These were creeds written to protect followers from being misled by charlatans, that is, people who were taking advantage of those who were grieving."

"But that doesn't answer the question of why it was considered a disturbance to the work that spirited beings were perceived to be doing."

"It was based on the misconception that we in Spirit are more powerful or more important than you in physical form. And just as a child hesitates to knock on the office door of an adult for fear of interrupting and being reprimanded, the spiritual leaders were also afraid of interrupting or disturbing beings whom they perceived as more powerful. These fear-filled creeds were created during a time of misunderstanding about the Spirit world. The instructions you referred to reflected the times in which they were written. The broader, more comprehensive message is that we are all equals."

"I appreciate your insight. I heard you say that the instructions reflected the times in which they were written. Can you offer an analogy?"

"If you wanted to mail a letter today, and you tried to follow instructions written in the 1800's, you'd be waiting for the Pony Express."

Death is a taboo subject in our culture; it's no wonder that people are afraid. When I was learning to lead corporate training sessions, I was told never to bring up the subject of death unless I wanted to lose my audience.

As you read these conversations, I encourage you to listen with your heart. The heart hears the whisperings of the soul better than the mind. Check in with yourself and see if what you're reading feels true. Notice how it resonates with you. My sense is, you'll find these conversations do more than provide insight into the hereafter. They illuminate life.

My purpose in writing this book isn't to convince you of an afterlife. In fact, I don't want to convince you of anything. I am inspired to contribute to a universal paradigm shift that fundamentally impacts the way we choose to live by clarifying the underlying misconceptions we have about death. Let's start with a conversation. As Zaydeh, my grandfather said, "When a child is afraid of the dark, the loving thing to do is to turn on the light and explore the room, discovering together that there's nothing hiding underneath the bed or in the closet."

Jana and my loved ones have turned on the light and explored the room with me. We've looked underneath the bed and peered into the closet, and in the process, love has rushed in and filled the places once occupied by fear.

Irene Kendig

ABOUT THE MEDIUM
JANA ANNA

My father tells me that when I was a child, I "talked to the air." Alone in my bedroom, he and Mom heard me talking, laughing, and singing. They assumed I had created imaginary friends. One day, when I was four, my parents heard me shouting and screaming and then saw me running out of my room in tears.

"Let her cry," Mom said. "She'll get over it."

Dad nodded and returned to his print shop.

That was the last time they heard me talking to the invisible world.

Four and a half decades later—after splitting with my life partner and going through a deep, dark night of the soul—I began sensing, hearing, seeing, and feeling non-physical beings again. As a massage therapist, I began seeing spirited beings in my mind's eye and feeling their relationship to the person on my table.

During the early re-emergence of my intuitive ability, one experience was particularly powerful. While giving a massage, I had an overwhelming sensation of a mother's love for my client. Never having had children myself, the feeling was unfamiliar and profound. I heard a woman's voice say, "I am very proud of you." I relayed the message to my client, and he confirmed that his mother had recently died and that this was a message he really needed to hear.

To test my intuitive accuracy, I asked friends if I could tune in to the world of Spirit and read for them. They were happy to oblige. Pleased with the results, they began referring friends. This is how I met Irene Kendig. As she writes in her introduction, she quickly scheduled a second session after the first—and this time she came prepared with questions. The answers we received were both fascinating and transformative. Excited about what we were learning, we agreed to collaborate. Our intention was, and is, to share a fundamental and profound learning: we are eternal beings living in a beneficent universe. It is this knowledge that allows the fear surrounding death to disappear.

What a perfect match we've been for this project! I'm like a skilled diamond miner, using my intuitive gifts to extract magnificent stones from the world of Spirit, while Irene, through her spiritual insight and love of writing, transforms these diamonds-in-the-rough into gems. Fueled by enthusiasm and inspiration, she's worked tirelessly to bring this book into the world. I am grateful for her ability to translate the images, sensations, and stiff channeled phrases into clear, compelling text. Each of the seven conversations has a unique energy signature and style. I pray that you, as the reader, can sense this subtle but distinct difference as you move from one conversation to the next.

Connecting with these non-physical "authors" is a gift unlike any other. I feel their emotions move through my body. It's visceral. At times, I am overwhelmed with love and moved to tears. I feel their energy expand as they move beyond individual expression into a deeper understanding and wisdom. This expansion isn't unique to the Spirit world; there are moments in our physical lives, as well, when we surprise ourselves with our own wisdom as we access an expanded version of ourselves.

This book is more than words on a page. It is more than concepts and perspectives. It has an energetic imprint that, if you allow it, will change you. This material has the power to connect you to your soul and to strengthen your own expression of Beneficence.

Channeling this book has been a blessed journey. I am more alive than ever before. My fear of death is gone, and my discomfort with change has diminished significantly. My appreciation for life has grown, and I welcome all that life has for me. I've learned that life is experience orchestrated by a beneficent force of love. What can go wrong? This book reminds me that there is no wrong or right. There is only experience.

The work I do brings me great joy. Whether I am working with an individual or a group, love reaches through me and heals the fears that distract us from expressing our authentic selves. My work is being a bridge, connecting people to their loved ones who've crossed over. I am filled with gratitude. As Jerry says, "There aren't two worlds, one spirited and one physical. There isn't a heaven and an earth. Earth is another expression of heaven, one that vibrates slowly and appears dense. It's all heaven. It's all Spirit. There is no *here* and *there*."

Indeed, heaven is here and now. We don't have to let go of our physical bodies to be transformed. Let this book change you. Refocus now. Fall in love with your life, and live heaven on earth. May you be so blessed.

Jana Anna

Jana Anna is a clear and conscious channel, uniting the spiritual with the physical for the empowerment and expansion of humanity. To schedule a private session or group event:

www.janaanna.com
connect2u@janaanna.com
(812) 369-6060

Notes to the Reader

We have many word choices when we talk about death. We say someone died, passed, passed away, passed on, crossed, crossed over, departed, transitioned, perished, croaked, expired, is at peace, is no longer with us, has gone home, went to heaven, went into the light, made the big change, met their maker, bit the bullet, bit the dust, bought the farm, cashed in their chips, is dead as a door nail, and kicked the bucket—to name a few. I've chosen to use a couple of different words. The first is *refocused*. It most accurately describes the process of shifting our energy from one state to another, from a physical body to a spirited body and beyond. We're simply *refocusing* our energy. I'll also be using *transitioned*, as it, too, describes a process of changing from one state to another. Let's not get hung up on semantics, though. Feel free to substitute whatever word or phrase is comfortable for you.

The same thing applies to the word *God*. If it's not a word you're comfortable with, replace it with something else. During the conversations, the following terms are often used interchangeably with *God* whether they're capitalized or not: *life, Truth, love, All-that-Is, light, Awareness, Beneficence, intelligence, the oneness, Spirit, Power, the infinite power of love, Source, divine infinite intelligence,* and *the Infinite One Mind.*

In service to clarity, I refer to *Physical* Jerry when referring to Jerry as I knew him on earth, and *Spirited* Jerry when referring to Jerry after he refocused. The same concept applies to all of my loved ones.

Last, the English language doesn't have a word that works well as a pronoun to refer to a person of unknown gender—like *someone, student,* or *child.* Some writers use "he or she," which seems awkward. Some use "he" or "she," which seems sexist. Switching between the two is confusing. "S/he" is impersonal, and "one" is archaic. I've chosen to use "they." While this choice breaks a grammatical rule by using a plural pronoun with a singular antecedent, it allows the conversations to flow naturally.

"When you transition, you shift your energy from the physical body to the spirited body and beyond. Transitioning is a refocusing of your energy."

—Jerry

JERRY

1937 – 2005

One night when Jerry was nine, he awakened with a question on his mind. How could people love each other and yet act in such unloving ways? He wondered how Jesus could have loved the people who nailed him to the cross.

Jerry had a transcendent experience that night as love effortlessly poured through him. He understood the distinction between loving someone and being a vessel of love. In that moment, Jerry dedicated his life in service to God.

He graduated from the University of Minnesota and went on to complete a Masters in Divinity at the Lutheran Seminary. Over the course of his life, he worked as a parish preacher, a radio commentator on social injustice issues, a reporter, and a counselor. Jerry studied and explored various expressions of spirituality, and in his later years was drawn to Zen Buddhism. He traveled frequently to Japan, where, over the course of a decade, he studied with a Zen Master.

Diagnosed with a brain tumor at age sixty-eight, Jerry was told he had two months to live. With the ever-present love and support of his wife, family and friends, he spent his remaining time completing unfinished business and saying goodbye. He was ordained as a Buddhist priest three weeks prior to transitioning at home, in his own bed, confident that he was moving toward loving expansion.

JERRY

CONVERSATION ONE

Irene: Jerry, what did you experience when you released your last breath on earth?

Jerry: I kept breathing, but my body wasn't responding. My release was gentle; I practically *melted* out of my body. I felt cold just before losing consciousness in my physical body, and then warm again as I transitioned into non-physical form. It was different from feeling warmed by an outside source, because this warmth came from *within*. I was surprised that I kept breathing; I thought breathing was limited to the physical body.

Irene: You kept *breathing*?

Jerry: It surprised me, too. Breath is a function of life, and the nature of life is expansion. It's the nature of life to expand itself into greater and more creative versions of itself.

Irene: What about contraction?

Jerry: Contraction is necessary in order to receive the energy that expands us further. Breathing *in* causes the diaphragm to contract; breathing *out* relaxes and expands the diaphragm. We're always changing, growing, and moving into a greater, more expanded version of who we are. With every inhalation we receive the energy of life, and with every exhalation we contribute. That makes our next inhalation a new experience. No two breaths are ever the same. Every moment is a new one.

Irene: What are you breathing *in*?

Jerry: Life force. Pure potential. It's the raw material of creation, the fuel for the manifest result of thought. On a non-physical level, breathing isn't for the purpose of maintaining the spirited body; it serves the purpose of connection: inhalation is receiving the oneness and exhalation is giving back to the oneness. It's a unifying process.

Irene: I never, *ever,* considered the possibility that we'd continue to breathe after transitioning. (Pause) I'd like to look something up in the dictionary. Can you give me a minute?

Jerry: (Laughing) I can't give time or take time, but *you* can take all the time you need.

Irene: (Pause) I looked up the word *spirit,* and—guess what? It originated from the Latin *spirare,* breathe.

Jerry: Truer words were never spoken.

Irene: Jerry, do you remember the actual moment you left your physical body?

Jerry: No. It was like moving from one room to another through a doorway. I wasn't conscious of the doorway, only of having changed rooms.

Irene: What happened next?

Jerry: I became aware that I could propel myself upward, and I did.

Irene: Were you in a body?

Jerry: It was a contained form, but not the spirited body I'm in now. I'd describe it as a loosely contained, yellowish-white light. It was pure energy.

Irene: *Then* what happened?

Jerry: I realized I wouldn't be seeing my body again. I returned to look at it, studying it as if I were going to draw it: the way my flesh outlined my bone structure, light giving way to shadow, and the lines carved on my face, sculpted by a lifetime of laughter and worry. I observed the position of my head and thought, *I will never be able to move my head again; it will have to be moved.* I felt sad that I wouldn't be able to breathe that body again, but it didn't last long because I felt the presence of someone—an old friend. We came together as one in a profound depth of love I'd never felt while in a physical body.

Irene: Can you describe it further?

Jerry: The illusion of separation disappeared. We merged, becoming one unified being with a greater capacity to love.

Irene: What was *that* like?

Jerry: The closest earthly reference I have is when I looked into the eyes of my newborn daughter, fresh from the world of Spirit. I connected with her wholeness, creating an unconditional bond. The depth of love I felt with my friend was also an unconditional bond. We looked at my body—laughing at the temporary state of the flesh—and then propelled upward and out into a great light with which we became one.

Irene: What did that feel like?

Jerry: I still felt like myself, but I also felt like the light. Vast and expansive, I was no longer limited by the boundaries of form. This is the union that we experience in Spirit; it is the ecstasy of rejoining the whole, of coming Home.

Irene: There was no individuated you?

Jerry: No. There *is* no individuated form—physical *or* spirited—that could possibly experience this Power.

Irene: Can you describe the ecstasy of rejoining the whole?

Jerry: How do you describe being consciously aware—all at once—of everyone and everything, while simultaneously feeling unconditional love and beneficence of a magnitude so great that it's beyond the comprehension of the physical mind?

Irene: I can only begin to imagine. (Pause) What happened then?

Jerry: In order to focus, I pulled myself back into the same loosely contained light form I'd initially experienced.

Irene: How?

Jerry: (Laughing) Shift happens. The process is difficult to describe because knowing how to shift one's focus is instinctual.

4

It's like having a great conversation with friends: there are some moments during the conversation when you're focused outwardly on your friends, and other moments when you're focused within—contemplating, perhaps, what someone said or relating what they said to your own experience—a shift in focus.

Irene: I can relate to that. You mentioned you're in a spirited body now. How would you describe it?

Jerry: It's similar to a physical body, but it's translucent and much lighter; it responds easily and naturally to my thoughts, and I can change form quickly. Having a spirited body that closely resembled the physical form I'd just left was comfortable; I still thought of myself as Jerry, and form follows thought. In that instant of changing form, I remembered I could do it because I'd done it in Spirit many times before. In every seemingly new experience was the remembrance of having done it before.

Irene: Given that form follows thought, were you thinking about being a loosely contained energetic light form after leaving your physical body?

Jerry: My thought was one of freedom, but it was more than just a thought; it was a feeling of being unrestricted and free of physical form. I found myself in this somewhat formless state because I was focused on freedom.

Irene: What happened after you pulled yourself back into a form?

Jerry: The friend who had greeted me took me on a tour. We visited an expansive library, and as we walked down corridors with rooms on either side, I could hear bits and pieces of telepathic conversations between people. I became aware that I was feeling the immense joy that *they* were feeling. It was overwhelming; everyone was enthused and excited about life. The heaviness, sadness, and stress I'd experienced in my physical life were gone.

Irene: What do spirited beings look like?

Jerry: As Physical Jerry, I'd imagined that everyone in spirited form would look similar. What I noticed, though, was diversity in appearance—different ages, skin colors, and sizes; some even appeared overweight. That surprised me. I later learned that choices are based on personal comfort, and some spirited beings are more comfortable appearing overweight. (Laughing) There's no such thing as being *out* of shape when you're in a spirited body. *Any* shape is *in* shape.

Irene: (Laughing) A lot of people are going to be happy to hear *that*. Do spirited beings appearing overweight *feel* overweight?

Jerry: No. The strain of carrying weight is limited to a physical body; there's no strain on a spirited body.

Irene: Please, continue with the tour.

Jerry: I visited learning centers where I saw groups of individuals reading, studying, and talking. Throughout the tour, I passed people who were engaged in recreational activities—dancing, singing, and playing. It was like visiting a college campus and walking from one building to another, seeing students lying on the grass—eating, listening to music, playing cards, throwing a Frisbee—like that. I also saw beings who were experiencing various self-created scenes: sitting on the beach near the ocean or meditating by a stream. It was truly Heaven: Home of God, *my* Home.

Irene: What do you mean by *self-created scenes?*

Jerry: Rather than going to a *place* called the ocean, those wanting to be near the ocean brought the ocean to where they were.

Irene: Is this a *mini* ocean?

Jerry: No. It was a scene like you'd see if someone were sitting on the beach by the ocean. There were others on the beach, as well.

Irene: So, you're going along on this tour, visiting the library and learning centers, and people are outside, like on a college campus. That all sounds pretty similar to what I might experience here. But then you've got a full-blown scene of someone sitting on the beach by the ocean or someone else sitting by a stream. I'm having difficulty seeing how that fits in.

Jerry: That's because the physical world and your relationship to it have their limitations. When you have a desire to visit the ocean, you're subject to physical laws. Given the way your life is structured, maybe you feel limited by time, so it requires that you create the time for your ocean experience. If you live a hundred miles from the ocean, physical law requires transportation; your mind isn't capable of physically bringing the ocean *to* you because the ocean itself is subject to physical laws—and your neighbors wouldn't appreciate tons of water appearing in the yard. Because creation here doesn't require material, it comes into form quickly. If someone wants to be near the ocean, they think about being near the ocean, and there it is in front of them.

Irene: I can close my eyes and imagine myself at the ocean, but what I'm hearing you say is that you have the thought of the ocean and it *is* the ocean.

Jerry: Yes, yes, yes. And that's because the ocean exists as pure energy. If I were to wade into it, it would feel wet because I'd expect it to feel wet and because both the ocean and I are nonphysical. If I wanted to experience the mountains on the tour and they weren't available through someone else's experience, I'd have to focus on my desire in order to manifest and experience them. It's not that I'm bringing the mountains *to* me. It *is* travel, but it's travel through thought, not over distance.

Irene: So, back to the people on the beach who had manifested the ocean through thought: if you were to jump in, would you be jumping into their *thought* of the ocean?

Jerry: No. With their permission, I'd be jumping into the *manifest result* of their ocean thought. It was *their* thought that made the experience of the ocean available.

Irene: Might you see someone creating a scene that conflicts with someone else's creation?

7

Jerry: Given infinite space, it would be disrespectful to interfere with someone's creation.

Irene: Why would someone create an ocean scene by the learning center?

Jerry: It wouldn't be here if it weren't a harmonious creation. Everyone's aware of being connected. If human beings were aware of their connection to each other, they'd know it isn't harmonious to play a boom box near someone who desires serenity. If they were aware of their connection, they'd take the boom box and play it next to someone who would enjoy it. When you're in harmony, you're aware of everyone's thoughts and desires, and you're drawn to those who share yours.

Irene: If someone who transitions is unaware of being connected and therefore unaware of their impact on others, do they suddenly get this awareness as a result of transitioning?

Jerry: No, they don't suddenly get it; they're still framing life through their most recent physical perspective, which includes their beliefs. In truth, everyone *is* connected, and in this connection, everyone *is* in harmony. An individual may, however, refuse to feel the oneness: freedom of choice. Based on past experiences of not feeling safe, someone might even create a structure that keeps them separate from others. Because unconditional love and harmony surround them, their fear can't be sustained, though. The unifying truth—that there is no separation—becomes their reality.

Irene: What if their creations are a disturbance to others? What happens to their inharmonious creations in the interim?

Jerry: Not only is there a great capacity for compassion and understanding here, there is also infinite space. You can always remove yourself from an experience in which you don't wish to participate and create something else. It's one of the benefits of infinity.

JERRY

CONVERSATION TWO

Irene: What happened after the tour?

Jerry: I began celebrating with family and friends, some from my lifetime as Physical Jerry and some from other lifetimes. Many of us have shared biological connections, and some of us never have; many have been friends and some have been adversaries. But we're all family here in Spirit. This was the beginning of my life review in an informal social setting.

Irene: Life review?

Jerry: Yes, but it's nothing like you could ever imagine from the perspective of an individuated being. As I reviewed every moment of my physical life, I experienced how *I* felt and how I affected everyone and everything around me, from *their* perspective. I experienced myself through them. I shared their thoughts and felt their feelings: people, animals, plants, and all sentient life. And how do you put *that* into words?

Irene: Wow. I'm inspired to live consciously and respectfully—to live my most loving life *now*.

(Pause) How did your life review unfold?

Jerry: I decided to sit in the studio I'd used as Physical Jerry. It was comfortable and familiar, and having always been inspired there, it was the perfect place to review my physical life. Once the review started, everything disappeared except what I was viewing—only I wasn't merely watching: it was happening through me and around me. I watched myself and I *was* myself. I watched everyone and I *was* everyone. Every moment lived was there for me to see, feel, and re-experience. There's nothing on earth like it.

Irene: What an extraordinary process. It's challenging enough to fathom reliving every moment of my life; to also imagine experiencing myself through those around me—with their history, their beliefs, their thoughts, and their feelings—well, it's astounding. (Pause) What surprised you most about your life?

Jerry: I was surprised by how jaded I became to the magic of life as I aged. Life was new and exciting through my five-year-old eyes. Ants crawling on the sidewalk captivated me in a timeless world. People fascinated me. I'd stare at them, studying their faces and wonder: *Do they have kids or dogs? What does their house look like? What would it be like to be their son? I wonder why his nose is so big; I hope mine doesn't get that big.*

The world of adults didn't allow for time spent in wonder. It wasn't part of the schedule. There were meals to eat—whether I was hungry or not—and school to get ready for. When I was caught up in the reverie of staring at someone, my mom would place her hand on my cheek, redirect my face, and whisper, "Stop your staring." I'd still sneak peeks at people, but I'd glance away in shame when I was caught staring. My curiosity waned with each passing year, and I noticed less and less. By the time I was grown, not only was I *not* captivated by ants, I was stepping on them, unconscious of where my feet were landing, my mind busy with thoughts about yesterday and tomorrow.

Irene: Did you have regrets as you reviewed your physical life?

Jerry: No. Regret requires judgment, and I had no judgment about what I was viewing. I was studying my life and assessing my evolution. My feelings served as a guidance system, leading me back to the thoughts and beliefs that were the source of my feelings. This helped me understand why I had responded the way I had in any given situation.

Irene: Can you provide a specific example?

Jerry: Yes. I was watching myself ask a girl out on a date when I was sixteen. I was beyond nervous—I was scared. My feelings of fear pointed me in the direction of my thoughts: *She'll never go out with me. I'm not attractive enough or popular enough for her.* These thoughts were generated by my beliefs: *I'm not enough. I'm not worthy.* My feelings led me to my thoughts, and my thoughts led me to my beliefs, where I discovered the judgments and limitations I'd placed on myself. (Laughing) I wish I'd had this awareness at sixteen; not only would I have felt better about myself, I would have had a lot more dates. She turned me down.

Irene: Ron, my mentor and friend, frequently reminds me that it's an inkblot world. "Outer experience is a reflection of inner reality," he says. So the girl who turned you down was a perfect match at the time because she mirrored what you believed was true about yourself.

Jerry: Your friend Ron is accurate. We're always interpreting our experiences based on what we believe. The universe responds in kind.

Irene: What immediately comes to mind when I consider my own life review is the emotional pain of my early twenties. I wouldn't want to relive it.

Jerry: You wouldn't relive the pain as "frightened, twenty-something Irene," who was judging herself, the experience, and those around her. You'd be witnessing and experiencing it without judgment, in a state of wisdom, compassion, and unconditional love. You'd also have the support and assistance of guides and helpers. I was reminded during my own life review that I could speed things up, slow things down, or stop the process altogether. I always felt unconditionally loved and supported.

Irene: No worries then. Jerry, knowing what you know now,

11

how would you live differently if you were in physical form on earth today?

Jerry: That's easy: loving, loving, and more loving. Loving me, loving all, loving everything I come in contact with. Not being afraid of being ridiculed or looking foolish, I'd shout from the mountaintops, "Love is endless!" To love, love, love—to spend my days writing about love, preaching about love, and breathing *in* love, for life itself *is* the energy of love.

JERRY

CONVERSATION THREE

Irene: When individuals transition, who greets them?

Jerry: It's a custom fit for the individual whose time it is to pass, determined by what is most loving for them. It isn't limited to one specific being; whole groups have met individuals who've recently transitioned.

Irene: Each transition is unique to each individual.

Jerry: It's as unique *as* each individual. There are no two people who believe or expect exactly the same thing. Your beliefs and expectations create the initial experience when you exit your body. Having faith in the continuity of life, and knowing that love and beneficence are its foundation, makes acclimating to this environment a peaceful experience.

Irene: What did *you* expect?

Jerry: I expected to experience what I believed, and I believed I would enter a state of oneness. I believed I would be coming Home, and I expected to feel loved and welcomed, as if returning from a long journey. I also expected to be surprised; I believed in the Mystery, but I didn't fear it.

(Pause) Because of the ease of my own transition, I've chosen to facilitate newcomers and, much like a midwife, assist them by being present and "beaming" love. I like to see fear replaced with the innocence of a newborn baby, fresh from the womb. By innocence, I mean *trust.*

Irene: What could we say in written form that would create more trust during transitioning?

Jerry: If people can read about the experiences of different individuals, they'll see that the experiences are as individual as each person. There is no set structure and no levels of purification, where one needs to do *a, b,* and *c* before entering the Kingdom of "Heaven." Just as naturally as the infant comes through the birth canal, so too does the life force enter the Spirit realm, which some call *Heaven* and I call *Home.*

Irene: Is the life force the same as the soul?

Jerry: The soul is an expression of the life force, just as your personality is an expression of your physical life. Everything is an expression of life force; it's a matter of capacity. A molecule of air, for example, expresses the life force in a smaller capacity than your physical body, which expresses the life force in a smaller capacity than your spirited body, which expresses the life force in a smaller capacity than your soul.

When the life force is released from your physical body, it joins your soul. Your physical body isn't currently capable of maintaining the full power of the life force, so the life force is reduced in order to support your physical body while still providing access to the power of your soul.

Irene: I'm not sure I understand.

Jerry: Let me provide an analogy. When you turn on a lamp at home, the lamp is receiving energy from a transformer, which holds greater amounts of energy than the lamp. The transformer is receiving energy from a substation that holds even *greater* amounts of energy. In order for the lamp to receive energy from the substation via the transformer, the substation reduces the high voltage transmission so that it doesn't blow out the circuitry of the house and short circuit the lamp. In each connection—from the substation to the transformer to the lamp—there's a reduction of energy. If the lamp in your home has a twenty-watt bulb, then twenty watts is all it's requesting. If you need more light, you'd replace it with a higher wattage bulb, and the transformer would comply by empowering *that* amount. The bulb's wattage is your choice. You can apply this metaphor to your life by not limiting your requests. Don't go through life making it harder than it needs to be. Ask for what you need.

Irene: That's a good reminder that we are the only ones who are limiting ourselves. By the way, why the "quotes" around *Heaven?*

Jerry: Because heaven isn't a place. Heaven is what we make of our lives, regardless of whether we're focusing through physical or non-physical form.

Irene: What's the difference between how you create heaven in spirited form and how we create heaven in physical form?

Jerry: As Physical Jerry, subject to the laws of the physical dimension, I felt separate, even in close relationships. I felt limited and alone and had to work at inclusiveness, not only with others, but with God as well. This sense of isolation is part of physical existence on earth, and just as I abide by the rules when playing a board game, I also do so when playing the physical game. When I stepped out of my physical body, I stepped away from physical limitations and was no longer subject to the rules of the physical dimension. There are no physical barriers here. Being in union with others is natural. Connection is built-in to the rules of this non-physical, spirited dimension.

Fears are magnified in isolation. When you feel separate from one another, you feel separate from your power, and when you feel separate from your power, you're fearful. You take your fear with you when you transition because it's energetic and part of your energetic body; it doesn't decay with your physical body. But once you feel your power here and experience union with others, the fear dissolves. Connection with others strengthens our power and turns on the light that can banish fear.

Irene: But I can be sitting alone and still create a heavenly state by feeling the power of love.

Jerry: *Feeling* alone and *being* alone aren't the same. You don't often *feel* alone, even though you frequently choose to *be* alone. You let love in. You feel the love of Spirit, of your family, your friends, and your Self. Some people feel alone even when surrounded by others because they're not letting anyone in. They may not even love themselves. Isolation could be written: i-soul-a-tion: noun; a sense of *I* that is separate from the soul. And: i-soul-na-tion: noun; a nation of people feeling alone and separate from their souls, engaged in a survival paradigm of every man for himself.

Irene: Beautifully expressed.

(Pause) It reminds me of a question posed my friend Ron: "How can you be separated from that which you are?" It's impossible. How absurd to think we could somehow disconnect ourselves from Spirit as if we were electric appliances—like toasters!

JERRY

CONVERSATION FOUR

Irene: I'm still curious about what it's like to *breathe* in a spirited body.

Jerry: As the breath comes in, I feel individualized, and as the breath goes out, my focus expands and becomes unified.

Irene: Can you elaborate?

Jerry: When you take a breath in physical form, material particles are taken into your body: oxygen, dust, pollen, and pollutants. Because of the body's requirements, some of these components need to be filtered out, and others need to be processed for nourishment, both of which require energy. Because the breath nourishes both the physical body *and* the spirited body, the energy in the breath is divided between the two. When your physical body is ill, it requires more nourishment from the breath, so the spirited body receives less. That's why people who are struggling with their physical health tend to be less inspired and more withdrawn from life; it's the breath that connects us to Spirit and unifies us with life.

Irene: I'm hearing you say that we have a spirited body even while still in physical form.

Jerry: Yes. Everything is in a state of wholeness.

Irene: Why can't I see it?

Jerry: Because it's moving too fast for your eyes to perceive.

Irene: It never occurred to me that the breath could be nourishing both the physical body *and* the spirited body. How does it feel to breathe in a spirited body?

Jerry: Lighter, lighter, lighter. As Physical Jerry, the elements in the air were important for the maintenance of my physical body: the inhalation brought in oxygen, and the exhalation released carbon dioxide. Yet, it seemed like the upper half of my body was doing all the breathing. When I'd focus on breathing consciously—taking deep breathes into my belly—I never thought about taking deep breaths into my legs or feet. I'd fill my belly and my chest, but there was no movement of breath below my waist. Most of the time, I wasn't even aware of breathing; it was something my body did for its own maintenance, without any conscious attention on my part.

There are no restrictions in a spirited body, so it's as if my whole body is breathing. And because the life force is no longer being shared with the physical body, there are no physical components. As I breathe in life force, it mixes with my own unique individuation, and when I exhale, that mix is my contribution to the oneness. Breathing is a rhythm that flows naturally in spirited bodies, just as it does in physical ones. Each physical breath, subtly nourishing and tangibly refreshing, is different from the previous one, and each one changes you. Physical breath is just as miraculous as spirited breath; it's simply easier in Spirit to be aware of the magic and the miracle of it. The breath awakens you to a new moment, providing an opportunity for change. It brings in the new and releases the old.

Irene: Do you breathe through your nose?

Jerry: No. The inhalation takes place throughout my body: feet, legs, belly, arms, and chest; it's like having a diaphragm that controls my entire spirited body. If you use your imagination, you can do this in physical form by breathing in through your feet and up through your entire body. This is how the spirited body is nourished, and it requires no conscious effort. It's the insistence of life expressing. As I inhale, I strengthen my being, and as I exhale, I add strength to the whole by sharing my experience.

I now fully recognize that my breath was, and is, a channel for energy.

When I was involved in a project as Physical Jerry, I often felt detached from my body; my breathing was shallow, and I seemed to take in only enough breath to maintain my body. While I was aware of the power available through the breath, I was lazy about applying what I knew—like using a 40-watt bulb for reading because I didn't feel like getting up to put in a 100-watt bulb, even though I knew it would make reading easier. Focusing on my breath would have allowed me to remain present in my physical body by adding power—in the form of inspiration—to what I was doing. Spirit connects with the physical body through the breath: my spirit supplied the energy, and my physical body did the work of breathing. When my spirit withdrew the energy from my body, my body no longer breathed.

There are times here in Spirit when I'm busy with a project and I'm not focused on each unifying breath. It may appear that I'm unconscious of the breathing process, but I'm always aware of the role the breath plays in connecting me to whatever I'm doing. When I'm involved in projects as Spirited Jerry, the unifying breath empowers me. It is always a full breath; there are no shallow breaths. All the energy I'm receiving from the breath goes directly to my spirited body and into whatever I'm doing.

Irene: What recommendations might you have regarding our awareness of breath?

Jerry: Make a concerted effort to *feel* the breath going in and out of your body at various times throughout the day. Keep the word *breath* in mind so that, as you're doing your daily activities, you can focus on at least one breath every now and then, which will create a habit. The breath will always take you into your body and fully into the moment.

Irene: You mentioned being involved with projects. What kinds of projects?

Jerry: I'm involved with projects that are designed to keep the memory of Spirit intact when we resume physical form. (Laughing) This book is one such project.

Irene: I'm delighted to be included.

(Pause) Jerry, is there an awareness of time where you are?

Jerry: (Laughing) There are no clocks, watches, timers, or beepers. Life here is one continuous flow of inspiration and action.

Irene: I'm not sure I understand what you mean by *one continuous flow.*

Jerry: My life on earth was divided between things I wanted to do and things I had to do. In order to be an artist—what I wanted to do—I had to find a way to support myself financially—what I had to do. These two weren't always in alignment, and I often had to step outside my heart's desire. Even choices on earth about everyday activities created a schism between following my heart and fulfilling my obligations. Rarely was I fully present with what I was doing; when I'd sit down with my journal, in the back of my mind I'd be thinking about the dishes in the sink.

Here in Spirit, there is *only* my heart's desire. When I participate in an experience, I'm not aware of any other experiences. There are no distractions. There's nothing I *have* to do—like the dishes. There *are* no dishes.

The closest experience on earth that I can compare this to was when I took action on my heart's desire. For me, it meant picking up my camera and going for a walk without any distractions. It was just me, the camera, and my intention to capture inspiring images on film. If my mind distracted me with thoughts of why I couldn't or shouldn't take action on my heart's desire, I was out of my heart's flow and into doubt. These distractions were consciously and unconsciously generated by fear. I was afraid I wasn't good enough. I was afraid of failing which, in my mind, would have proved I wasn't good enough and confirmed my fear-based belief. So even when I had the time to follow my heart's desire, I often found myself tempted to do any number of other things.

Irene: Writing this book is *my* heart's desire.

Jerry: Your heart's desire is always the highest priority in life.

Irene: I've never felt happier. I can't wait to wake up in the morning and go to work; I know I'm aligned with my soul's purpose.

Jerry: The quality of energy you experience—your enthusiasm—is evidence of that.

Irene: Let me look something up. (Pause) *Enthusiasm* comes from the Greek *enthous* and originally meant, "inspired by God." That's exactly how I feel.

(Pause) I heard you say previously that your fears transitioned with you. Is that accurate?

Jerry: (Laughing) I wanted to leave them for the yard sale, but I couldn't—they followed me; they were mine, after all. In my spirited body, I clearly recognize fears as separate from who I am. I'm fortified by the love of this spirited community, and as my love for myself grows stronger, the fears become weaker.

Irene: Do you have obligations?

Jerry: Yes, obligations that flow from my heart and in which I'm completely immersed. They're obligations to my Self, choices I make for the purpose of my own growth and expansion. My heart's desire is my momentum and it fuels my choices. When I participate in these obligations, I'm not shutting out any part of myself, which is something I frequently did on earth.

When I'd do the dishes as Physical Jerry, for example, a part of me would shut down; I wasn't fully present because I would have preferred doing something else. Something would tug at me, the way a little boy tugs at his mother's clothing to get her attention.

Because duality is the dominant consciousness on earth, even love can be perceived as having an opposing force. When you love someone, for example, present in the love is what you *don't* like about them—specific behaviors. When you react to those behaviors by withholding your love, the reaction is always based in fear. You may not like the fact that your partner is disorganized. Why? Maybe being organized makes you feel safe and in control, so your partner's disorganization brings up fear of being out of control. Fear restricts the flow of love. It doesn't mean that love isn't available; it just isn't flowing through *you* because your fear-based reaction is restricting it.

Although duality gives you a choice—sometimes conscious and sometimes unconscious—to allow the flow or constrict it, the flow of love is always available. You can choose love and allow the flow, or you can choose fear and constrict it. I constricted the flow, for example, while doing the dishes. Many people spend their earthly lives making choices from a place of fear, setting themselves up to constantly choose between what they love doing and what they have to do in order to survive. Working at a restaurant so you can earn money to do what you really love is a roundabout way of getting to your heart's desire. Some people close the door completely on what they love and live life segmented between things they *should* do and things they *have to* do. This is survival. Survival thoughts attract survival experiences. Fear attracts fear. Life becomes a struggle instead of a flow.

In the world of Spirit, there is no survival paradigm. There is no duality. It's *all* love. Every choice is between what I love to do and what I love to do. And my deep connection with this power of love guides me to what would most serve me in each choice. I may choose to sit near a stream, yet I could just as easily choose to study spiritual principles in the library, something I love doing equally as much. But through my connection, I'm guided to the stream, which provides me with the most nourishment in the now. I flow from one joyous experience to the next, guided by wisdom.

Irene: I'm so glad that, in *this* now, you're guided to participate with us.

Jerry: It's as nourishing for me as it is for you or I wouldn't be participating.

Irene: (Pause) Is there any message you'd like me to give your wife?

Jerry: Tell her to open her ears to the silent place between breaths and realize that I'm alive and present, talking to her all the time. I'm excited about where I am and what I'm learning, and want to share it with her. (Laughing) There's no need for her to hurry getting here, though. Our souls' journeys are synchronized. We'll always find each other.

JERRY

CONVERSATION FIVE

Medium: He's tan and vibrant. He says he's got that just-off-the-beach look and wants you to know he's robust and feels good. He appears young—in his late thirties. (Jerry was sixty-eight when he transitioned.)

Jerry: It's one of the benefits of being able to create instantaneously. Just as *you* choose an outfit from your closet that matches, changes, or enhances your mood, I do it with my spirited body. I choose an appearance that matches my objective.

Irene: How soon after you transitioned were you able to do this?

Jerry: (Laughing) I'm laughing at the "how soon" part of your question.

Irene: I keep forgetting that you're not sharing in the space-time continuum.

Jerry: It's evolution without time. To answer your question, as I saw others changing their appearance, I knew I could do it, too. I remembered the skills it takes to manifest when manifestation began to happen. Once I acknowledged I could do it, I did it.

Irene: Frankly, I'd be a bit concerned if I could manifest instantaneously. What if I manifested something that was simply a fleeting thought and potentially hurtful to someone?

Jerry: First of all, you can't hurt anyone who doesn't agree to be hurt; it's the same on earth.

Irene: That's true. I'd like to come back and explore that idea further after completing this train of thought. What if I think a fleeting thought that's hurtful to *me*?

Jerry: You'd simply change the thought. Only dwelling on that particular thought would allow it to exist; anything that's not in harmony with the consciousness of love isn't sustained unless the one manifesting it keeps it in existence. Some people expect to see hell when they transition—and so they do—because that's their belief, their reality. It requires a lot of effort on their part to keep that reality alive, though, because it's inconsistent with this unconditionally loving environment.

Irene: And because this is a beneficent universe, if someone chooses to create hell, the universe complies. (Pause) So if hell only exists if we choose to create it, what happens to suicide bombers who believe they'll be rewarded with seventy-two virgins when they transition?

Medium: He's laughing and holding up a sign that says: *Virgins This Way*.

Jerry: Everyone who transitions—without exception—immediately experiences whatever they believe they're going to experience. They also control the sustainability of that reality; the more inconsistent their reality is with this environment, the sooner it disappears.

Irene: So a suicide bomber would initially experience seventy-two virgins—and then what? I guess my real question is, if the suicide bomber believes his actions are for the good of all, but they're really not, what then?

Jerry: Everything that's done *is* for the good of all because everyone involved has agreed to play their part and is fulfilling their agreement. The "suicide bomber" eventually grows tired of being with seventy-two virgins and starts to wonder what else there is, which creates an opening for spiritual guidance. Every being re-experiences their physical life through a life review, and it's during this review that "suicide bombers" experience the consequences of their acts, including all the ramifications of the bomb.

Irene: Why the "quotes" around *suicide bombers*?

Jerry: "Suicide bomber" is simply the role this person chose to play. It's not who they are.

Irene: If we've all agreed to play our parts and fulfill our agreements, and if, therefore, there are no victims, then why, during the life review, do we experience someone else's hurt if it's theirs to own?

Jerry: You choose to feel their hurt in order to understand them. By understanding *them* you understand more of *you*. In truth, it isn't *them* and *you*. We're all One. We're all in the process of understanding and reuniting.

Irene: Okay, back to your previous statement, that you can't hurt anyone who doesn't agree to be hurt.

Jerry: People are drawn together by wounds that fit like a hand in a glove. These wounds are passed down from generation to generation. While no one is to blame, each of us is responsible for healing our own wounds.

Irene: I know how true that is from having done so much self-healing.

Jerry: Tell me about it.

Irene: Neither of my parents knew how to love themselves. How could they model self-love for me if they didn't know what it was? I grew up unsure of my identity, yet certain that *unlovable, inadequate and unworthy* were words that described me. I suffered for decades as a result, trying to *do* enough so I could *be* enough. But no amount of doing could ever change the fact that I already *am* lovable, acceptable and worthy. These are qualities intrinsic to *being*. (Laughing) Lovable, Acceptable and Worthy: LAW of the universe.

(Pause) My parents weren't to blame, though. Their parents

didn't know how to love themselves . . . and their parents' parents didn't know how to love themselves . . . and on and on it goes, everyone in the same unloving boat.

Jerry: Now, that's a boat with no paddles.

Irene: You're not kidding. Not loving ourselves is the mother of all diseases, and it's a worldwide epidemic. Instead of healing this disease within—the only place it *can* be healed—I looked outside myself, mistakenly thinking that love was to be found there. And all the while, I blamed others for not giving me what I needed.

Not knowing how to love ourselves is why we overeat, overspend, overwork, overindulge, and are sex-crazed shopaholics, desperate to be in relationships and yearning to succeed.

Jerry: Well-said, Irene. *Epidemic* is an accurate description. Lack of self-love is why the planet is in the condition it's in. No one can treat another—including the earth—better than they treat themselves. People try, thinking it's the right thing to do, but it's a strain to sustain. Love can flow only when you unleash it from within. Loving yourself is like priming the pump so that the love that's already there can flow out into the world.

Irene: And so it is. It reminds me of the airline safety instruction about putting on your own oxygen mask before putting one on your child. Being self-loving allows me to come into relationships *giving* rather than looking to receive.

Jerry: And what you're giving is coming *through* you. You have to receive it yourself before you can give it.

Irene: That's so true. (Pause) The days of not knowing who I am or how to love myself are over. I no longer need someone's love to prove I'm lovable. I don't need to succeed to prove I'm acceptable. And I don't need outside approval to know that I'm worthy. Loving myself unconditionally while knowing that I am an eternal being having a human experience is like playing the game of life after already having won.

Jerry: Every moment is complete and fulfilling. That's an example of loving yourself as God loves you.

Irene: The good news is that if *I* can do it, so can anyone else who wants to heal this mother of all diseases—the true original sin—for which no one is to blame.

Jerry: The mother of all diseases is the illusion of separation. Not loving yourself is a symptom.

Irene: That's profound. (Pause) I'm reminded of my friend Ron, who says that if the entire *Diagnostic and Statistical Manual of Mental Disorders (DSM IV)* were reduced to one single code, it would be "*Perceived* separation from Spirit."

Jerry: It would certainly simplify things.

Irene: (Pause) I'd like to go back to what you said earlier, about how we can't be hurt unless we agree to it. It implies that we've all agreed to experience whatever we're experiencing. There are no victims. It's all by agreement.

Jerry: It's true. You're not only a participant in your life; you're an active creator. No experience is ever forced on you. It's always by choice. Life isn't happening *to* you, it's happening *through* you. By the very nature of it coming *through* you, you're in agreement to experience it.

Irene: I was sharing this concept with a woman who recently experienced a miscarriage. "So, you're saying that *I* created the miscarriage?" she asked in disbelief.

"That's not helpful," I said. "You have to approach it from a bigger reality. You've defined the miscarriage as bad, and you're asking, 'Am I responsible for this bad thing that happened?'"

I invited her to release the judgment—that this was a bad thing—and to consider the possibility that the baby's soul had its own agenda and curriculum and had fulfilled it while in the womb. "Why heap judgment on an already challenging situation?" I asked. "It's time to cherish, nourish, and be tender with yourself."

Jerry: I know from experience how challenging it must have been for her to wrap her physically focused mind around such a concept, but it's true. Individuals choose their experiences based on wisdom that's beyond the logic of the physical realm.

Irene: This is such a powerful concept. Let's use another example. What if I'm mugged at gunpoint. Would you say I've chosen that?

Jerry: I'd say the confusion lies in your limited and narrow definition of "I." When you say "I," you're talking about Irene. Would Irene ever want to be mugged at gunpoint? No, of course not. Would another aspect of Irene—one that's non-physical and has a greater perspective—have reason to choose a mugging experience? Yes. It's from this Greater You that these choices are made. This is an important concept, so I'll say it again: Individuals choose their experiences based on wisdom that's beyond the logic of the physical realm. Life is eternal. There is no death. The main focus of the soul is expansion through experience.

Irene: And experiences aren't good or bad, right or wrong— they just *are*. (Pause) Okay, what about an event like 9/11?

Jerry: When an event like 9/11 occurs, it's not just the individuals involved who are affected; the whole world is affected and has an opportunity to grow. While there is no right or wrong way, there *is* a way that's in alignment with the highest good.

Irene: What would be an example of an action that's in alignment with the highest good?

Jerry: You can choose to get to the root of why someone would fly a plane into a building full of people—which means getting to the root of how you've contributed to this act—as individuals and as a nation.

Irene: Outer experience is a reflection of inner reality.

Jerry: That's accurate.

Irene: A friend recently told me about a woman who,

recognizing outer experience as a reflection of inner reality, chose to take responsibility for terrorism in the world by owning and transforming terrorism within her own consciousness. I was inspired and motivated to do the same, looking within to see where and how I was still waging war with myself, and healing it there.

I remember what it was like to live in an internal war zone, my intellect at war with my emotions on the battleground of my body. I'd feel an emotion followed by a judgment, and the judgment was always a variation on the theme of, *It's not okay: It's not okay to feel that. You're wrong for feeling that. You shouldn't be feeling that.* These thoughts were the result of limiting beliefs like, *There's something wrong with me,* and *I'm not good enough.* Whew! There are those of us living in areas of the world that are battlegrounds, while others of us are living in peaceful regions and allowing battlegrounds to exist *within:* we're continually in conflict, critical of ourselves, thinking negatively, and holding on to anger and resentment. (Pause) The most important work I do is being kind, loving, and compassionate with myself on a moment-by-moment basis. Being at peace within continues to be my contribution to peace on the planet.

(Pause) I guess some people who read this will be outraged by the thought that they contributed to the events of 9/11.

Jerry: As long as individuals and nations of individuals assume the role of victim, they'll continue to create similar scenarios. Expressing wholeness as an individual means expressing power. In order to express power, you have to take responsibility for all the events in your life.

Irene: I can choose to change within so that I'm no longer contributing to the energy that brings these kinds of events to fruition.

Jerry: Yes.

Irene: I contribute to these kinds of events whenever I create opposition, and I create opposition when I separate myself from others by focusing on our differences rather than on our similarities; I create opposition when I try to *not* be like my mother; I create opposition when I march *against* war instead of *for* peace, which supports a survival paradigm of "me versus them."

(Pause) Anyone who could justify killing someone in order to make a point would have to feel separate. And because the motivation for separation is always fear, I'm adding fear to the mix and contributing to the same energy of separation whenever I place judgment on others. When I marginalize or disavow an aspect of myself and project it onto someone else—judging *them* for what I'm unwilling to accept in myself—I'm contributing to the energy of separation. I do this, for example, when I judge my husband as wrong for not being able to repair things in our home instead of compassionately embracing the places in my own life where I'm not as capable as I'd like to be. My judgments contribute to the same energy of separation that fueled the events of 9/11.

Jerry: The consciousness of the planet is like a pot of soup. With every thought, feeling, word, and deed, you add something to the mix. The more rooted these are in separation and the more consistently you focus this way, the more you're contributing *that* to the pot and strengthening those feelings in everyone. The more present these feelings already are in someone, the stronger they become as a result of what you've contributed.

Irene: It's like complaining about the water quality while peeing in the pool.

Jerry: Well said.

Irene: Placing judgment on a group of people contributes to the experience of separation.

Jerry: There's always good to be found in the ways that people choose to express life. It's your job to look for the good and focus on that. A culture is a group of people who are choosing to express themselves in similar ways. Look for the good in that culture rather than looking for what makes them separate and different. Whenever people come together in a group, there are pockets of fear and pockets of love. It's your job as a healer to look for the pockets of love and focus on those; that's the only way to heal the pockets of fear. The only way to make a dark room light is to add more light. The only way to heal fear within a group is to increase the love.

Jerry

Conversation Six

Irene: Jerry, what suggestions might you have for someone who has an intention to transition with grace and ease?

Jerry: Relax into the body. Accept it where it is in each dying moment. I had a loving relationship with my body. I worked *with* my body and that carried through to the end.

Irene: What suggestions might you have for someone who's just transitioned?

Jerry: Ask for help. Newly transitioned ones often struggle because they don't ask for help. There's no difference between how you behave in a physical body and how you behave outside that body. If you were one to ask for help while in a physical body, you'll ask for help when you're outside it. If you were flexible, that flexibility will carry through, and you'll adapt easily and find your way with grace. I could go on and on with qualities that are present in flesh that are present without the flesh, but I think you get the drift. Develop a loving relationship with your body while in the flesh. My pride often prevented me from asking for help when I was in a physical body. Start asking for help on a regular basis *now.*

I'm also excited to tell you that I take care of my body here. My spirited body appears just as real here as my physical body did there. I'm doing yoga, and I don't need any accouterments—no mat, for instance, since I can create any surface I want so that my feet don't slide.

Irene: Are there consequences for not exercising your spirited body as there are with a physical body, like *use it or lose it?*

Jerry: No. I choose yoga and various other disciplines because I enjoy them. Joy is an attribute of love. Since I choose to be joyful, I do what brings me joy. Exercising the physical body is joyful when you choose practices that you love. Love motivates everyone and everything. Love is the prime mover, because it's the energy of life itself.

People who don't enjoy physical exercise often don't fully enjoy being in their bodies and may even feel trapped in physical form. They haven't connected being in their bodies with *loving* being in their bodies. The key to loving being in your body is to discover what you love doing in your body. Exercise motivated by fear of what will happen if you don't do it turns it into drudgery—and usually leads to doing someone else's good idea of exercise. It may be good for that person because it's joyful for them, but if it doesn't bring *you* joy, it won't work for you, no matter how good it is for them. Exercise without joy results in further resentment of the body, and it's about as much fun as dragging a child to the dentist; exercise and the discipline of self-care become obligations to fulfill: you resent being in a body so you don't want to do for it, in much the same way that doing something for someone you resent is more challenging than doing something for someone you love. Loving your body is what guides you to the exercise that brings you joy.

Irene: I understood you to say that self-care of the body is important throughout life as well as beyond transition. But does your body still require self-care if it's no longer dense?

Jerry: Self-care is the same as self-love: when you're caring for yourself, you're loving your Self. Self-care isn't so much about taking care of the form; it's about caring for Self, the energy that *empowers* the form—the creative focus that's the true embodiment on the spiritual plane. The mind is powerful. What you think here manifests instantly. Taking care of your Self is being mindful. Being aware of others and how you're affecting them is also Self-care. As you evolve here at Home, you understand with greater clarity the effects you have on others and their effects on you. When you take care of your Self, you're contributing to the care of others.

When you first arrive here at Home, it's easier to embody a form similar to the one you embodied on earth because your mind is accustomed to creating and moving in that form. And because it's familiar, spirited loved ones can interact more easily with it.

Part of my reason for caring for my body is that I enjoy Self-care. I want it to be ingrained in my memory so I'll continue the practice when I'm in flesh again. I see so much abuse of and disregard for the body. I did my fair share, resenting the constriction of it and the time involved with maintaining it. Because all spirited beings in this dimension have had a physical body at one time, it's easier to connect, socialize, and relate to one another in this familiar form. It's like feeling more confident in your favorite clothes.

The image of my body that you're holding in your mind isn't my only choice; I can change at will into other expressions that suit my mood. I find it amusing sometimes to take the form of other beings and experience life from a different perspective. With just my thoughts, I can go from being the Jerry you know, to a small child, to a four-legged animal, to a fish in water—and back to Jerry—and I can do it all in one of your seconds.

The difference between a dense body and a spirited body is vibratory speed. The spirited body vibrates faster, so it can change form quickly. The physical body, because of its slower vibration, isn't capable of conducting this kind of energy. It would be like trying to run a car on AA batteries. The potential to change forms while in a physical body is, however, part of human evolution.

Irene: What do you learn from changing form?

Jerry: Perspective, perspective, perspective. It's the most efficient way to experience more of life. God looks through many different eyes. What better way to understand God?

Jerry

Conversation Seven

Irene: What's the process for returning to physical form?

Jerry: There's an opportunity prior to refocusing into physical form to practice with the spirited version of the physical body we'll use in that lifetime. We fine-tune our relationship with it in order to be in harmony. We create an imprint, a song, a tone that's uniquely ours and draws those we love to us, those who will be our family and friends. This is why meeting those we love in physical form for the first time feels so familiar. We—this community of friends and family—come into physical life synchronistically so that we can go through life together.

We gather in Spirit to plan and arrange our time on earth together, practicing in the spirited version of the bodies we'll occupy in physical form. Similar to a dress rehearsal, we don our costumes and laugh, play, sing, joke, dance, merge, and talk about the fun we're going to have. We talk about the challenges we'll face and how real it will seem—how we'll miss knowing the truth, and how hard it will be to experience forgetting. We speak of how challenging it is to drape the Light, our shining Selves, but how necessary it is for our growth and our service.

Some say they'll remember—they really *will* remember—who they are and where they've come from. How could they ever forget such a powerful experience? There's excitement and anticipation about experiencing the ecstasy of birth, the beauty of the jewel, the shining jewel of that gorgeous planet that gives herself so freely.

Irene: Why is draping our shining Selves necessary for our growth and our service?

Jerry: It's not a requirement. There are no rules or mandates. It's necessary in the context that it's what we desire. Life flows from desire and choice. It's our nature to explore and experience life, which is synonymous with God. Playing roles and connecting with others is one way of doing that, but it's only one of an infinite number of ways to express and explore God. Draping our shining Selves strengthens our ability to choose to express the light within, no matter what.

Irene: Why do we need to strengthen our ability to express the light within?

Jerry: The light within is synonymous with God. The process of evolution is driven by the desire to fully express God in every experience. It's what drives life.

The earth experience reflects diversity and individuation, but it includes a caveat: forgetfulness. It's easier to express your uniqueness when you've forgotten that you're all One. It's this unique expression that expands God. Each unique expression is a new experience that expands the whole.

You and Jana can have a similar experience, for instance, but you can never have the same experience. You can walk into the same room, see the same people, and even breathe the same air, but you'll each have a different experience that is unique to who you are. *That's* diversity. That's unique expression. That's the expansion of the whole.

When you question and doubt your heartfelt desires, you deny the expression of your God Self. When you hold back your truth by worrying about what others will think of you, you're denying the expression of your God Self. Authentic expression equals God Self. Your authentic expression is your unique and creative signature.

Irene: I'd like to hear more.

Jerry: Being authentic is being true to your Self and making decisions based on love for yourself. Choosing a livelihood that brings you joy, for instance, is living authentically. Choosing to be around loving, supportive people is living authentically. Being loyal to your friends and family is living authentically. Treating yourself and others with love and respect is living authentically. Being courageous and taking risks in support of all the things mentioned is living authentically. If you're earning money and not enjoying what you're doing, you're not living authentically, and you're not being true to your Self.

As Physical Jerry, I thought being in a physical body was something I needed to evolve *beyond;* I thought the earth experience was small potatoes and that bigger, better, and more spiritually refined things were available. What I know now is that having a physical form while conscious of being God is a new phenomenon. To be wrapped in the veil of forgetfulness and the fog of unconsciousness that exists on earth, and to remember who you are in the midst of that—a whole and complete expression of God—has never been done before.

The earth is uniquely able to support diverse expressions of life. It's the *appearance* of diversity that contributes to the illusion that everyone and everything is separate, which is part of the unconsciousness. Decisions based on perceived separation, like "every man for himself," are unconscious and contrary to life. Conscious decisions are made with the awareness of unity.

This awakening is as important as the discovery of fire; it's an evolutionary moment that catalyzes growth throughout the entire planetary system. Whatever happens on earth exponentially increases the evolution of the whole. Humans are the only unconscious beings on the planet. Animals, plants, and the rest of sentient life know who they are. They remember. They're not in the veil of forgetfulness.

Irene: When you say that all sentient life forms except humans know who they are, what is it they remember? When a giraffe knows who it is, for example, what does it know?

Jerry: It's not a *knowing*. It's a *being*. A giraffe isn't discontent. It's not thinking it needs to be something else or somewhere else. It's not concerned about what it did or what it will do. It doesn't even know it's a giraffe. It just *is*. It responds to life flowing through it and around it.

Irene: Ron, my mentor, said something funny to a friend of mine, and I'm reminded of it now. My friend was complaining that he wasn't living up to what God intended for him. After talking with him for several minutes, Ron said, "You don't hear a rose saying, 'I should have been a squirrel.'" This happened months ago, and it still makes me laugh.

(Pause) Given the importance of remembering who we are while having a human experience, have you decided to refocus into physical form at some point and put what you know into practice? (Laughing) Earth is where the rubber meets the road, you know.

Jerry: I haven't decided yet whether I'll choose to re-enter human form. I may choose to be someone's guide or teacher—a consultant, so-to-say, whispering in the ears of those I love the truth of who they are and the power they command.

Irene: And what would you whisper?

Jerry: I would—I do—remind these beautiful ones how much they're loved. I tell them of the power they have to create their lives as their hearts desire, and I remind them that it's through the heart that the soul speaks.

It's easy to remember my power here. What's challenging is to witness the perceived powerlessness of someone dear to me in the physical realm and to watch them stumble over their own mess. But then I see myself as you saw me, in the same human struggle, and I have compassion. The evolutionary leap now is to remember that we are Spirit having a human experience. Expressing the attributes of love—forgiveness, compassion, wisdom, kindness, peace, joy, enthusiasm, and truth—strengthens our consciousness of Spirit because these are all unifying attributes. It's lack of unity consciousness that separates the Spirit realm from the physical realm. When all life on earth consciously unifies, the veil will disappear, the fog will lift, and heaven and earth will unite as one vibration.

JERRY

CONVERSATION EIGHT

Irene: Your wife told me that your life changed as a result of a transcendent experience when you were nine.

Jerry: Yes. I awoke in the middle of the night, thinking about an argument I'd overheard my parents having and wondering how it fit in with love. I knew they loved each other, but I didn't understand how they could treat each other so unkindly. Did they put love aside and stop loving each other while they argued? Could they love each other and *not* love each other at the same time? These were questions I was contemplating.

I thought about Jesus and wondered how he continued loving the people who'd nailed him to the cross. Maybe love was like a blank piece of paper and the "not-love" was like a layer of grime on top; the "not-love" didn't make the love go away; it just covered it up. *Love is always there,* I thought, *and everything else takes place on top of it.* I wondered what it would be like if nothing were on top. *What if there was just love?* I realized that that's what it was like to be Jesus. In that moment, I saw and felt Jesus and the pure love—without anything on top covering it up—and I knew that, no matter what anyone said or did, love was always underneath. Nothing could stop it from being. My parents could love each other and still argue and act unloving toward one another. Loving is who we are; *un*loving is how we sometimes act.

How the other kids behaved didn't bother me as much after that, because I knew they were just acting unloving. Their actions were like the layer of grime, but the pure love—the white paper—was still underneath. It was the same with my caregivers, who said they loved and cared about me but often didn't act like it. When I saw people acting in unloving ways, I'd close my eyes and think of the white paper and remember how it felt to experience love as Jesus had. While there were times throughout my life when I forgot, they were short-lived. Once you feel the power of unconditional love, you always come back to remembering.

Irene: How sublime. I know how challenging it must be to elaborate on a transcendent experience, but would you?

Jerry: Boundaries dissolved. My consciousness expanded, and I was aware of the bigger picture. It was no longer the world *and* I. I *was* the world, and I knew it was all good.

Irene: How did you know?

Jerry: I knew from the feelings of joy, peace, and love. It was a moment of being; there were no thoughts about what I was experiencing. It's challenging to describe a pure feeling of unity. If you, Irene, were to have this experience, your description would be different than mine and mean something different to you. These are experiences for the poets to describe.

I understood that sometimes people acted contrary to their true nature, contrary to this goodness I'd seen that was everything. Confusion turned to compassion. After the experience, I was able to connect with the goodness and love in my caregivers. What they said or did no longer affected me in the way it had; it didn't have the same power over me. I was reminded of this experience throughout my life: love is a constant presence in everyone and everything, regardless of how things appear.

Irene: The power of a transformative moment. Thank you for sharing. (Pause) Can you choose to be in the presence of Jesus now, and if so, how does he appear?

Jerry: He appears in scenes that are conducive to conversation and connection: sitting under a tree or at a dinner table, for instance. His appearance always meets my level of expectation, and my expectations have changed as I've adapted to the Spirit realm. When I first met him, I expected him to look like the pictures and paintings I'd seen of him, and so he did. As I freed myself of expectations, though, he was free to express himself as he desired—in ordinary-looking street clothes for example, or in feminine form—even though there's no gender here. It's the essence of his being that matters, not how he appears. This is a lesson for physical life: allow others to be who they are and don't expect them to change to meet your expectations.

Irene: How do you recognize him if his form is always changing?

Jerry: I feel him. I recognize his energetic signature. We change form all the time, depending on our mood and with whom we're associating. The world of Spirit isn't form-focused; we recognize the energy of others, regardless of their form.

Irene: Can anyone choose to be with Jesus?

Jerry: Yes. Jesus isn't a celebrity here. His ability to embody unconditional love draws others like a magnet because they want to love as he loves.

Irene: He's learned to embody unconditional love.

Jerry: He hasn't *learned* to embody unconditional love. It would be more accurate to say that he's developed the capacity to maintain greater levels of love for longer periods of time by holding faster frequencies without getting distracted.

(Pause) I enjoy being with the masters—male and female—who hold the wisdom of the ages in their energetic fields, and in whose presence my consciousness expands.

Irene: Male and female? Isn't the Spirit world genderless?

Jerry: We *are* genderless. I'm guided to insert male and female images because masters are often portrayed as male, especially in the earth's history over the past ten thousand years. It's also important to picture female masters.

Irene: What's it like to be in their presence?

Jerry: When I'm in their presence, I feel an indescribable love, a fortifying power that expands my capacity to experience greater depths of beauty, harmony, and joy. They make their power available to you on earth, as well. It's a free-flowing energy that anyone can use at any time, like electricity in your home. It's more powerful when I'm in their presence because I'm consciously focused on it. People on earth often pray with underlying doubt, which causes a dissipation of power. When I'm in their presence, there is no room for doubt. Stories tell of the words that Jesus spoke, but his presence was far more powerful than his words.

Irene: How are Jesus, Buddha, Mohammed, and other spiritual masters similar, and how are they different?

Jerry: Their similarity lies in their capacity to express the qualities of love. What makes them unique are things like *when* they chose to appear on the earth and *how* they chose to communicate. Their differing communication styles—word choice, syntax, and allegories, for example—attract different people.

Irene: Aren't they also unique in terms of *where* they chose to appear on earth?

Jerry: No, it doesn't matter. Their presence on earth affected not only the earth, but the universe and beyond. Their presence remains active through their words, their stories, and in the prayers that are spoken in their names.

Irene: Haven't some of the words and concepts in these sacred books been mistranslated and misinterpreted?

Jerry: The spirit of the truth can't be altered. The words, like the physical body, are temporary. The truth, like the soul, is eternal, and always seeking expression. Truth seeks and finds people who are seeking *it,* and they find the words that best express its essence. Some people read the Bible and it feeds their fear. Others read the Bible and it feeds their love. It's their choice. It's free will.

Irene: Jerry, given that you're in touch with your power and we're here, having forgotten some of the things you're talking about regarding our true nature, how might we support each other so that it's mutually beneficial to ourselves, to you, and to the whole?

Jerry: You're already doing it by demonstrating that there is no separation between worlds. There is only one world, and that's the world of Spirit. The earth is an expression of Spirit, one that vibrates slowly and appears dense. It's *all* Spirit.

You're receiving my formless thoughts and using words to translate them into form. It's a spirited connection; my spirit is connecting with yours. It's like the spaces between the colors of the rainbow, each one containing a bit of the other. I reach through the veil, so to speak, and we clasp hands, reminding you of your power and reminding me that it's possible to merge with form while remaining conscious of being formless. There is no *here* and *there*. We're simply using these terms to distinguish states of being. In reality, in truth, it's all *here* always.

Irene: Would you elaborate?

Jerry: What distinguishes physical reality from spirited reality is the speed of vibration. Physical vibration is slower, so it appears solid. The faster, spirited vibration can pass through it, which is how they exist simultaneously. The faster vibrations seem invisible because of their speed. Everything exists *here,* with one moving faster than the other, like notes in a chord that form one sound; all are expressed in the same moment, but they vibrate at different speeds. The faster-moving, spirited vibrations and the slower-moving, physical vibrations are evolving into harmony. There's an invisible line between the two worlds—like a veil—that makes it easier for you to focus only on the more dense vibrations, as if that's all there is.

Everyone born onto the planet has agreed to bring fear with them from all over the universe. This fear is an accumulation of energies that will be transformed by accelerating its vibration. The earth has agreed to be the playground where discordant energies can harmonize.

Irene: We're all in service. Each of us on the planet is serving the whole when we allow love to be greater than fear, when we allow unity to prevail over separation, and when we love ourselves instead of marginalizing aspects of who we are. Fear is strengthened into love when we love ourselves, fears and all.

Jerry: It's like the white paper with the layer of grime that I spoke of previously. We've chosen to cover ourselves with grime. Once the grime is removed, it'll no longer exist in our universe, which is one of an infinite number of universes.

Irene: And to reiterate, the grime represents . . .

Jerry: Energies that aren't in harmony with the truth.

Irene: The truth that we are unified, that we are One, that we are Love expressing Itself, that we are God expressing Itself.

Jerry: Yes. Everyone on earth is there to strengthen love so that fear can't exist in its presence. By the way, fear and love aren't two separate energies.

Irene: Fear exists within a greater context of love.

Jerry: Right.

Irene: It reminds me of the analogy you previously gave of light and dark. Darkness exists within a greater context of light. If you want to reduce the darkness, increase the light. If you want to reduce the fear, increase the love.

Jerry: In order to be fearful, you have to pretend there's no love. Strengthen the love until you can't pretend anymore.

Irene: Love is always present.

Jerry: Yes.

Irene: Jerry, why go through all of this expressing and experiencing?

Jerry: There are many answers to that question, but there are more questions than answers, for the All-That-Is is vast, and the *why* is like asking why the sun continues to shine or why we continue to love. The sun shines because it's filled with sun shining-ness . . . we continue to love because love is who we are . . . we continue to *be* because being-ness is all we know . . . we're driven to express because it's our nature. While there are an infinite number of choices about *how* to express, we have no choice *but* to express. The *why* is not answerable. I don't know why. I know the power I feel when I'm expressing, and it evokes a deep trust in this process. It's nourishing, and I'm drawn to it as a baby is drawn to its mother's breast. It's instinctual. Not biologically instinctual, but greater and deeper: it's *intuitively* instinctual to express. At the point of knowing God, you're so overcome with feelings of love that you don't ask why. In the bliss of your lover's arms, you don't ask, "Why are we together?" That comes when you're experiencing conflict or separation.

As an individuated expression, I'm not capable of sustaining the power of love to which I'm referring. When I'm in a group meditation, though, and we're focused on the qualities of love, the power that goes through my spirited body is immense and ecstatic. It shows me what's possible, yet it's only a small portion of what's available. I'm trying to appease your logic and satisfy your curiosity, but all I can say is that, as a group expression, I've experienced the vast Beneficence. In this experience, I don't care why I'm expressing. When in ecstasy you don't ask why.

JERRY

CONVERSATION NINE

Irene: What are the options in choosing our next physical existence?

Jerry: To give you an idea of what's available in terms of options, imagine yourself standing in the center of an immense circle, filled with lines *so* dense that they appear to be melting, one into the other. Each line represents a different lifetime experience on earth. This gives you an idea of the vast number of choices. At the center, where a line originates, there's a preview of that life experience projected onto a screen; it's a preview of the options available for the growth and expansion of the soul. It's an infinite menu, and I feel overwhelmed when I consider the possibilities. Fortunately, a lot of guidance is available.

It's very interesting and something I never would have envisioned—as wise as I was in the ways of Spirit—that the technology would be so advanced as to project infinity into a finite focus. This amazes me. You've only begun to scratch the surface of technology on earth.

By previewing each line, I see the potential for my soul's growth: option after option after option, outcome after outcome after possible outcome of all the possibilities that are available to me, projected onto a screen. This system picks up my imprint and focuses on me as an individual. If another being were to explore the same option, the projection on the screen would be suited to them and totally different. This system is used as part of the incarnation process on earth; it is part of the orchestration of planning your life, which is just one line out of infinite possibilities. I'll call these lines *advancements,* because they advance outward into infinite possibilities, infinite experiences, and infinite ways to love and be loved.

Irene: Wow. That's amazing. How is your imprint picked up?

Jerry: Your individuated mind, the individuation of the One Mind, records all of your experiences. It's like a computer that takes in all the data pertaining to your soul's evolution—all the needs that have been met, all the healed and unhealed places within you, and all the action in need of consequence, which is frequently referred to as karma. This individuated mind connects with a system here that's similar to a huge, sentient database. This sentient database receives input from the individuated minds, determines what each soul needs, and projects onto a screen all the possibilities available to potentially meet those needs. This database is an impressionable, sentient being that's capable of receiving, generating, and processing energy. It expands and evolves with the input of the experiences of all the individuated minds. It's aware of everything. If you had this level of awareness in physical form, you'd be able to feel a hair follicle falling off your arm or the cells in your body dying and being regenerated: that's the awareness of the One Mind. It's the One Mind within an even greater mind.

Irene: If it's within an even greater mind, is it the *One* Mind?

Jerry: Have you ever seen Russian nesting dolls? Each one fits inside another, yet each one is whole and complete. Now, imagine those dolls existing infinitely. Would you be able to call any one of them the *One?* The bigger it gets, the more challenging it is to conceive. Just like a physical object, it can get so big you can't take in the whole of it; you can't see behind it or below it or above it. This is the perceptual limitation I have as I attempt to share with you the concept of One Mind. I can only perceive so much.

Irene: Wow. Thank you for sharing this. It's amazing. (Pause) I love you, Jerry.

Jerry: In all my oneness, I love you, too, Irene.

JERRY

CONVERSATION TEN

Irene: Where does the individuated mind exist?

Jerry: It exists in every cell of your physical body and in every particle of light that you are. All the energy that remains after the release of your physical body contains the mind.

Irene: If the individuated mind exists both in the physical body and in every particle of light that I am, then what happens to the part that belongs to my physical body when it dies?

Jerry: The individuated mind doesn't belong to the physical body. A portion of the energy that you are animates the physical body, which is pure energy, too, just in a denser form. When it's time to release your physical body, that energy is withdrawn and refocused in your spirited body. It's not segmented into physical energy or spirited energy; it's all one, and an aspect of that one energy is focused on commanding the physical body.

Irene: Would you elaborate on the One Mind?

Jerry: Just as the individuated mind focuses energy in order to animate the physical body, the One Mind focuses energy to animate the individuated minds. We're always connected to the One Mind, because each individuated mind is a holographic expression. It's another reason that, when many individuated minds come together, there can be an increase in power: what's coming together is more of the One Mind. Just as multiple physical bodies are capable of more physical work, multiple individuated minds are capable of generating more energy for whatever the chosen creative endeavor. Each individuated mind offers a different perspective of the One Mind.

Irene: To make sure I'm getting this, I'm going to run this back by you, starting with what you said previously about the circle and the lines—which reminded me of a colossal wheel with countless spokes. I heard you say that this circle is filled with lines so dense that they appear to be melting into each other as they advance outward into infinite experiences and possibilities for loving and being loved. You called these lines *advancements*. At the center of the circle—where these advancements originate—your imprint is picked up through your individuated mind, which contains all the information about your soul's evolution. It's picked up by a system that resembles a big, sentient database, which could be referred to as the One Mind within the Infinite One Mind. This sentient database evaluates your soul's needs and shows you all the possibilities available to potentially meet those needs, projecting them onto a screen as a preview of what making that particular life choice would mean for the growth and expansion of your soul. Each person sees a different preview, which is unique to them and based on their needs.

Jerry: Yes. One spoke represents one individual's possible lifetime on the earth. As you view the screen, you see your fullest potential for expansion realized—the maximum available from that life. You see your life lived to full capacity: a perfect life with all strengths and gifts fully expressed. This registers as a knowing that you take with you when it's time to incarnate, much like you take a shopping list to the grocery store so you can take full advantage of the trip. It's a preview of your best life, fully utilizing your God-Self and imprinted in your knowing. The sentient database connects you with your entire soul family: along this projected advancement is every encounter you could potentially have, along with how that encounter could potentially affect you and could potentially affect them, as well. This is the wisdom and the awareness contained in this sentient database being.

Irene: (Laughing) It's astonishing. Should *sentient database being* be capitalized?

Jerry: With that kind of power and capability, it deserves capitalization.

Our individuated mind is aware of everything that goes on in the physical body and uses this information to command all the processes taking place. The individuated mind knows how to balance the physical body for optimum health. It's aware, for example, of hormone and chemical levels. It works to harmonize all of the systems within the physical body: circulatory, digestive, endocrine, immune, lymphatic, nervous, reproductive, respiratory, and urinary.

Irene: If the individuated mind knows how to balance the physical body for optimum health, why aren't we all healthy?

Jerry: The individuated mind is influenced by individual, cultural, and collective beliefs. When these beliefs aren't in harmony with optimum health, they impede the physical body's receptivity. (Pause) Illness can also serve the soul's purpose.

Irene: Okay, I get it. And the individuated mind is a microcosm.

Jerry: Yes. In the same way the individuated mind strives for balance within the physical body, the Sentient Database Being strives for balance within and between individuated minds. When your physical body is in balance, you're able to channel love with greater ease. It's the same when you get all the minds in balance; there's a greater ease and capacity to channel love.

We communicate more through feeling in this realm. In order to communicate clearly with your spirited self through your intuition, it's important to be aware of your feelings. Be willing to feel them. Spirit communicates through feelings. When you feel an aversion to a person or a situation and you know something's not right, that is an example of Spirit communicating with you through your intuition and providing feedback for how to proceed, just as it does when you feel inspired and know you're on the right track.

Your spirited loved ones also communicate with you through your feelings. When you think of your transitioned loved ones, be aware of what you're present to—grief, joy, anger, hurt—because your feelings are your link to them. Be receptive to your loved ones. Talk to them. Allow yourself to feel comforted by them. Allow yourself to express whatever you're feeling. You're transparent to those in Spirit, so why not do yourself a favor and release whatever feelings are present? Being true to yourself includes being true to your feelings.

JERRY

CONVERSATION ELEVEN

Irene: What are the possibilities beyond the earth experience?

Jerry: There are many planetary systems from which to choose, and each one operates within a different paradigm. Just as the earth has rules of engagement in its paradigm—polarity, free will, and individuated physical bodies that give the appearance of separation—so, too, do other systems have their rules of engagement. I haven't chosen to live in any other paradigm, but I've visited.

Irene: Can you describe what you've experienced?

Jerry: Yes. One vivid experience involves a system that operates as a group in a group mind. They are individuated in form yet consciously linked telepathically with each other. There are no private thoughts; the entire group receives each individual experience. If you and Jana were in this paradigm, you, Irene, would have experienced what Jana did when she went swimming in the lake earlier this week, and in turn, Jana would have benefited from your retreat in the redwoods. Your loss would be her loss. Your gain would be her gain.

One of the reasons I chose to visit this planetary system is that it's similar to the earth experience. Everyone on earth is linked, but you're not conscious of it, and you haven't the energetic capacity to receive the input from all the individuals on the planet. The beings that live in the planetary system I mentioned have a very refined nature. When you're aware that your thoughts affect the whole, you're mindful of what you think. You think through your heart.

56

Irene: Does this planetary system have a name?

Jerry: It does, but the name would be meaningless to you.

Irene: What do these beings look like?

Jerry: They have translucent bodies.

Irene: Do they look like us?

Jerry: Yes, although individuals don't have the varying characteristics that you do on earth. They all look like they're from the same family. Everything is a milky color: skin, hair, and even their clothing. Because there's no duality, there's also no gender. They walk gently, practically skimming the surface.

Irene: What does their world look like?

Jerry: It's monotone; there's no contrast. The universe is filled with infinite opportunities to experience life. Just as you're drawn to experience situations and people on earth that match your vibration, so, too, are whole systems available throughout the universes that match the vibrations of soul families. We choose to experience paradigms, not as individuals, but as groups.

Irene: Would it be accurate to say that I previewed my current life during the Preview of My Potential Life you mentioned earlier, and chose it out of all the possibilities?

Jerry: Yes and no. What you saw, or more specifically, what *I've* seen, is that each moment holds many choices, and each choice holds many experiences. If it were laid out, as you say, at each point there would be only one choice and one outcome. But that isn't the case. There's never only one choice. So as you view this potential life, you have an idea, a sense, a general impression, but you don't know exactly what you'll choose. A finite number of choices are suited to your particular pattern; they are the ones that will meet the specific need you have to further your capacity to love.

Irene: If what we're seeing is the optimum outcome available, why aren't we always making optimum choices?

Jerry: Fear. It begins at an early age and creates an unhealthy environment that clogs our memory. We're often taught to be fearful from the moment we take our first breath; we sense the fear of our mother, father, and those who greet us as we emerge from the womb. We learn to be afraid, and fear distracts us from the truth. As we make decisions, we may have a strong urge to go left—remembering that, in our soul's vision, *left* had the greatest potential for our growth and the greatest gifts for us—but if our fears have become louder than the memory of our soul's calling, we may go *right* instead, choosing what appears to be the safer way.

If we're not ready in that particular moment for the challenge, we'll have the opportunity again. We'll always have opportunities to expand and to grow. We can choose the challenges that offer the greatest growth, or we can choose to play it safe, allowing fear to override our soul's voice—and that's okay, too. It's not wrong; we're still growing, just not as quickly. There is no *right* or *wrong* choice or *right* or *wrong* way. There are just choices, and your soul expands through it all. Even *not* choosing is a choice that empowers and expands. It's like the grocery store analogy: you have an intention to follow your list and get everything you came for during this one trip, but it doesn't always work out that way. You may be in the grocery store and notice that it's about to rain; fearful of driving on slick roads, you may choose to leave before getting everything you came for. Choices made from fear-based beliefs distract us from our soul's agenda.

I encourage you to take full advantage of your lifetime in physical form. Inside each of us is our soul's memory of how to fully maximize this life. It's a question of remembering that we're more powerful than any fear. There's a distinction between what we're taught to believe about ourselves and who we are.

JERRY

CONVERSATION TWELVE

Irene: When I look around, I see my desk, a flower, a bottle of water, my hands, my body . . . What do *you* see when you look around?

Jerry: (Laughing) I see your desk, a flower, a bottle of water, your hands, your body, my hands, and my body. But I'm also able to see more. With your permission, Irene, I can see some of the lives you've lived.

Irene: You need my permission to see my past lives?

Jerry: I wouldn't be able to see the details without your permission. It's a bit like knocking on your neighbor's front door; you might catch a glance of the interior when the door opens, but you wouldn't be able to see the details unless you were invited in.

Irene: Do you have five senses as you did when you were in a physical body?

Jerry: The primary reason for the five senses in a physical body is survival, yet there's so much more available to experience through the senses, and it's this "so much more" that we in Spirit can more easily access.

Irene: Would you elaborate?

Jerry: Depth of perception varies from individual to individual. You, Irene, can smell a flower and have a deeper appreciation of its fragrance than someone else. It's the appreciation that connects you more deeply with Spirit. While Maya could stroll past a garden without noticing the lilies, Sarah would stop and take in their fragrances, vowing to plant some in her garden. What varies is the degree to which people experience life through their senses.

Everything in physical form has a spirited aspect, and it's the spirited aspect that I access here. Trying to share with you what it's like to experience the senses from this perspective would be like you trying to explain your experience of a work of art to a friend. When you're deeply moved by a painting and your friend asks what you're experiencing, it goes beyond the senses, beyond a description of the colors and textures. The physical senses are portals that provide access to Spirit. As your eyes see the painting, something within you responds. That "something within you" is your Spirit. The response is as unique as you are, and that's the part that's difficult to share with your friend. Since I don't have a physical body, nothing needs to pass through the physical senses in order to get to Spirit. I have a spirited response to all experiences, which is more immediate.

Maintaining a physical body requires substantial energy. When you refocus your energy into spirit form, that energy is freed and can be used to delve deeper into Spirit, deeper into the essence of an apple, or deeper into anything else you can imagine.

Irene: I wonder if you'd be willing to expand on how you experience each of the senses in Spirit.

Jerry: Sure.

Physical vision requires a series of complex processes. In the absence of these physical requirements, I'm able to go beyond simply seeing a tree. I can access its spirited body and know its experiences.

It's the same when I use my sense of touch to merge with someone. I can know everything there is to know about them— every life they've lived and every experience they've had—simply by holding their hand. It's easy to connect because there's no physical barrier. When mutually agreed upon, our hands become one, and the connection is made.

Irene: How do you hold someone's hand if there's no physical barrier?

Jerry: Form matches form. Spirited bodies vibrate at the same rate, so they can embrace one another just as two physical bodies can.

Irene: Does one hand disappear into the other, or do they merge as one hand that's a combination of the two?

Jerry: Spirited hands embrace like physical hands and become one in the same way two physical hands do. It's a matter of visual perspective.

Irene: What's your sense of smell like?

Jerry: Since I'm not limited by the physical requirements of a nose, the energy is freed up, and I can smell with my entire being. When I connect with a rose, I not only smell its fragrance, I have access to the pleasure every being has ever experienced while smelling a rose—and access to the life force that created it.

Irene: *A* rose or that *specific* rose?

Jerry: *A* rose. What I'm connecting with are the collective memories and experiences associated with the smelling of a rose. Smelling is a way of accessing these collective experiences, just as it is in physical form. When you smell a rose, for example, it may remind you of being in your aunt's garden or remind you of the corsage you wore at your senior prom. These are the kinds of collective memories and experiences I access.

Irene: What about hearing?

Jerry: The process of hearing is similar in that I receive vibrations just as you do, but I receive them in a pure form, and they literally vibrate my whole being. Just as with the other senses, I don't have the physical process to distract from the experience; receiving the sound doesn't depend on my ability to process it through the body.

When I listen to a stream, I feel the essence of the water. I can tune in to the way it changes as it runs over a rock. I understand the way it feels as it carries a leaf or a stick. I don't just listen to its movement; I'm a part of it. The leaf allows the water to carry it, for without the water, the leaf would be immobile. There's joy in the leaf's movement, just as there's joy when you catch an ocean wave and allow it to carry you. The leaf experiences joy, and as the water shares the leaf's joy, it celebrates its service to creating *more* joy. There's also joy in the sounds of leaves rustling in the wind. The wind creates an opportunity for the leaves to move, and the rustling sounds are the leaves celebrating joyous movement. It's all a dance.

Just as I can merge with friends and family and become aware of their thoughts, feelings, and experiences, I can also merge with the elements and become aware of their place in creation. Because they don't have thoughts, I'm aware of their consciousness, so it's different than merging with a person. The senses are gateways into the essence of everything, whether in spirited or physical form.

Irene: Does this ever become overwhelming?

Jerry: I become aware of as much as I choose to become aware of. It's no different in physical form.

Irene: I know what you mean. As I was driving home from the vet's office yesterday, I stopped at a traffic light in my neighborhood, one that I've stopped at hundreds of times before. It's a long light—five minutes—and, as I sat waiting for the light to change, I decided to become conscious of what I'm normally oblivious to. I looked around and saw trees along the center divider that I'd never noticed before, their outline framed against the twilight sky. I realized that if someone had previously shown me this silhouette of trees and asked me where I'd seen it, I would have said I never had—even though I'd stopped there countless times. I'm oblivious to so much of my everyday surroundings.

(Pause) Would you elaborate on how you communicate with one another?

Jerry: We don't use our voices here and people's mouths don't move. They try, and their mouths sometimes move, but when they do, it looks like a dubbed foreign film where mouths and words are out of sync. The voice here is telepathic: thoughts are exchanged instantaneously. It takes practice to control, though, and I have to go very slowly to communicate with Jana because her mind isn't accustomed to picking up thoughts, feelings, and images that travel this quickly. She also has to translate it all into words!

Irene: So you communicate with Jana through thoughts, feelings, and images?

Jerry: I communicate with both of you. I merge with each of you in order to access your memories and experiences for the purpose of clear communication. I use your experiences to convey the message. I'll remind Jana, for example, of a quote she already knows that would go nicely in the book, or I clarify a concept by referencing an experience you've had. When the two of you have chosen words that most accurately match the concepts and thoughts I want to convey, I confirm it, and you both resonate with it.

Irene: While I don't physically feel you merging with me, it's as if a light goes on and I get what you're saying. It's an "aha" moment and there's a surge of energy.

Jerry: You don't have to be in spirit form for this to happen. When Pam, for example, shares a new awareness with Mike, something she's excited about that has expanded her consciousness—and Mike *gets* it—they become *one* in that aha moment of expansion. The surge of energy is the result of expanded consciousness.

Irene: Jerry, when you merge with me, why don't I have access to all of *your* experiences?

Jerry: The physical form doesn't yet have the capacity. It's like a computer that doesn't have enough memory to run a new application. The application called "Running the Physical Body" takes a lot of memory. That's changing through evolution, though.

Irene: Continuing with our conversation about the senses, do you eat? If so, what's that like?

Jerry: The purpose of eating, whether in a physical body or a spirited one, is to consume the energetic essence of the food and make it part of you. Let's use an apple as an example. Digesting an apple in a physical body requires an expenditure of energy. In a spirited body, there are no physical components to break down, no fiber or sugar to process, and no nutrients to absorb. It's simply the pure consumption of the apple's beautiful essence. Satiation occurs—both in the physical body and in the spirited body—when sufficient life force has been received through the food. In order to become satiated, we have to consciously connect with the life force in the food, and that's easier to do in a spirited body.

While I enjoyed eating food as Physical Jerry, I rarely ate consciously; often, I'd eat on the run, thinking of everything except the food all the while I was consuming it. I seldom thought of food as being alive; food was something I pulled out of the fridge and quickly prepared, never considering its life force. Even though I'd stop eating when my belly felt full, I wasn't necessarily satiated. In fact, I often experienced indigestion after eating and blamed my discomfort on the food instead of taking responsibility for the unconsciousness with which I'd consumed it. Because I rarely felt satiated, I craved and consumed sugary, salty, spicy, and highly refined foods. I was seeking satiation through the sensations these foods offered rather than through connecting with the life force of the food. Consciousness regarding food and its preparation is at a low level on the earth right now. Foods are processed for convenience and marketability, and the life force is processed right out of them.

Irene: I understood you to say that your body is as real as mine, yet you also said you can't digest an apple.

Jerry: My experience in this body is as real as I want it to be. I can hold my arm up and, as I move it, my arm feels as real as my memory of moving my arm did when it was covered with flesh.

Irene: If you wanted to pick up something in material form, would you be able to lift it?

Jerry: When in Rome, do as the Romans do. I'd need to be in sync with that object, and we'd need to be of a similar vibration. If what you're asking is whether my picking up that object would be the same as you picking up that object, the answer is *no*, not any more than you could successfully wrap your arms around me and feel flesh. I could, with focused intention, move that object with my mind.

Irene: What would that look like to me, the observer?

Jerry: The object would look as if it were magically moving from one place to another without any visible cause. In order to make their presence known, spirited beings often move objects for their physical loved ones. Rarely are the objects seen while in motion; they're simply found in a different place. This is one way spirited beings communicate with their physical loved ones. In order for me to pick up an object with my hand and move it, I'd require a physical body. All movement in Spirit takes place with the mind, as does spirited communication.

Irene: Back to eating: knowing what you know now, if you were in physical form today, how would you choose to eat?

Jerry: I'd connect with the life force of the food before putting it into my mouth. I'd eat consciously and in communion with the food, knowing I was consuming energy and not just material sustenance. I'd remember that every particle of food has a history and getting it to the table required an expenditure of energy on the part of many: the earth, the sun, the animals, the insects, the farm laborers, the truckers, the manufacturing crews, the grocery staff—it's a long list. I'd acknowledge and give thanks for all those involved in this blessed process.

If I chose to eat processed food, I'd spend even more time adding life force to the food by blessing it with prayers of gratitude before taking it into my body. Even the most processed foods can be enhanced through a blessing of appreciation.

Eating is an energetic and sacred act. I'm honored and blessed to be able to share this information with you, information that can literally change the world by increasing health and vitality. Appreciate the experiences your physical senses provide; you connect more consciously and deeply with Spirit through appreciation.

Irene: I didn't hear you mention God.

Jerry: God is all of that. God is the energy *and* the form.

JERRY

CONVERSATION THIRTEEN

Irene: I'd like to talk about funerals.

Jerry: What's the definition of *funeral*?

Irene: Let me look it up. (Pause) It says: the ceremonies honoring a dead person, typically involving burial or cremation.

Jerry: A funeral is all about the dead, and there is no such thing. A memorial, on the other hand, is a celebration of the newly departed during which they're remembered and acknowledged for the difference they made.

Irene: Let me look up the word *memorial*. (Pause) Here it is: something, especially a structure, established to remind people of a person or event.

Jerry: A memorial is both an acknowledgment of the impact a person made and a celebration of the eternal Self. Grieving the physical loss of our loved ones is part of that celebration and helps us adjust to the change that physical loss creates. It's healthy to grieve. Crying is cleansing and prepares us for the new. At a soul level, however, we all know that there is no such thing as death, and that what appears to be loss, is simply change.

Irene: If you were designing a memorial for a loved one, how would it look?

Jerry: I'd choose a place that was special to the person, a place they liked; this is, after all, *their* party. People would bring mementos that reminded them of this person: pictures, music, food, and above all, stories. I'd create a comfortable and relaxing ambiance, with natural lighting, soft colors, and comfortable seating. I'd make a sign that read, *All feelings are welcome here.* I would encourage people to stand up and share stories. The point of a memorial is to honor the person who's passed.

Irene: What special consideration would you give the body?

Jerry: The body, whether buried or cremated, needs to reunite with the elements of the earth. Every element of the physical body comes from the earth and should return to the earth. This is a coming home for the body.

If the body were to be buried, I would have it wrapped in a cloth made of natural fibers, and in a color that my loved one would have chosen. If a casket were to be used, I would choose one made of materials that are in harmony with the earth, such as pine, so the body could be easily released and complete its cycle.

Irene: What about cremation?

Jerry: Cremation is another option. Ideally, the ashes would be returned to the earth rather than deposited in urns and kept on mantels. I would choose to make a ritual of this by spreading the ashes in a place that had special meaning for my loved one.

Irene: (Pause) Are some ways to transition better than others?

Jerry: (Laughing) Let me first say that there isn't an unsuccessful way. Some ways are more graceful than others. The most graceful way to transition is to imagine a loving scenario. Form follows thought.

Irene: You spoke of being something of a midwife for those who are transitioning. I'd love to hear more about that.

Jerry: When an individual is ready to refocus their energy from a physical form to a spirited one, and if their vibratory signature is a good fit with mine, I receive a telepathic communication from their physical body. Helping people transition is one of the many opportunities to serve in the realm of Spirit. I embody the essence of love, comfort, and compassion and support their chosen beliefs—even if their chosen belief is hell. I honor and respect their beliefs, without judgment, and, like a beacon, maintain the power of love until they remember the truth.

Irene: The truth . . .

Jerry: The truth of the existence of a unified beneficence. The truth that all is love. Through my sessions with the masters, I've learned how to hold the vibration of love for extended periods of time, much like the sun continues to shine regardless of clouds in the sky. If someone who's refocusing from physical to Spirit has imagined a loving scenario, I, along with other spirited beings, add to the power of their creation. Our presence shows them the love.

Irene: Let me see if I understand. If they believe they'll see Jesus, you take on the form of Jesus and present it to them?

Jerry: The form has already been created through their beliefs. I infuse it with the love that's expected.

Irene: That's just great. I can hear readers now: "Do you mean to tell me that instead of getting Jesus, I'm getting Jerry?"

Jerry: They're getting neither; they're getting love. Love is formless, and so is Christ. Christ is a particular frequency of energy that is pure love. Jesus is the form that demonstrates the power of that energy through instantaneous healing and seemingly miraculous manifestations.

Irene: So, if I'm expecting to see my mother, is it actually *her*?

Jerry: Yes and no. Her spirited body will respond by assuming the appearance that's most comforting to you. She may enjoy looking like her nineteen-year-old self, but that's not how you'll see her because that's not the mother you knew. She's embodying love for you. What's important is the love.

Irene: Would I still see her if she's already reincarnated and living another life?

Jerry: Family members are drawn to the power of love connecting each to the other. If your mother is occupied with living another life and can't be fully present to greet you, there's still a part of her that remains in Spirit. There's a part of each one of

CONVERSATIONS WITH JERRY AND OTHER PEOPLE I THOUGHT WERE DEAD

us—our individualized source—that remains in Spirit.

Irene: Can you elaborate?

Jerry: The sun is the source of a light beam, yet there's more than one light beam coming from it, just as there's more to you than one physical expression.

(Pause) You create an image of your mother's form based on both your need for comfort and your expectation. The aspect of her that remains in Spirit, along with the unconditional love of those in assistance, animates the form. Love is *love;* it doesn't matter how it's individualized. You'd probably be getting more *mom-ness* than you ever got from your earthly mom. It's your mom minus all her fears—unless you were also expecting her fears, in which case that's what you'd get.

The full presence of Jesus, Buddha, Mohammed, or any of the other spiritual masters would be as overwhelming to a newcomer as the midday sun would be to someone exiting a dark cave.

Irene: Overwhelmed by . . .

Jerry: Overwhelmed by so much love. It's my job—along with others who share in this service—to meet newcomers where they are: "meet and greet," you might say.

Irene: Are we all existing in multiple dimensions simultaneously?

Jerry: Multi-dimensionality is a constant occurrence there as well as here. Each personality has a connection to the moments in time and space of each of their incarnations. Everything they've ever experienced is still available. The moment itself holds the representation—like a stage set—and you can visit it and animate it.

I lived in ancient Rome, for instance, and participated in the senate. That personality is alive and real. I can focus my essence into that reality from here and experience it in this present moment. I was also a young princess in Greece, and I can visit and experience *that* life as easily as walking onto that stage set in this present moment. The purpose for this is to remind us of our experiences. Once something is created, it always exists.

Irene: Nothing is ever gone.

Jerry: No. Nothing is ever gone.

Irene: Energy can't be destroyed.

Jerry: No, energy can't be destroyed. It can re-form. Creations—all creations—hold the essence of All-That-Is and are honored. Just as a priceless masterpiece is hung in a museum and revered, so, too, is every creation throughout infinity. You may call these *incarnations* or *dimensions* because they all have a certain tone, vibration, or song. Dimensions are as infinite as the universe, as is the Heart of God.

Irene: Can we visit these stage sets while we're in physical form?

Jerry: No. They require more fluidity of form, like that of a spirited body.

Irene: I'm assuming the terms *God* and *All-That-Is* are interchangeable.

Jerry: Yes, that's true. What's in a name? That which you'd call a rose by any other name would smell as sweet.

Irene: Shakespeare knew what he was talking about. (Pause) Have your beliefs about God changed since you transitioned?

Jerry: God is larger and more personal now. As Physical Jerry, I felt confident in my perception that God was infinite and lived in everyone, but I lived a lot of what I knew in my head. I was only skimming the surface of the depth of love I feel now. When I no longer needed to expend the energy required to maintain my physical body, my consciousness—in relation to my perception of God—expanded. I was able to go beyond any imagined notions or beliefs and get to the essence of Truth seeking expression. Truth is another word for God, as is Life. Truth is pure potential that seeks creative expression through form, whether physical or spirited. We're driven to express Truth. It's in our spiritual DNA.

Jerry

Conversation Fourteen

Seven months elapsed between Conversation Thirteen and Conversation Fourteen, during which I was communicating with other loved ones.

Jerry: I'm excited to be here with you. A great big loving hug to you, Irene!

Medium: He's simultaneously wrapping his arms around you and the world.

Jerry: You're a microcosmic representation of the macrocosm. When I wrap my arms around you, it's one world wrapping its arms around another.

Irene: Thank you, Jerry, and a loving embrace to *you*. (Pause) How have you expanded since our last conversation?

Jerry: I've taken in more of the experiences available to me. As I shared previously, I enjoy sitting in the presence of masters. I'm now able to absorb more of their perspective.

I've also connected with many newcomers to the Spirit world. Much like reading a book provides a new perspective, merging with another and becoming *one* is like taking in a whole library! I experience everything they've experienced: the people, love, limitations, breakthroughs, and joys. This is the expansion that's available when connecting without form.

Irene: I guess the way to prepare for that on earth would be to accept another's experience without judgment.

Jerry: Start by being truly present with another. Our thoughts distract us from our ability to be present. Quieting your mind and truly listening is the closest you can come to this kind of connection. Your focused presence encourages the expression of their wisdom.

Irene: Are you fully present with the masters as well as with others?

Jerry: I've been practicing being fully present; I haven't perfected it. Even here, I find ways to distract myself.

Irene: Really? How?

Jerry: Pain, be it my own or another's. The inability to touch and be touched in those places where I'm still wounded prevents me from being fully present and allowing love into the experience.

Irene: Would you be willing to share how you're still wounded?

Jerry: It's not being wounded per se; it's being impatient when I see how unconscious others are to the love that's available. It's like watching a person who's starving and there, next to them, is a bowl of fresh fruit. The sustenance they require is at hand and yet they refuse to see it. My shortcoming is not being patient enough to connect with others where they are. This was also challenging for me as Physical Jerry; my impatience blocked the love that would otherwise have flowed *to* and *through* me. To love someone is to accept that person exactly as they are, even if it means watching them in pain, in fear, or doing without. I've learned that love has no boundaries or limitations. Love has no exceptions. Love allows. Love is so great that it allows even *not* being loved. When I don't fully accept someone, I marginalize an aspect of them, which also marginalizes that same aspect within myself.

Irene: May I offer a suggestion for your consideration?

Jerry: I welcome your input.

Irene: Given that outer experience is a reflection of inner reality, are there ways in which you might be unconscious to what's available? In my experience, when I compassionately embrace an aspect of myself that I've marginalized, it's no longer an issue when I see it reflected in others.

Jerry: Yes, projection is a powerful tool and a reminder that when we're looking at others we're also looking at ourselves. It's a tool I've used and will continue to use. I'm being healed of this perceived separation as we speak. Anytime we marginalize an aspect, we're participating in the illusion of separation.

Irene: Like my friend Ron says, "It's an inkblot world." (Pause) Jerry, is it in any way distracting or disturbing when Jana and I contact you?

Jerry: It's a pleasant interruption. Say you're busy with an enjoyable task at home, which for you, Irene, might be preparing one of your delicious meals. The phone rings and you see that it's someone you love or someone you haven't heard from in a long time, so you make a choice to stop what you're doing and connect with them. It's the same here. I may be engaged in a joyous experience, yet, when I hear the call and it's an old friend or someone whose heart I resonate with, I'm glad to put aside what I'm doing; I can always come back to it. I choose being in your presence and fully embodying the experience of our exchange because no experience is greater than another. It's my receptivity that determines which experience takes precedence for me. What determines my receptivity is how desirous I am of serving the whole. When I receive that individual's call through my heart, I know I'm being asked to a greater service and will benefit optimally by heeding the call. There may be some hesitation, just as when—during a crucial moment in cooking—you say, "I'll call you back in ten minutes." I, too, may have to complete what I'm involved with in order to be fully present.

Irene: I previously understood you to say that you're guided by wisdom as you move from what you love to what you love. I recall the example you gave of sitting near a stream or going to the library. While you would benefit from either one, wisdom guided you to the library because that was for your highest good. I'm now hearing you say that what determines whether the experience is optimal or not is your receptivity to serving the whole. Would you clarify?

Jerry: Everything I choose to experience has value and expands me. Your call regarding this work is wisdom calling me and I experience optimum growth and expansion when I follow it. Every experience provides gifts for growth and expansion; the wisdom of my heart takes me to the experience that I'm most receptive to. It's never just about me as an individual; it's always orchestrated for the gain of the whole, so that, when I heed the call to come and assist you and Jana with this book project, I'm serving not only myself, but also the greater good. All signals from the heart are signals from the whole. When you follow your heart, you're serving the whole.

Irene: It's wonderful to know that when I'm doing what I love—writing, speaking, and coaching—I'm simultaneously contributing to myself and to the greater whole.

(Pause) On a different note, I've made a commitment to accept myself, others, and life *as is*. It requires vigilance and a willingness to release my judgments of how anyone or anything *should* be.

Jerry: Life is experiencing ourselves through, with, and in others. It's also experiencing others through, with, and in ourselves. Your energy field is in a constant state of expansion, stretching beyond imposed limitations. When we refocus our energy from physical to spirited form, a shift in focus occurs: we become aware of others as extensions of ourselves, as aspects of ourselves, as being one and the same, because our physical form, which makes each one of us distinct, *disappears*. What's left is pure energy that may have the appearance of form, but you realize that you don't have to speak to someone in order to communicate. I immediately know the depth of what you're expressing by what you're feeling; you don't have to explain it to me. By simply focusing on you, I'm able to experience as much of you as you're willing to reveal.

Irene: That's the merging you spoke of previously.

Jerry: Yes. I feel your feelings as if they were mine, and you feel mine as if they were yours. This is the greatest expression of empathy available.

Irene: What would I do differently if I were in your presence and I preferred not to reveal anything about myself?

Jerry: I would hear your thoughts of wanting privacy and feel your feelings associated with those thoughts. Your thoughts and feelings regarding privacy would become my own, and I'd respect them as my own. You can easily provide what someone needs when you know their thoughts and feelings.

JERRY

CONVERSATION FIFTEEN

Irene: Good morning, Jerry!

Jerry: Good morning where *you* are.

Irene: Don't you have morning where you are?

Jerry: No. Not the way you on earth experience morning.

Irene: Would you elaborate?

Jerry: There's only light where I am. This light doesn't come from the sun, though. It arises from the inherent illumination of all things. Darkness isn't necessary here. That doesn't stop me, though, from creating a beautiful sunrise or sunset, or a star-filled sky, complete with a bright, full moon for ambiance.

Irene: Darkness doesn't exist where you are?

Jerry: Day and night are aspects of the earth experience, because the earth herself requires darkness on some part of her body at all times to accommodate her nocturnal residents. Darkness is available here as a personal choice. I could create darkness, for instance, by choosing to sit in a darkened room. Some beings are overwhelmed by the intensity of light as well as by the transparency of thoughts and so they choose to retreat in order to feel solitary. Others create the cycles of the sun until they adjust to this constantly light environment.

Irene: I'm confused. You said previously that there is no *there*. Everything is always *here*. Yet you say it's good morning where I am, and not where you are. So how can it all be *here*?

Jerry: It's all *here now*. Outside the perception of time, it's all *here*, and it's all *now*. What creates the perception of *there* is the earth's paradigm of duality and the way your mind functions within those parameters.

Let's use an example. You're *here* in your home office. Existing in the same *here* is everything in your home and everything outside your home. At this time in your physical evolution, your mind is limited; you're unable to focus on all those other things simultaneously, so your mind separates them from you and that creates a *there*. So, if someone were to ask, "Where are you?" you'd say, "I'm *here*, in my office." If someone were to ask you where Jana is, what you'd know is that she's outside your physical focus and therefore not present in your *here*. [Jana and I live in different cities and do our work by phone.] You might even answer by saying, "Well, she's not *here*." Given the nature of duality, if she's not *here*, she's somewhere out *there*. This is all a matter of living within the parameters of time and space. If you were both proficient in telepathy, she'd always be in your *here* because of your shared ability to connect through your focus.

Irene: (Laughing) What if I didn't choose to have her in my *here*? She'd be *there*, wouldn't she?

Jerry: You may not always choose to communicate, but she'd always be *there* with you in your *here*. (Laughing) It's a function of availability. If you could consciously connect with Jana at any time, she'd be consciously in your *here*. It's the inability to connect beyond your *here* that creates the *there*. It's the perceived separation that creates the *there*. It's the inability to use the mind to its full capacity that creates the *there*. In Spirit, everyone's always accessible. The connection is overt. The mind only knows *here* because the mind knows unity.

JERRY

CONVERSATION SIXTEEN

Irene: I know a woman who, after a year of grieving the loss of her husband, found a loving partner. He had been a close friend of the family and was godfather to their children. It almost seemed as if her spirited husband had orchestrated the situation so that his wife would see this man with new eyes. They've been married now for twenty years. Do you have the ability to assist in orchestrating such unions?

Jerry: *Facilitate* would be a better word. This can be done in a number of ways, one of which is to surround your physical loved one with even more of who you are, which is love.

As physical beings, we're often limited in our capacity to love even those to whom we've given our hearts through marriage or partnership. When we refocus our energy into Spirit, we experience a boundless field of love. This is who we truly are. When we remember, we're able to fully love our physical partner, wife, or husband; and with this love, they begin to love themselves more.

As their love expands, they begin to recognize the gifts and the shortcomings inherent in the relationship with their transitioned loved one. Their focus becomes clearer through contrast, having experienced life *with* their partner and now without. Some people experience a sense of freedom from ways they'd been accommodating their partner, so they begin to expand in ways that the partnership hadn't allowed. When a tree that's been shading the ground is removed, the earth beneath it is able to flourish in new ways. As the person on earth experiences the love of their refocused partner, they have their own realizations about themselves and the relationship; these combine to provide a shift in perspective that allows them to attract someone else, if that is their heart's desire.

Irene: If the husband, wife, or partner who transitions was controlling or possessive, can they get in the way of their loved one moving on with another partner?

Jerry: No, because that's a violation of free will. What *can* get in the way are the energetic patterns within the person on earth that allowed a controlling and manipulative person into their life in the first place. Until those patterns are healed, they'll probably attract the same kind of person. Depending on their level of consciousness, they'll either wake up to their responsibility in this attraction or they'll continue to blame the other person. They may even think that their loved one on the other side is messing with their life.

Irene: (Pause) Jerry, do you have responsibilities?

Jerry: I don't have responsibilities as you think of them on earth. I don't have to make money or "have to" anything. Responsibility is simply responding to each moment and what I desire to do with that moment. There's no judgment of others. You on earth often do things in response to what you think others will think of you, especially when it comes to judgments of *not* doing. Here, we honor those who choose to do nothing; it's what their soul is calling them to do—sometimes for eons. Others are overwhelmed by the infinite possibilities and don't know where to begin, so they do nothing but take it all in. Even when I say someone is doing *nothing,* they're never without the presence of love. We're always expanding; nothing is ever still on earth or here at Home.

Irene: What's the next step in your evolution?

Jerry: There is no *step,* as in the linear concept of one thing after another. It's continuous expansion. Evolution is constant, whether you're in body or not. Evolution is simply expansion of your presence, your understanding, and your perspective into the One. Instead of *steps,* it might be more accurate to say *taking-in.* What is your capacity to *take-in?* I'd liken it to entering a room full of people. How many people are you able to be fully present with? As you evolve, you're able to be fully present with more people at one time. With the level of consciousness that you'd call *Christ Consciousness,* for instance, you'd be fully present with everyone in the room, experiencing people, not as individuals, but as a group of individuated experiences. Evolution is the ability to be with many experiences simultaneously. You begin by being fully present with yourself, aware of what you're thinking, what you're feeling, how you're responding to life, and aware of your feet on the ground in each moment. And then, when you're with another, be fully present with them by first being fully present with yourself.

JERRY

CONVERSATION SEVENTEEN

Medium: He's here, and he's smiling from ear to ear.

Jerry: Indeed. I am expressing what is. And what is—is *joy*. You don't see it as clearly in physical form because you're constantly straining to see what's real, like trying to see through fogged windows in a car. When you come Home, you see the truth in all situations. And the truth is: there's nothing *but* joy. The creative process comes through your heart, is at your fingertips, and is always there to please you. Heartfelt desires are designed to bring joy into your life. When you do what you love, manifesting your heart's desires, you're contributing to the whole.

Irene: I see it more clearly every day. (Pause) Jerry, on a different note, we don't suddenly evolve as a result of transitioning, do we? In other words, I won't suddenly become wiser when I transition, will I?

Jerry: Your level of consciousness remains the same. What changes is the awareness of Self that comes from the freed-up energy when you no longer need to maintain a physical body. It's like being in a play where you spend three hours in character and then step off the stage: you no longer have to use your energy to maintain the character, so you can now focus on the person *playing* the character.

The more you focus on Self, the more aware you become of your Self. Spirited friends and loved ones who are also focused on Self strengthen you by relating to you as the being who has just finished playing the character. And you may, for a while, see *them* in the role that was most familiar to you; but through interacting with them and through your own Self-emergence, you see beyond their roles, as well. As you remember your true nature—the power behind all the characters—you evolve, becoming more aware of the wisdom that's been available all along.

Irene: It sounds like Dorothy in *The Wizard of Oz.* When she pulls back the curtain and reveals the source of the wizard, she becomes aware of her own wisdom and uses it to complete her journey. The wisdom, however, had been there all along.

Jerry: Exactly.

Irene: What prevents us from accessing our innate wisdom?

Jerry: Beliefs fueled by fear. If you believe that you'll be judged when you transition, for instance, then you'll create a drama based on that belief; you'll play the role of the one being judged while others do the judging and you'll move from one stage to another. The more conscious you are of Self—on earth, right now—the more conscious you'll be of Self when you transition. The more trust you have in the process of life and the more conscious you are about your true nature—the being who plays all the roles—the sooner you'll step into that being. So, in answer to your question about whether you suddenly evolve: the act of releasing your body doesn't suddenly make you aware of your wisdom.

Irene: Jerry, what makes the bigger difference: being in a loving state or doing good deeds motivated by obligation? Let me give you an example. I love being home and writing. It's blissful. I don't interact with many people, but when I do, it's usually from a loving place. My friend Janet does volunteer work that's motivated by a sense of obligation; it's what her religion dictates.

Jerry: Expressing love is the primary force for change and can make the biggest difference. I know you've felt the difference when someone's doing something motivated by love as opposed to obligation. As Physical Jerry, being assisted by a sales clerk who loved their job was a pleasant and often joyous experience; they were caring, solicitous, informative, and eager to meet my needs. But I also had many an unpleasant encounter with a sales clerk who *didn't* like their job. Either way, their attitudes were contagious. When someone lovingly and enthusiastically greeted me, I was influenced by their joy, making it easier for me to express joy back to them or to the next person I met. In turn, when the clerk was frustrated and angry, resenting their job and resenting me—as if I were to blame—it was easier to become frustrated and angry. When I was spiritually centered, I remained grounded in love and compassion and didn't let it influence me; but if I was on shaky ground, it was easy for me to respond in kind to them or to the next person I encountered. How we choose to *be* influences everyone around us. So, in your example, if you're in a loving space with yourself and you bring that to all your encounters, that makes a bigger difference than the number of good deeds you may do: quality over quantity.

Irene: Are you ever on shaky ground in the Spirit world? Are others ever grumpy or not enjoying what they're doing?

Jerry: No. The feelings that create "shaky ground" can't be sustained long enough to throw me off balance. Unloving feelings are fleeting; they are diluted by the power of love. Discord doesn't last here.

Irene: Are you saying that everyone in the Spirit realm is happy and loving?

Jerry: No. Everyone has free choice. But it's difficult to sustain unloving expressions in this loving environment, because the unloving expression isn't reinforced; instead, it's recognized as a wound that needs healing.

Irene: But what if two beings come together who share similar wounds?

Jerry: Here in Spirit there are never just two beings, because everyone is aware of everyone else. Even when two beings are focused on their wounds, they're surrounded by love.

Irene: Could you be alone with someone if that's what you desired?

Jerry: Yes, of course.

Irene: (Pause) Jerry, we're so accustomed to the comfort that physical form provides—our bodies, cars, homes, and routines—I'm wondering how we can gracefully release the familiar when the time comes to refocus our energy from physical to spirited form.

Jerry: The ease with which you release the familiar depends on your willingness to experience more than what you perceive yourself to be. I've seen people transition who continue to project what was most familiar about their living and working environments. They create the home and the job they just left, resuming their lives as if nothing has happened. They even create their families and co-workers! I want to take a moment to remind you of how powerful you are that you can create in this way.

Transitioned family members and friends participate in these scenarios, gently helping to bring awareness of the change that's occurred, because until the previous existence is released, the life review can't take place. Personal evolution slows and this affects the entire soul family. It's like a family vacation with Aunt Gloria, who slows everyone down because she's lingering longer at the Louvre while everyone else wants to see the Eiffel Tower.

When *I* transitioned, I was more attached to what was beyond the physical world. I wanted *out* of the physical world, so it didn't occur to me to recreate it. I was excited by the adventure of something different, of life beyond the physical. I was open to The Mystery. I wanted to be surprised, and I was prepared to be surprised. The physical friends and family who surrounded me held a similar vision and weren't afraid of the unknown or concerned about where I was going. And even though there was sadness around my passing, there was also an underlying sense of joy for my release. I believed I was going Home. The physical environment I was leaving was a place I'd been visiting. When I transitioned, I had the feeling I'd often had after returning from a vacation: pleased with my experiences yet glad to be home.

JERRY

CONVERSATION EIGHTEEN

Irene: Jerry, each time Jana has contacted my spirited mom, Beba, she's been playing cards—an activity she very much enjoyed when she was on earth. She's not in some sort of perpetual card game, is she?

Jerry: She's quite a gal! She accomplishes a lot in this kind of social environment. She discusses things in depth with many people while she plays cards; it helps her focus her energies—like someone who knits while talking. Remember the quilting parties that created a revolution? That's what Beba does with cards. She not only loves playing cards, she loves connecting with others. Don't underestimate what goes on during these games; I've had illuminating and productive conversations while playing. We often share about the specific patterns we've worked through, as well as strategies for living productively. These conversations are *evolutionary* rather than revolutionary. (Pause) I sense you have a judgment about Beba.

Irene: Yes, I guess I do. I judge her as shallow for playing cards as often as she does.

(Pause) I'm completing an M.A. in Spiritual Psychology, and its cornerstone is the willingness to take one hundred percent responsibility for any disturbance going on within, without blaming it on anyone or anything outside.

Jerry: Taking responsibility gives you the power to restore peace, a state of being that can be maintained only from within.

Irene: Exactly.

Jerry: The spiritual aspect needs to be added to *all* the sciences. Tell me how adding it to psychology changes its structure.

Irene: The word *psychology* originated from the Greek words, *psyche* and *logos,* meaning, *the study of spirit, soul, mind;* but current psychology, as studied in colleges and universities, doesn't address the spirit or soul at all.

Spiritual Psychology, on the other hand, begins with the premise that we are spiritual beings having a human experience. It asserts that earth functions as a school for the evolution of consciousness. Everyone has their own spiritual agenda and is conditioned accordingly.

Jerry: Tell me about conditioning.

Irene: Well, the way we're conditioned is truly extraordinary, because our basic personality structure is laid down by age five, but it's not until age seven or so that our cognitive development is concretely operational and we can reason logically.

Jerry: So reasoning processes aren't in place until *after* the personality has been laid down.

Irene: Exactly. The best we can do as our personality is forming is to make associations. As an example, if little Eddie is standing in his crib and Mom comes in with outstretched arms, he knows loving is coming his way. But let's say the phone rings and Mom leaves. Eddie may associate *loving* with *leaving.* This could be the beginning of a pattern in which Eddie creates abandonment by his partners later in life. But he'll only make this association if it's part of his spiritual agenda.

Jerry: Women in abusive relationships were once little girls who associated intimacy with abuse.

Irene: Precisely. Traditional psychology looks at these dynamics and describes them, but can't offer an explanation. Spiritual Psychology asserts that we have spiritual agendas and everyone will be conditioned according to what they're here to learn.

So, in the example of Eddie pairing *loving* and *leaving,* he'll only form that pattern if it's part of his spiritual agenda. If it's not, he'll make other associations that *are.* We can't protect our children from their spiritual agendas, nor would we want to; it's why our children came here, and it's what they're here to learn. Differing agendas explain why two children from the same family can grow up in the same environment, have the same parents, and yet turn out so differently.

Jerry: And children choose parents who will help them accomplish their spiritual agendas. They choose their parents, not only for their consciousness, but for their *un*consciousness as well.

Irene: That should help take some of the pressure off of parents.

(Pause) Traditional psychology addresses the physical, mental, and emotional aspects of a person, but not the spiritual aspect. Spiritual Psychology calls this aspect the Authentic Self, an integral facet of our being that's beyond personality, beyond the ego, and beyond duality; it is the essence of who we are. It's our authentic nature. It's a state of consciousness characterized by such qualities as acceptance, love, peace, joy, compassion, kindness, gratitude and wisdom.

Jerry: Feelings of separation dissolve at the level of Authentic Self, and we are One. This reflects the shift in consciousness, from duality to unity, that's taking place on the planet.

Irene: Indeed. We're participating in the transformation of human consciousness. What an extraordinary time to be on the planet.

(Pause) Spiritual Psychology recognizes that the goal of the ego is to be right and to make others wrong, and we call this *judgment.* Since we're all divine beings having a human experience, and we don't know what anyone's agenda is, we're not in a position to judge. When we think we know more than we do and we place a judgment—on ourselves, on another, or on a situation—it feeds

JERRY • CONVERSATION EIGHTEEN

the ego, or the "small" self. The moment we enter into judgment, we've entered into duality, creating painful feelings of separation. Have you ever noticed that making someone or something *wrong* disrupts inner peace?

Jerry: Absolutely. As you separate yourself from someone as a result of judgment, you're disrupting your connection to the Authentic Self.

Irene: Yes. And judgment is always at the root of an inner disturbance. When our ideals are violated, for example, what's violated is the way we think things *should* be, which is usually the way we were brought up to think is the *right* way. From the perspective of the Authentic Self, however, there *is* no right or wrong. There *are* no judgments. There are simply choices and consequences. This is not to condone "bad" behavior; it's simply that, identifying the judgment and letting it go allows us to grow spiritually.

If we don't know what we or anyone else is here to learn, then we're in no position to place judgement on ourselves, others, or situations. And if we're not in a position to place judgment on anyone, then we never have to forgive them—for anything—because in order to forgive, we first have to judge. I don't have to forgive my spouse, my children, my parents or my siblings. I don't have to forgive them because they never did anything wrong. (Pause) It took months for this concept to sink in when I first heard it.

When I take one hundred percent responsibility for any disturbance going on within, without blaming it on anyone or anything outside, the only person I ever have to forgive is myself—for the judgments I've placed. It's always about *self*-forgiveness, because I can't forgive anyone else if they didn't do anything to me. There are no exceptions to taking one hundred percent responsibility—not child abuse, rape, or murder. It's all part of the spiritual agenda. It doesn't mean we agree with or advocate these things; it means that, as spiritual beings, we're all here to learn different lessons.

Jerry: We block the flow of love and create unnecessary suffering when we judge. Love is always available and always flowing. The question is, are we allowing it or blocking it?

Irene: Precisely. Self-forgiveness allows us to compassionately apply love to the places inside that hurt, which allows the flow of love. It's a powerful tool in service to healing. When I place a judgment on someone—in this case, Beba—and I forgive myself for having placed the judgment on her in the first place, I move out of duality and into acceptance.

And so, I forgive myself for judging Beba as shallow. I forgive myself for judging card games as a waste of time. I forgive myself for having bought into the misinterpretation that I know what's best for Beba—or anyone else, for that matter. I release these judgments, recognizing that I have no idea what she's in the process of learning or what circumstance will best serve her. I pray for her highest good and the highest good of all concerned.

Jerry: Judgment stops the flow of feelings. So-and-so is wrong for this or that, and you're right for this or that. It usually means you're closing the door on something. You make a statement that so-and-so is wrong, you get angry at so-and-so for doing what they're doing, and then you sit with it. And you usually wait for and attract someone else who'll agree with you, so that both of you can be in this place of agreement, of feeling right. But it closes the door on so-and-so, because suddenly so-and-so is over there and you're over here. So-and-so is wrong and you're right. You've separated yourself.

Irene: Judgment creates separation.

Jerry: It's only a *perception* of separation; it's impossible to create separation except in your mind. That perception can become very strong, though.

Irene: And when we're judging ourselves . . .

Jerry: Then you've separated yourself from the expression of yourself that behaved a certain way. Forgiveness starts the flow of feelings again. Forgiving: *for giving*. You're giving yourself acceptance. You're giving acceptance to another person and acceptance to that moment in your own experience. You're opening your arms and allowing everything to be the way it is. And you love yourself just the way you are. And you love *them* the way they are. It's forgiving. It's for giving to your self or for giving to another, and what you're giving is acceptance.

Irene: Yes. And, once we're clear that nobody knows what anyone is here to learn or how they've chosen to learn it, there really is no choice but to experience acceptance. That doesn't mean being a doormat, and it's not resignation.

Jerry: Accepting yourself allows you to accept others. It's an expression of unconditional love.

Irene: Absolutely. (Laughing) I'm glad we got *that* cleared up! (Pause) I'd like to talk about something else that's on my mind.

Jerry: Yes?

Irene: I love being in the comfort of my home. I'm concerned, though, that comfort is becoming a pattern in my life. I'm wondering whether it might be useful to shake things up a bit so I don't get too comfortable.

Jerry: Your inner comfort is constantly being challenged. You're always growing and changing within, and the home environment you've created is simply a place where the inner work can happen. A seed in the ground is constantly changing and depends on the stability of the ground around it so it can grow. The beautiful home you've created is your stable ground; you've included the things you need to nourish yourself so that you can do the inner work you've been doing.

Irene: Thanks. That rings true for me. (Pause) I'm realizing that, not only had I placed a judgment on Beba—judging her as shallow for playing cards—but also on myself, judging myself as shallow for desiring comfort. And so, I forgive myself for judging myself as shallow for desiring comfort. I forgive myself for buying into the misconception that enjoying comfort isn't spiritual. I forgive myself for the misinterpretation that spirituality and material abundance don't go together. The belief that's more appropriate, given who I am today, is that spirituality is *inclusive,* not *exclusive.*

Jerry: You're right. *Everything* flows from Spirit. Form is Spirit manifest, whether rich and abundant or poor and impoverished. It's *all* Spirit.

Irene: (Pause) Jerry, do people have themes to their lives?

Jerry: Not themes. Each life has an agenda. Each person has both an individual agenda and a group agenda. The agenda isn't dictated, though, and there are no requirements. In the spirit of cooperation, those who are going to incarnate choose to strengthen certain virtues and attributes for the greatest good of all concerned. The individualized agenda expresses itself in each person's freedom to create the experiences that strengthen their ability to give and receive love.

Many of these experiences revolve around family conflict. Learning to cooperate with your biological family or with your partner strengthens your ability to live harmoniously with others. You may choose to be born into a family in which you and your mother are in constant conflict, for example, and by working through these issues with your mother—and sometimes not with your mother, but with others who represent your mother—you learn to strengthen your ability to give and receive love.

Irene: So, no matter what circumstance we create, the learning is always about love?

Jerry: It's not *learning* so much as it is strengthening your ability to express and receive love and all its attributes. That's the goal. Some people create anti-love situations in order to strengthen their love muscles.

Irene: Can you offer an example?

Jerry: Creating challenging people or situations—neighbors, in-laws, losing your job, bankruptcy . . . individuals often choose challenging beginnings—abusive parents or being orphaned—in order to grow in their ability to love relentlessly. The sooner the person recognizes how their situation is serving them, the sooner they can benefit and move on. This recognition takes them from being a victim to being a creative force in their own life and in the lives of others. The greatest challenge is loving ourselves.

Irene: What about people living in areas where genocide is occurring?

Jerry: This is an example of an extreme obstacle course that's been chosen in order to strengthen the love muscles: compassion, optimism, empathy, forgiveness, joy, patience, and wisdom. There are many group experiences on earth that challenge people's love muscles and each person made the choice to be born into such a situation. The ones who understand this are the ones who find love soonest. Individuals know, before they incarnate, which attributes need to be strengthened through their life experience and they choose their situation accordingly. People who face the greatest challenges seem to be the most inspiring. Others think, *If they can do that, so can I!*

Irene: Absolutely. I'm reminded of Viktor Frankl, a Jewish psychiatrist who survived the concentration camp experience. He realized that there was one thing that could never be taken from him: the freedom to choose his own attitude. He chose love and compassion. His story now inspires millions.

Jerry: Love is like glue. It holds everyone together. When you're together, you're all stronger and more powerful. Fear divides. Love unifies.

JERRY

CONVERSATION NINETEEN

Irene: Hi, Jerry! What have you been up to?

Jerry: I'm assisting spirited beings in planning their journeys into the earth plane in much the same way a guidance counselor helps students plan their class schedules.

Irene: You've also served as a midwife to those coming into the Spirit world. Do you participate in other helping professions?

Jerry: I prefer to call it *being of service* rather than *helping professions.* There's no sacrifice in this kind of service. It's always win-win. I share my wisdom and love with every connection I make; I open my heart to them, and they open their hearts to me. We're sharing the wealth, serving up platters of love and wisdom to each other.

My specific service has been to assist people coming out of the earth plane; now I'm helping them go back in. While these seem to be opposite, they're actually similar. When beings come into non-physical reality after living in the forgetfulness of the physical, my service is to remind them of where they are now. I lovingly assure them so that their experience isn't dominated by any fears they may have brought with them. If someone has thoughts of going to a hellish place, for instance, free will allows it to be created. It's the job of those offering assistance to affirm the reality of the Spirit realm and to remind them that it's loving and familiar. It's Home.

When spirited beings are in the process of returning to the earth plane, I help them remember the truth of unity as they slip back into physical form. I also serve as a counselor by looking at their soul's goals for expansion in this journey on which they're embarking. It's easier to help those who are returning to the physical plane because they already know the truth; their memory hasn't been diminished. When they're arriving *from* the physical plane, sometimes it's like going against the tide, because people's thoughts about what it is to transition can be so indoctrinated with fear that it takes a lot of energy to maintain the truth. I still participate in both services, and I continue to return to the presence of the masters for nourishment. That's my food here.

Irene: Do you ever assist spirited beings in going somewhere other than earth?

Jerry: No, although I know it's a service that's available. I choose to remain with my Spirit family. Since they're connected to the earth, I choose to perform services that allow me to have contact there.

Irene: Why do we choose to incarnate on the earth instead of going elsewhere?

Jerry: The earth has a lot to offer. The sensual delights of physical form are a main attraction. The human body is a huge receptor. Just sit still for a moment with your eyes closed. Feel the air against your skin. Listen to the sounds around you. Smell the air. What does the inside of your mouth taste like?

Irene: I see what you mean.

Jerry: That's just the beginning. Another reason the earth is so attractive is that it's a diverse environment that allows for creative opportunities not found elsewhere. It's like choosing a buffet instead of a single entrée; everywhere you turn there's an opportunity to experience something else.

The earth also offers the opportunity to experience contrast. The most efficient way to understand something is to experience its opposite. You know what *cold* is through the experience of *hot*. Where would *up* be if there were no *down*?

Returning to physical form on earth to be of service is another compelling draw. The potential for paradise on earth is great. When I say *paradise,* I'm referring to the potential for widespread diversity to live in harmony, ruled by love, peace, compassion, and joy.

Another unique feature is free will. When you're on the earth, it's like being a child let loose in an amusement park. Since your true essence can never be harmed, you're safe to do whatever you desire. You may choose to spend a lifetime on one ride because you think it's the only ride available or because you want to experience every aspect of that particular ride. You can ride it over and over again and it'll never be the same. (Laughing) There are no reruns in creation. God bores easily. As *we* expand, the whole of creation expands.

Irene: Free will isn't unique to the earth, is it? Don't we always have choice, regardless of whether we're on the earth or elsewhere?

Jerry: Free will is a universal experience except when one chooses to have free will withheld.

Irene: Why would someone choose to have free will withheld?

Jerry: Some individuals don't want a wide variety of choices; they want it narrowed down—a main entrée instead of a buffet.

Irene: I just realized something. We've been given free will about everything—with one exception: we can't choose to *not* exist. Wow. What an amazing realization. We may change form, but since energy cannot be destroyed or created, we will always exist.

Jerry: Well said. I concur.

Irene: What about my consciousness? Will my consciousness continue to evolve and expand?

Jerry: There is nothing that *isn't* energy, including your consciousness. The nature of energy is expansion, because all energy is God, and God is constantly expanding into a greater expression of Itself. Everything is expanding, including inanimate objects. That's why they wear out—to break free of that form and assume another. Couches, chairs, cars . . . they're all energy in motion, God in form.

You attract objects into your life to serve you. The consciousness they have is the consciousness you give them through their service to you. Everything in your environment has a signature that's uniquely yours. It's called your *style* and it's an extension of you: the furniture you have, the car you drive, the artwork on your walls; they embody your consciousness and come and go as you evolve. This evolution is sometimes conscious, such as when you decide to redecorate your house and get all new furnishings, for example. Sometimes it's more *un*conscious, like when that old couch you've been sitting on for three decades wears down and no longer supports your body. The couch is done with serving *you,* and you're done with serving *it.* Resistance to letting it go is a reflection of resistance to your own evolution. Go through your home, go through your things, and ask yourself, *Is this item serving me? Do I still love this? Is this couch comfortable?* Let go of what no longer serves you.

JERRY

CONVERSATION TWENTY

Irene: Does the earth have an intention for her own evolution?

Jerry: Yes, she does. Her soul has an evolutionary agenda, which is the same as ours: to express more and more God essence. She is a massive energetic presence; when we live in harmony with her, we increase our ability to evolve our own agendas. It's all one agenda: to focus only on what's in harmony with God's essence, which is love.

Irene: What distinguishes each agenda?

Jerry: What distinguishes each agenda is the available set of experiences. If your agenda for the day is to have fun, you'll choose experiences that, to you, represent fun. Each person chooses different experiences to fulfill the agenda of fun; one person may choose a baseball game while another chooses a museum.

Irene: How can the earth accomplish her evolutionary agenda to express God's essence when so many of her human inhabitants are at war? Why doesn't she shake off what's not in harmony with her, like a dog shakes off fleas?

Jerry: The violence of war is part of their cleansing process.

Irene: How so?

Jerry: It's a manifestation of the inner conflict that's present in the collective consciousness.

Irene: If we were all doing our inner work of healing the warring aspects within ourselves, there would be no war.

Jerry: Yes, that's true. By taking responsibility for our feelings and circumstances, we have the power to change our lives.

We give away our power to change when we blame others. When we're at war, we're trying to affect change outside ourselves, thinking that if we get rid of *them,* our inner problems will be solved and we'll be okay. War is blame magnified, taking place on a massive scale that everyone can see. Using war as a strategy for change is like going into someone else's home, gutting it, redecorating it, and expecting *your* home to change.

Irene: Not even Martha Stewart could make a winning strategy of that. (Pause) You said the earth assists us in evolving our own agendas. How?

Jerry: She assists by example, by inspiring you with her natural beauty. Whether you're aware of it or not, your energy is elevated in her presence: when you stand barefoot on the ground, she stimulates inspiration by sending love and appreciation through you. She's always giving. When you're appreciating a beautiful sunset, for example, your appreciation is magnified by her appreciation of your appreciation. (Laughing) It's an uplifting spiral that has the potential to harmonize your body. When you start thinking about what time it is or what you have to do, your thoughts break the cycle. Stay present with appreciation and miracles happen.

Irene: *Miracles?*

Jerry: Miracles don't have to be dramatic. A subtle miracle—a realization or a shift in attitude—can change your life.

You also have the capacity to inspire others by expressing your unique beauty through your thoughts, words, actions, and creations. You can choose to speak in a way that uplifts others, you can inspire others with acts of kindness, or you can find a vocation that allows you to express your gifts and talents. Your perspective is your unique signature. You are the only one who can look through your eyes.

Another way the earth serves by example is through constant

renewal. She uses everything and wastes nothing. By-products become resources; trees, for example, utilize carbon dioxide and provide oxygen, while decaying fruits fertilize the seeds contained within them. If systems like transportation, electric power, and waste management were set up to utilize the by-products they produce, you'd experience better health and that would uplift your energy.

The earth's nature is one of giving and receiving. She's constantly sustaining life by giving all that life requires—oxygen, water, food, shelter—and at the same time, she's self-sustaining. No one fertilizes the forests on the planet; they're part of her self-sustaining system. When an apple falls to the ground and decomposes, it contains the nutrients that will nourish the tree from which it fell.

What you experience as a storm, an earthquake, or the eruption of a volcano is the earth ridding her body of toxins as part of monitoring her health. The consequences of these events can affect her physical surface by decreasing the population in an area and lightening her load. They can also create the opportunity for you to change on a variety of levels—physical, mental, emotional, and spiritual: you may be forced to move, your attitudes may change, or your capacity to experience compassion may expand to new levels. These kinds of changes afford you the opportunity to expand your perspective. After such events, people re-evaluate and re-prioritize their lives to include more of the attributes of love: gratitude, compassion, goodwill, joy, peace, and courage.

The movement to save the earth isn't about *saving* her—it's about *appreciating* her. Saving would imply that she's a victim and that you have control over her. Neither is true. The control you *do* have is over how you choose to respond to the flow of life. Are you responding with love or with fear? Your response strengthens one or the other. The green movement is quickening and expanding the consciousness of love through harmonious living. Your response either supports the quickening or slows it. This isn't about saving anything. It's about coming into harmony with the earth and recognizing that you're an integral part of her.

The green movement is more than living in harmony with the earth; it's also about living in harmony with each other. The earth is a model of efficient, synergistic, and harmonious living. This is what she's showing you. This is what her presence does for you in service to the whole.

From where I am, the earth looks like a radiant sphere of love. Her presence and power transform everyone who chooses her as their home.

JERRY

CONVERSATION TWENTY-ONE

Irene: I have a friend who says he wants to experience life in a better, more evolved place than the earth. He's hoping his personal evolution will provide forward movement in this regard.

Jerry: There is no forward movement. There are opportunities from which to choose. Choices are based on individual needs, and needs are based on the growth and expansion of one's soul.

Irene: Doesn't one naturally make choices that expand the soul?

Jerry: Yes. Always. Every choice leads to expansion, even when the choice is contraction. Beings may choose to contract in order to help others by reflecting areas where love is constricted; they may choose a path that goes against their nature in order to be of service, which sometimes entails being a villain in the drama.

Irene: Given that we all have free choice, what if someone chooses *not* to expand—even by contracting?

Jerry: Whenever someone makes a choice, it's an expression of power, and they expand.

Irene: So even choosing *not* to choose leads to expansion?

Jerry: Yes. Every choice is a creative process and therefore expansive. No one can choose *not* to expand because, by consciously choosing not to expand, they've made a choice, and the choice itself leads to expansion. So it's not about whether they're going to expand or not; it's about how much they're going to expand. It's like the breath in the physical body: you can't consciously choose not to breathe for any sustained period of time; you can, however, choose how deeply you're going to breathe. Some people go through life taking shallow breaths, never expanding their lungs to full capacity, while others choose to breathe deeply. Once you've experienced how nourishing and calming it is to breath deeply, you no longer want to restrict your breath. This is also the way of the soul and its choice to expand; expansion feels good because you're bringing more of your true nature into your experience.

When you breathe consciously, for example, your breath deepens, your sense of well-being increases, and your body benefits, so you want to continue. Likewise, once you express and experience acts of love and kindness, your sense of well-being increases. You and everyone around you benefits, and you want to continue. Love is your authentic nature, so it's your nature to express the virtues of love. When you choose to express compassion, kindness, and forgiveness, there's a comfort that makes you want to express more. It feels good to be your Self.

The word *good* is universal in its meaning, yet it doesn't mean the same thing to everyone. People look for the good in things. They want something that's good tasting and good for them. They want good friends. They look for the goodness in life. The interpretation of *good* varies with each individual: some think a good experience is watching a football game, while others think a good experience is listening to the symphony. The interpretation of what's good is unique to each individual; but good *feelings* are universal and the good feelings we seek represent our true nature, our soul's influence, and our God-Self. To feel *good* is to feel *God*. *Good* and *God* are interchangeable.

I know what you're thinking, Irene: God is interchangeable with everything. That's true, but it's the degree of pure expression that separates one thing from another and one feeling from another. It's like gold jewelry; you can wear a gold bracelet and, indeed, there's gold in it, but how much and of what quality? Fourteen karats? Twenty-four karats? It's the same with self-expression. While all expression is God, how much "gold" is in the expression?

Irene: You're referring to the attributes of love as the "gold" in expression?

Jerry: Yes. Doing our best to express the essence of God/good in our lives is expansion; it is expansion through refinement. Refinement is the process of removing impurities or unwanted elements from a substance; it's the improvement or clarification of something by making small changes. As you express more love in your life, all that is *not* love comes forward to be purified. Love is like the sun, transforming darkness by the power of its presence. Love, by its virtues, transforms that which is unloving. Indeed, it's all God, but some expressions capture love, truth, and joy more effectively than others. God captures the essence of pure love, pure truth, and pure joy in ways that are more harmonious with your own nature and the nature of those around you.

JERRY

CONVERSATION TWENTY-TWO

Irene: Can you describe the relationship between the physical body and the spirited body?

Jerry: The physical body is an appendage of the spirited body. The physical body receives information from the physical world and relays it to the spirited body through the aura. The spirited body then responds by providing intuition and guidance to your physical body.

Irene: I have the image of a figure eight.

Jerry: Yes. It's a figure eight in motion.

The physical body and the spirited body provide access to different kinds of information. The physical body uses the senses: What color is that? What does that taste like? What am I receiving intuitively?

The spirited body has access to all the information derived from the experiences you've had and are having as Irene, as well as information about probable future choices as Irene. Once you've transitioned, it provides information about your most recent life, which includes access to the experiences of others while they were in your presence. During the life review, that's how you're able to experience yourself from *their* perspective and know how you affected them.

Irene: Does the spirited body have an aura that connects it to something else?

Jerry: Yes. It has an aura that connects it to the spiritual body. The spiritual body not only provides access to all the information derived from your experiences as Irene, it also provides access to all the information derived from your experiences in all your lifetimes.

Irene: It reminds me of the Russian nesting dolls you spoke of previously: each one fits inside the other, yet is whole and complete in itself.

Jerry: That's the pattern of infinity. There's never an endpoint. It's infinite and whole in all directions, from the microcosm to the macrocosm.

The spiritual body provides access to experiences from all the lives you have had, are having, and potentially will have. It also provides access to all the interactions you have had, are having, and potentially will have with others. When you access this information, you receive it with a personal focus: it's for the purpose of your own growth and expansion.

Let's use you and Jana as an example. Your spiritual body, Irene, contains every lifetime you have had, are having, and potentially will have, and all the interactions within all those lifetimes. Some of those interactions include Jana. You, Irene, would have access to Jana's experiences in all those lifetimes, but only as they relate to you.

Just as the physical body accesses the spirited body for the purpose of gaining a broader perspective from which to make informed choices, so, too, does the spirited body access the spiritual body. If you, Irene, in spirited body, wanted to understand more about why you chose your lifetime as Irene, you could access the spiritual body and gain the perspective of all your lifetimes. You'd know how the lifetime as Irene makes sense in the greater picture of You.

Irene: (Laughing) My mind is being stretched. I assume my spiritual body also has an aura that connects it to something else?

Jerry: Yes. The *oversoul* provides access to even more information. It provides access to all your experiences from all the lives you have had, are having, and potentially will have, as well as access to all the interactions you have had, are having, and potentially will have with others in relation to you. But it also includes all *their* experiences and interactions from their perspectives, whether they relate directly to you or not.

Again, let's use you and Jana as an example. When you, Irene, access the oversoul, it contains every lifetime you have had, are having, and potentially will have, as well as all the interactions within all those lifetimes. Some of those interactions include Jana. You, Irene, would have access to all Jana's experiences in all her lifetimes, even those not directly related to you. When you access this information, you receive it in consideration for the expansion of the group. If you, Irene, in spiritual body, wanted to understand more about how each of your lifetimes contributed to the expansion of the group, as well as how each of *their* lifetimes contributed to the expansion of the group, you could access the oversoul. You'd then know what was needed for the group to evolve more efficiently and effectively. It's like a corporate meeting where the various divisions are brought together to determine how the company is doing: "Let's hear from accounting, from sales, from marketing, from product development; let's hear from all divisions so we'll know how we're doing as a whole." You gain the perspective of how each whole contributes to the greater whole, and you know how all of your lifetimes make sense in the greater picture of the group.

It's all about information. These energetic systems—the physical body, the spirited body, the spiritual body, the oversoul—all store information in greater and greater amounts. Each one offers a broader and more inclusive perspective than the previous one.

Irene: Let me check understanding. In the *physical* body, I have direct access to information through my senses. In the *spirited* body, I have direct access to information about my last life, which includes the experiences of others while they were in my presence. I have the opportunity to experience how I affected them—from *their* perspective. In the *spiritual* body, I have direct access to information about all the lives I've ever lived, which includes the experiences of others while they were in my presence in all those lifetimes. Here I have the opportunity to experience how I affected others throughout shared lifetimes— again, from *their* perspective. In the oversoul, I have direct access to information about all of my lifetimes, which includes all of the experiences of others in all of their lifetimes as they relate not only to me, but also to each other and to the group. I not only have the opportunity to experience how I affected others in all of those lifetimes—from *their* perspective—but also how they affected others within the group throughout all of those lifetimes.

Jerry: Yes.

Irene: What form do these bodies have?

Jerry: The spirited body is a malleable form that is capable of shape shifting. It's a form that expands as other realms are explored. If you were to merge with the spiritual body, the spirited body would expand in order to fully access the information. Then you would be a spirited body expanded into the spiritual body.

Irene: What does it take to merge with the spiritual body?

Jerry: It takes an intention to fully access the information stored there. We always have access to information from all the bodies, because they're all *us.* Our physical body, however, is capable of receiving only small amounts of information from each body; full access would result in overload. When you first met your husband, Charlie, for example, he needed to feel familiar so that you would allow him into your life. That feeling of familiarity was received through your physical body from information stored in the other bodies.

Irene: Is the spiritual body also malleable and able to shape-shift?

Jerry: Yes. As it moves into the oversoul, however, it becomes formless. It's challenging to find the words to describe these concepts; it's like trying to describe the mind. It's important to note that these systems affect your physical life, and that your choices affect all these systems. You're receiving information from all these systems in the form of a relay; the information is modified through each system to make it accessible to you.

The level beyond the oversoul provides information about multiple groups and how they affect the whole. There are greater and greater groupings that include other star systems and universes, ad infinitum. Trying to understand the infinite is complicated, yet the process of evolution increases our capacity to understand more and more.

Irene: I think that, for the moment, I've reached *my* capacity. What an amazing journey we're on.

Jerry: Indeed.

Irene: (Pause) As we bring our conversation to a close, I want to thank you. I'm grateful for your loving presence and for your contribution to my growth and expansion as well as for your contribution to all who are reading this. Would you like to say something in closing?

Jerry: Everything is an expression of the Infinite Power of Love. The Source is always flowing and making love available to you. Every transition you make throughout life is empowered by love and encourages you to grow and expand. The process of transitioning from physical to non-physical form is a loving one, as are all of your transitions. Each time you expand, love rushes in to fill the space. The most important belief you can hold is that the universe is loving and beneficent and that all transitions are moving you toward a greater capacity to give and receive love. If that means a different city, a different partner, or a different body, it's all what's most loving for you. Not a moment goes by in physical existence during which something or someone isn't transitioning. Trust Life. I have thoroughly enjoyed conversing with you both.

JARED

1969 – 1999

Jared was nine years old when I first met him. My son David arrived home from school with his arm around Jared's neck, announcing, "This is Jared, my new best friend." Their friendship blossomed, and they continued to love and support each other throughout adolescence and into adulthood. They were the best of friends for twenty-one years.

Jared was like my adopted son. He practically lived at our house and even went on a couple of family vacations with us.

He injured his back when he was twenty-three. Unable to work and in chronic pain, Jared underwent two surgeries. He remained on narcotic pain medications and had little quality of life until he transitioned as a result of internal organ failure.

JARED

CONVERSATION ONE

Irene: Jared, what did you experience when you released your last breath on earth?

Jared: I was shot out of my body like a bullet out of a gun—but I was ready. I was chomping at the bit to be released. I'd been miserable for a long time.

Irene: Was it painful?

Jared: No, there was no pain. It felt like my physical body blew me out like an air gun. I didn't have any regrets about leaving my physical body. I was done with it. As I hovered three or four feet above it, I noticed how sickly it was in contrast to how good I felt—better than I'd felt in a long time; I'd been in terrible pain just seconds before. My physical face looked peaceful, and I thought, *My body wasn't the cause of the pain; it was me* experiencing *my body that was the cause. Without* me, *it can't experience pain—or anything else for that matter. I* am *the experience.* I suddenly got that I was responsible for everything that had gone on with my body.

I thought it odd that my mother was weeping, but I understood that, from her perspective, I *was* my body. I felt her sadness, but not through my body; I felt it in the air. I realized the air was like a membrane, connecting us. What *she* was feeling was being sent to me through this membrane, and I was feeling it like it was mine. When I realized I didn't need a physical body to receive her emotions, I thought that maybe I never had. I became aware of my connection to everything, and then I became aware of everyone in the room.

Irene: Were you aware of having a form or a body?

Jared: Yes. It was a body similar to the one I'd left, but pain-free and stronger.

Irene: How was it stronger?

Jared: I stood upright and tall, my shoulders back. I felt like I could do anything.

Irene: Had you lost the ability to hold yourself up straight and stand tall in your physical body?

Jared: My movement had been restricted by pain and I'd been struggling for some time.

Irene: What happened next?

Jared: I put my arm around my mother and comforted her as she wept. As I felt her pain ease, I realized my presence was making a difference. Then, in a flash, I was suddenly with my sister, experiencing *her* emotions as if they were mine. I wanted to reassure her, because the strongest emotion *she* was feeling was guilt, and I felt it as a cramp in my fluidity.

Irene: Do you know why her guilt felt like a cramp?

Jared: It was a kink in the flow of love I was experiencing.

Irene: I'm wondering why your mother's sadness didn't feel like a cramp.

Jared: My mother's sadness was the result of her love for me; she knew she'd miss me. My sister's guilt was the result of fear: she believed she hadn't done enough for me and was focused more on herself than she was on me.

Irene: But your sister would have had to love you in order to feel guilty about not having done enough for you, wouldn't she? Wasn't her guilt, like your mother's sadness, also the result of her love?

Jared: Everything comes from love. It's a question of how much fear is present in the love. In this case, there was more fear than love.

(Pause) In the midst of this, I became conscious of other

beings in spirited bodies like mine. I recognized someone from my childhood.

"Oh, Mr. Parker!" I said. "What are *you* doing here?"

And Mr. Parker said, "I might ask the same thing of you!"

We laughed and hugged. He took me out through a lit doorway, where I was peacefully embraced and eased into a gentle slumber. I'd never felt so peaceful. I drifted away into what I'd call sleep, yet it wasn't.

Irene: Who was embracing you?

Jared: It wasn't a being in a body; that's why I refer to it as a presence.

Irene: Can you elaborate?

Jared: If I were to take all the comforting memories of my physical life and energize them into one presence, it would only begin to describe what I felt. It was like the comfort of warm pajamas from the dryer, freshly baked chocolate chip cookies, my mom's reassuring hug, and millions of other comforting memories, all rolled into one. I had the feeling of comfort, but without the specific memories: I wasn't thinking about warm pajamas. This is the closest I can come to describing how I felt.

Jared and Jerry
Conversation Two

Irene: I have a question for Jerry.

Jerry: I'm at your service.

Irene: Jerry, I understood you to say that immediately after transitioning, you were focusing through a "loosely contained light form."

Jerry: Yes.

Irene: And Jared, I understood *you* to say that you were focusing through a spirited body that resembled your physical body.

Jared: Correct.

Irene: Can either of you elaborate on why you were focusing through different forms?

Jerry: While some beings are comforted by containment of the spirited body, I'd had enough limitation. I was ready to expand myself. I wanted the experience of joining the Whole and being *more*. My desire dictated my experience.

Jared: I'd read about the afterlife and had imagined that my spiritual experience would look like my physical experience. I'd read stories of people seeing apparitions of their transitioned loved ones, and because they appeared in a familiar body, I guess I assumed that's how it would be for me. I say, "I guess," because it wasn't a conscious thought, like, *I'll create a spirited body*. I just assumed that form.

Irene: Jared, did you experience merging with the Light?

Jared: Yes.

Irene: So, focusing through a spirited body immediately after transitioning didn't affect your ability to merge with the Light.

Jared: It didn't. I connected with other spirited beings and it was through them that I remembered all the possibilities here, which included joining the Oneness.

JARED

CONVERSATION THREE

Irene: You mentioned that you drifted into what you'd call sleep, yet it wasn't. How was it different?

Jared: I was in a neutral, peaceful state, but I had a heightened sense of awareness. I perceived that I wasn't alone. In addition to this calming presence, there were beings caressing and soothing me. It felt like they were recharging my body in the way the sun recharges a solar panel. I later discovered that residue from the illness was still lingering in my non-physical body and they were working to heal this condition.

Irene: Am I hearing you say that after years of experiencing pain in your physical body, your *non*-physical body was affected?

Jared: It's the other way around. Physical disease is first experienced in the spiritual body as a restriction in fluidity. The physical body is a mirror image. The healing that occurred after I left my physical body needed to take place in my spiritual body.

Irene: Why would anyone choose to experience illness or disease as part of their spiritual agenda?

Jared: The purpose of disease varies with each individual. For most people, disease serves to end physical life when the soul's agenda has been fulfilled.

Irene: An exit strategy.

Jared: Yes. Disease also helps people put things in proper perspective and discover what's really important.

Irene: My brother Joe comes to mind. Since suffering a mild heart attack, he's less judgmental and more accepting.

Jared: Precisely. Disease also serves to remind people that control is an illusion and that a greater Power is directing life, providing them with an opportunity to surrender to that Power.

Irene: That's a good example of why it's impossible to judge a situation as "good," or "bad." (Pause) In what other ways do illness and disease serve us?

Jared: When people are no longer able to do things the same way they used to, disease can lead to deeper levels of compassion for oneself, as well as for others who are facing similar challenges.

Irene: Sometimes we need a wake-up call to open our hearts.

Jared: That's true. As people begin to appreciate what they'd once taken for granted, disease can also assist them in accessing gratitude; maybe they hadn't stopped to enjoy the changing colors in the evening sky, or maybe it takes being home with an illness to help them appreciate their family.

Irene: It's all for our highest good.

Jared: Yes, it is. (Pause) Disease can also provide an opportunity to ask for assistance. People are forced to call on the service of others, who are given the chance to help.

Irene: That's *my* Achilles heel. I don't like to impose on others. Anything else?

Jared: Yes. People are often more receptive to the wisdom of their soul as a result of disease.

Irene: That's quite a list. I'll never think of disease in the same way. (Pause) So healing takes place in the spiritual body after leaving the physical body?

Jared: Yes. Once the energy is released from the physical body, it returns to the spiritual body, where it centers itself, creating healing and wholeness. My vibration had slowed considerably because of the restriction and pain in my physical body, so the peaceful, sleep-like state I mentioned not only provided the healing I needed, but also the opportunity to adjust and acclimate to my spiritual body.

Irene: When you refer to the energy being released from your physical body, are *you* that energy?

Jared: I *am* that energy—and so much more.

Irene: What were you aware of when this sleep-like state was complete?

Jared: I attended my memorial service. I realized I was capable of feeling much more joy. Even though I was witnessing the grief, sadness, and tears of my physical family and friends, I felt the joy and love within their sadness.

Irene: How beautiful that you were able to witness their grief within a larger context of love. (Pause) I'm curious about something. When Jerry was sharing his experience, he mentioned that he was greeted by a friend, went on a tour, attended a reunion, and participated in a life review. He didn't mention anything about attending his memorial, although you attended yours.

Jared: Each person's process is based on personal needs. Since the initial experience is determined by what an individual believes, one person might picture Jesus guiding them, while another might picture Buddha. Each person is leaving a different set of circumstances and holding a different set of beliefs about what they expect here in Spirit, so each one requires something different.

While everything you mentioned is available—being greeted, attending one's memorial, the reunion, the tour, and the life review—not all are necessary in order to process the physical experience. Some beings transition and go right into the life review without attending a reunion; their physical experience was so focused on their spiritual agenda that they just want to review their life, learn from it, and return to physical form. It's like your preference, Aunt Irene, to attend a spiritual retreat instead of sipping margaritas on the beach. There's nothing wrong with sipping margaritas on the beach; it's just that the retreat provides a specific structure of support designed to expand your consciousness.

So, some arrive here not needing to be reminded of their soul's agenda. When they transition, it's for the purpose of getting a new body and discovering ways to be more effective. Others who transition think they *are* their physical bodies or their personalities; they need to be reminded that they are much more. *I* did. So, there's a pause. A pause, Aunt Irene, that's challenging to convey without a time reference; it's like the slumber I spoke of previously.

Irene: Let me see if I understand. Not everyone needs the reunion; some people come off the physical playing field, experience their life review, get a little coaching, get a new body, and go right back into the physical game.

Jared: That's right.

Irene: When people are identified with their personalities or their bodies and are unaware of their essence or true nature, sometimes a peaceful pause may be most loving for them.

Jared: Yes.

Irene: I'm also hearing that everyone has a life review.

Jared: Yes, because it's an objective evaluation designed to facilitate your ability to accomplish your soul's agenda, the essence of which is giving and receiving love. When you give and receive love, you're expressing your true nature, which is God.

Irene: What about being greeted by a loved one? Does everyone experience that?

Jared: What happens initially is congruent with what you believe. Because I believed it, the experience manifested. Some people believe they're *nothing* once they pass out of their body, so that's their initial experience. When they feel the emptiness of nothingness and call for help, that's when loved ones appear to assist them.

Irene: You have to be open to the idea of being greeted in order to experience it?

Jared: Everyone has a greeter who patiently waits to be invited into the experience.

Irene: Do all who transition attend their memorial service?

Jared: No. The memorial is a reunion on earth that provides closure with one's physical life and an opportunity to comfort grieving loved ones.

Irene: Why wouldn't someone attend their own memorial?

Jared: There are people whose memorials are uneventful; they may not have had close family or friends. There's always a time, though, when the newcomer revisits their inanimate physical body for the purpose of closure. "Inanimate" isn't really an accurate description, because everything is filled with life. Even after I withdrew my energy from my physical body, it was still teeming with life in the form of bacteria.

Irene: I'm hearing you say that everyone who transitions participates in three processes. The first is witnessing their "inanimate" physical body for the purpose of closure. The second is being met by a greeter or greeters when it's what the person believes will happen or when the person chooses to invite a greeter or greeters into the experience. And the third process that everyone participates in is a life review.

Jared: There's one more: connecting with the soul family for the purpose of setting the agenda in the next life. Everyone sets an agenda in communion with their soul family because everyone in that soul family plays a part in the agenda. Some of the beings in the soul family are already in physical form, like the mother who's going to give birth to the new baby. It's like a soul meeting of the minds; everyone confers, some in physical form and some in Spirit.

Irene: How does the meeting take place for those already in physical form?

Jared: During activities that don't require full attention: sleeping, for example, or daydreaming.

Irene: So, when we transition, we'll experience four processes.

Jared: Correct. All other activities—the memorial, the reunion, and the tour—are optional.

Irene: Would it be accurate to say that some people who transition don't have another physical life?

Jared: Everyone continues in some form or another and assumes the form that best suits their intention.

Irene: Could I choose to be a rock or a cloud?

Jared: Yes, if being a rock or a cloud would meet your soul's agenda. There's no such thing as an inanimate object. Everything is alive. Everything is an expression of the All-In-All. Everything has life force that empowers it. We can be anything we want and express through any form we desire.

JARED

CONVERSATION FOUR

Irene: What happened after your memorial service?

Jared: There was a reunion here with my family and friends to celebrate my arrival and all the experiences I brought with me. Their unconditional love strengthened my awareness of Self as separate from the physical identity I'd held as Jared. It also provided a solid perspective from which to review my life experiences. Reliving aspects of my life—the pain and the times I'd withheld love—could have been distressing without the perspective of Self firmly in place.

Irene: What was your life review like?

Jared: Enlightening. My life was like a play, and I experienced every part. In each scene from my life, I experienced everyone who was present. I was in their skin experiencing me, while I was simultaneously me experiencing them. I missed so much as Physical Jared, particularly how my feelings affected others. By simultaneously being them and being myself, I saw how much we're always affecting one another.

Although I recognized my inability to give and receive love at various times throughout my life, there was no sense of regret, guilt, or punishment during my life review, because I understood fully what had led up to each moment. It all made sense on a spiritual level; each moment provided an opportunity to learn more about myself and about those who'd shared experiences with me. This applied even to people I hadn't noticed: people standing next to me in a grocery line and passersby on the street.

We all affected each other. I embodied each one for as long as they were in my presence, seeing through their eyes, thinking their thoughts, and feeling their emotions. I loved this. As soon as they were gone, I no longer experienced them.

Irene: While I realize the dimension of time doesn't exist for you, from *my* perspective it seems like this process would take a long time.

Jared: I have no frame of reference for the passage of time. Everything happens in a flash.

Irene: What do you mean, *in a flash?*

Jared: It's as fast as going from one thought to the next. It's instantaneous.

Irene: What happens as you have a specific thought?

Jared: If I think of a loved one on earth and I have a desire to connect with them, I'm with them—in a flash. If it's a thought of something I'd like to do, like go for a hike, I'm doing it—in a flash.

Irene: If you have the desire to connect with a physical loved one, do you need their permission?

Jared: Yes, of course. They have to be willing to receive me. If that's not the case, and they're preoccupied or they want privacy, I get the equivalent of a busy signal.

Irene: Do you ever regret having a specific thought?

Jared: No, although I've had a thought of something I *didn't* want. When I found myself experiencing it and realized what was happening, I changed the thought and changed the experience. There's no regret here. Regret requires a sustained consequence, and that requires time.

Irene: Can you elaborate?

Jared: If you, Aunt Irene, attended a party and then regretted being there, you would have already lost a certain amount of time and energy getting there. But if I find myself somewhere I don't want to be, I just think something different, and the scene changes. No time has been lost because there *is* no time. No

126

energy has been lost because energy is infinite and can't be lost.

Irene: Let's take a different example: let's say you were to have an angry thought and you slapped someone, immediately regretting your action.

Jared: First of all, there would need to be a next moment in order to feel regret. And second, it would be impossible for me to slap someone without feeling it myself. All consequences from actions are immediate, because there is no time lapse. Everything is now.

Irene: (Pause) Jared, what do you enjoy most about the Spirit world?

Jared: I love the deep way I can connect with others. When I was in physical form, getting to know someone took time and energy. Learning about someone and "feeling them out" was largely a mental process. It's different here. If I choose to merge with someone, we know each other instantly.

Irene: Do you ever merge with a spirited being and *not* enjoy it?

Jared: How could I not enjoy it? God is infused in everyone.

Irene: What if you merge with someone who's just transitioned and holds negative, fearful thoughts?

Jared: (Laughing) I'm going to let Jerry pinch-hit for me.

Jerry: Let's say I merge with Spirited Bob. The first thing I experience is the shared Essence of who we are. If I want to go deeper and understand how Spirited Bob came to be a unique expression of that Essence, then I merge with his experiences. It's all the same Essence, but everyone, through their unique experiences, rearranges the Essence in different ways. So, there's the Essence and there's the unique way the Essence is arranged, but it's all God Essence, and that's what I'm merging with, which is why it's a joy to merge with everyone.

JARED

CONVERSATION FIVE

Irene: What happened after your life review?

Jared: Rest and relaxation. I visited with others and leisurely explored my surroundings. I slept. I sought out gentle healing. I became reacquainted with all that's available.

Irene: And what's available?

Jared: Everything you can imagine: recreational activities, games, sports, music, classes of all kinds, and so much more. I especially enjoy hiking. And I'm learning how to remove discordant energies from people's non-physical bodies when they first transition, as was done for me.

Irene: Are you happy, Jared?

Jared: I'm very, very happy. I'm in a constant state of acceptance of myself and of everyone.

Irene: Did you ever experience that kind of acceptance as Physical Jared?

Jared: As a child, I fully accepted my circumstances. I accepted my parents and the choices they made as something I'd chosen, too. I was aware of my power and knew I was exactly where I needed to be.

It wasn't until I began comparing my circumstances to those of other kids that I started questioning my situation. Originally, I thought all families were like mine and abided by the same rules; I soon discovered that wasn't the case. Other kids had fewer restrictions than I did. As my perception of the world at large expanded, my perception of my own world contracted. I started pushing up against limitations imposed by my parents: what I could eat, how much television I could watch, which movies I could see—things like that. They often said *no* to things without including me in the decision-making process. My sense of power shifted. I started looking at them as being more powerful because they could usurp my choices. "Because I said so," didn't empower me to develop my reasoning abilities. It's up to parents to help their children understand the consequences of their choices.

Irene: Is the acceptance you're currently feeling similar to the acceptance you felt as a child, before you began comparing yourself to others?

Jared: It's similar. Because of the deep sense of unity here, my experience doesn't include comparisons. Unity is present when we first come into physical bodies and disappears as we grow up, replaced by the learned behavior of feeling separate. Our natural state is to feel one with all. It's easy for children, who are focused in the present; they accept things as they are, and don't compare them to the past or the future.

Irene: I'm confused. As Physical Jared, there was a time when, as a child, you fully accepted your circumstances because you didn't compare them to anyone else's. I also understood you to say that, as Spirited Jared, your experience doesn't include comparisons because of the profound sense of unity. Yet I also heard you say that these two experiences of acceptance are similar, yet not the same.

Jared: The acceptance I felt as a child was the result of *exclusion:* I accepted myself and I accepted my circumstances while excluding the experiences of others. As Spirited Jared, the acceptance I feel is a result of *inclusion:* it includes the perspectives of everyone. Knowing and feeling the experiences of others is unifying.

Irene: That's an interesting distinction.

(Pause) Do you have an understanding of why you chose to

suffer pain as Physical Jared?

Jared: There isn't a simple answer to your question because my physical life as Jared affected many people, and each of them had a different reason or purpose for experiencing me in the way they did. Experience is unified; everything we do affects everyone else, so our physical journey is planned as a group rather than as an individual. My life is still affecting my physical family and friends: when they remember Physical Jared, it means something different to each of them, and the memory—for that moment— changes them. Our effects are as infinite as we are.

Irene: You lived thirty years as Physical Jared. Did you choose your length of stay?

Jared: Yes. I wanted to make a difference and do it quickly. Sometimes a brief life has more impact on people than a long one, because people remember those who die young—and those who die young often live a lot in a short time. I chose a painful process to bring my physical life to an end, and now I can assist others who are choosing pain as their teacher. My mission is to work with people on earth who are similarly restricted by pain and assist them in seeing the gifts inherent in their experience.

Irene: How, specifically, do you work with people who are in pain?

Jared: My goal in this service is to help people take responsibility for their lives so that they can make changes. I work with them as they sleep, assisting them in seeing their experience from a broader perspective. I also work with the energy of the spirited and physical bodies, helping to ease the pain so they can focus on the spiritual aspects of their situation.

I also like working with friends and family in their dreams. I like to keep our connection strong by reminding them that I'm still present. By actively participating in their dream scenes, I assist them in working out issues in our relationship. I strive to convey that our relationship was perfect the way it was, and that what's important is the love we share.

Irene: What *are* dreams?

Jared: Jerry is standing by to answer that question.

Jerry: Dreams are where minds meet. What I mean is that dreams are where your individualized mind meets the universal mind. Everything exists in this universal mind. How you choose to use your dream time is a function of the conscious and unconscious aspects of your mind.

You choose the dream scene as part of the message of the dream, and it has universal as well as personal meaning. If you dream of a mall, for instance, there's the universal meaning everyone relates to—shopping—and a personal meaning that's unique to you: some people loathe shopping malls and others love them. The message relates to how *you* feel abut the mall and to how your thoughts and feelings relate to your physical life.

How your dream unfolds varies with your needs and your intention to meet those needs. Someone whose life is very stressful may use dream time to help release stress; their dreams may include a lot of sex, play, or relaxation. If people request healing before going to sleep, their dreams may be filled with symbolism that guides them toward making changes in their physical life, or it may include hands-on healing of their physical body from their own spirited Self. People who long to connect with loved ones may use their dream time to do so. What you do in your dreams is a reflection of your consciousness.

Everyone dreams. Spirit never sleeps; only the body sleeps. When people don't remember their dreams, their physical body simply isn't capable of bringing the dream time experience to physical reality.

Irene: I set a bedtime intention each night before going to sleep. I state my intention aloud a couple of times, and then I write it down on a pad of paper that I keep on my nightstand. I might state an intention as: "I ask that whatever can be healed by grace while I sleep be healed for my highest good and the highest good of all concerned," or "I want to know how best to proceed with x, y or z." I usually wake up in the middle of the night or first thing in the morning with a dream, which I immediately write down. Sometimes the answer is crystal clear, but more often than not, it requires contemplation. (Pause) Is it true that the soul needs the body to sleep so that it can experience freedom, its true nature?

Jerry: Yes, that's true. While the body sleeps, the soul can withdraw some of its energy and experience other realms. It's like the freedom parents experience when their young children go to visit someone and they have the house to themselves; they're aware of their children and they're within calling distance by phone, but they're free to put their attention elsewhere for a while.

Jared

Conversation Six

Irene: As Physical Jared, you enjoyed studying with Native American elders. Is that still true for you in Spirit?

Jared: Yes, although they haven't lived a long time, and that's what I think of when I hear the word *elders*. They're not any older than any of us, nor have they lived more lifetimes; they've simply made the most of each lifetime by staying focused on their spiritual agenda, which has enabled them to express more love and wisdom. It's like light bulbs: some generate a hundred watts and others fifteen; these beings are of the one-hundred-watt type.

When I sit in their presence, I feel the energy they're transmitting, and it awakens more of mine. Many of them choose not to return to physical form because maintaining the slower vibration of a physical body would be challenging. Instead, they visit the physical plane while focusing through their spirited bodies. They're frequently present anywhere people gather: temples, churches, mosques, sporting events, concerts, and rallies. Their lives are about service and they visit with the intention of raising the vibration of everyone present.

Irene: Can you be with them as much as you want?

Jared: No, I'm not capable of handling the intensity, yet. Even though I'm drawn to them, I respect my capacity. It's like being sensitive to the sun: you don't expose yourself to more than your body can handle.

Irene: Is there anything you miss about being in a physical body?

Jared: I don't miss anything, although I've spoken to others who miss certain sensual experiences that don't exist here, except in memory. I'm content. Everything I could possibly want is available here and now. I would like my family and friends on the physical plane to acknowledge my presence, although not because I miss it; I'd like it more for them than for me. I know I'm very much alive, but they don't. Because people can't experience me with their five senses, they think I don't exist anymore, and they assume there's no place to put their love for me. Loneliness is people falsely believing that no one is there to receive their love. It's our natural instinct to express love, and when we can't, it creates sadness. Being around people who miss me saddens me.

Irene: Help me understand why you're saddened when they're missing you.

Jared: It's my desire to share their experience in that moment, so I'm sad because they're sad.

Irene: I hear what you're saying. (Pause) On a slightly different note, I'm curious as to how you related to your feelings as Physical Jared.

Jared: I thought I *was* my feelings; I thought my feelings were part of my character, my persona. I didn't realize it was possible to allow feelings to move through me without being attached to them or owning them. I know now that I could have allowed my feelings to inform me by creating a pause between what I felt and what I interpreted the feeling to mean. It's during this pause that I could have chosen my response to the feeling. That's why it's wise to count to ten, especially with an emotionally charged feeling like anger.

Irene: That reminds me of something Victor Frankel wrote in *Man's Search for Meaning:* "Between stimulus and response there is a space. In that space is our power to choose our response. In our response lies our growth and our freedom."

Jared: Wise words. (Pause) As Physical Jared, brooding was familiar to me, so people expected a slight frown on my face. I had lots of excuses, justifications, and beliefs that kept my feelings in place, like blaming my family life and my physically challenged body. I held back on experiencing life because I was afraid of the "negative" emotions that might be part of a new experience. If I failed at something new, for example, it resulted in a critical inner dialogue and "negative" feelings that I would then suppress. Life easily flows through us when we're true to our feelings and express them freely. That's not what I did.

I learned to suppress the feelings that my parents were uncomfortable with: sadness, anger, frustration, and grief. They considered these "negative." Holding back what I was feeling consumed a lot of energy. When my cat died, for example, I stuffed my sadness and grief so as not to make my parents uncomfortable. I was never able to fully love a pet after that because I was so afraid I'd have to face those feelings again. Death and grief are as much a part of life as joy and enthusiasm. By holding on to unexpressed emotions year after year, my body reached a point of saturation. There wasn't room for restorative energy.

Irene: That's a good reminder that the way we get through grieving is to cry all our tears.

Jared: Even the people who are consciously aware that their transitioned loved ones are alive may still feel sad because they miss the physical aspects of the relationship. A woman may be very much in communion with her transitioned husband, talking to him every day and hearing his voice in her head, but when she goes to bed at night, she may miss his smell or the touch of his hand.

When a person is chronically sad, their beliefs may be fueling the perception of separation. They may believe that their loved one only existed in physical form and is gone forever, or that they will never see, speak, or be with them again. These beliefs keep their transitioned loved one from fully connecting with them—and it's this full connection that would ease the sadness. It's important for those who are grieving to fully express their sadness in the moment, and allow the emotion to move through them so that it doesn't get stuck in the body. It's also important to challenge the beliefs that may be the source of prolonged and unnecessary suffering.

Irene: That's the primary focus of the work I do. I faciliate people in releasing the beliefs that no longer serve them. Our beliefs generate our thoughts and our thoughts generate our feelings. If we want to *feel* differently, we have to *think* differently, which means that we have to challenge and change our beliefs. Releasing assumptions, limiting beliefs, conditioned patterns, misinterpretations and judgments allows us to grow spiritually. And when we change *within*, life has a way of showing up differently. I've said it before, but it's worth saying again: outer experience is a reflection of inner reality.

(Pause) What would you suggest to someone who wants to strengthen their connection to a transitioned love one?

Jared: I recommend bringing your transitioned loved one closer to you by remembering the loving times you had together. You'll know you've succeeded in connecting when you feel joy, which is the substance of Spirit.

Irene: I joyously—and unexpectedly—connected with my transitioned mother late one afternoon last year. It was the fourth of July, and the air was heavy with the scent of rain; I knew I'd be in the midst of a downpour within minutes. I was walking briskly past a restaurant in our local town center, adjusting the collar of my shirt, when I caught my reflection in the window. I wondered whether I was the one fixing my collar, or was it my mother? Something in my manner was hers. An overhead

loudspeaker played an instrumental version of *Autumn Leaves,*
one of my mother's favorites. I inhaled a deep, delicious breath of
rain-filled air. A red balloon floated upward in the darkening sky.
I experienced that moment—the music, the smell of rain, the red
balloon—in slow motion and with unparalleled depth. I thought,
*I feel your presence, Beba. Thank you for sharing this exquisite moment.
I enjoyed it all the more because you were here. I love you.*

Jared: That's beautiful, Aunt Irene. It's easier for me to connect
with physical loved ones and it's easier for them to experience
our connection when they believe in an afterlife. The specifics of
their beliefs don't matter as long as they believe that life goes on.
When people are quiet, perhaps sitting in meditation or taking a
walk by themselves, they're more receptive to my communication, and I often experience them experiencing me.

Irene: How do you communicate with them?

Jared: If it's my mother, I wrap my arms around her and I merge
with her. If she isn't already thinking about me, she starts to. If
it's a friend, I join them in whatever they're doing. Sometimes, if
they're studying or taking an exam, I whisper encouragement. If
they're challenged or in need of help, I coach them, telling them
how strong and wonderful they are. Sometimes they think of me,
and sometimes they don't. Either way, I've strengthened them.

JARED

CONVERSATION SEVEN

Irene: You mentioned previously that you like to hike. Do you create the mountain path through memory?

Jared: No, I don't have to remember a specific mountain path; all I need is the desire to hike on one. The mountain path is already here, waiting for desire to bring it into form so I can experience it. Desire is like a magnet, which is true in the physical realm, as well.

Irene: Can you elaborate?

Jared: Everything in the physical realm has its origin in the non-physical realm. When I hike on a mountain path here, it's the same mountain path you may choose to hike on there. Of course, it's vibrating faster here and doesn't contain physical material; I never have to worry about stepping on someone's discarded chewing gum or tripping over an aluminum can, because litter doesn't exist in this realm.

Irene: If what's in the physical realm has its origin in the non-physical realm, why don't you also have litter?

Jared: Litter may exist on the surface of the earth, and its components may be *of* the earth, but its elements have been rearranged so that the earth can't digest them: plastic, aluminum cans, disposable diapers, and cigarette butts aren't in harmony with her. They're not her creation. What *she* creates has its origin in the Spirit realm. I don't have to work at creating her creation; the mountain path is already here. This environment supports and sustains her creations through mutual love and appreciation. In

138

contrast, no matter how much I loved my favorite baseball cap, it didn't come with me and it wasn't already here. I can, however, create a spirited version from my memory of it and my love for it. My spirited baseball cap is *my* creation. When I return to the earth for another life, my spirited baseball cap won't remain here like the mountain path, unless I give it to someone who continues to love and enjoy it. In that case, their love will sustain it.

Irene: I'd assumed—and I don't know where this notion came from—that you had to keep imagining something in the non-physical realm to keep it present, but it sounds like once you create it, it remains as long as it's loved and appreciated.

Jared: Yes, it remains until the love is withdrawn from it, just like that favorite blouse in your closet. As long as you love it and keep choosing to wear it, it'll remain with you; if you stop loving it, you'll give it away and someone else will sustain it with their love. It's the same here.

Irene: (Pause) I'd like to hear about how you experience food.

Jared: While all I have here is the memory of the physical experience, I connect with food energetically. The closest thing I could compare it to would be "ingesting an experience." When I was on earth, I remember returning home after attending a retreat. Something inside me had shifted or expanded as a result of ingesting the experience. I had changed. I couldn't put words to the changes, but I'd changed none-the-less. That's what eating is like here: I take another spirited life form into my body, and it changes me. I ingest the experience of a carrot, for example, and it helps me understand the earth because I'm ingesting a part of her creation. I can taste it, but it's a spirited sensation rather than a physical one.

Irene: If the earth is there, litter-free and in all her splendor, why would you choose to come here?

Jared: The physical game. Most everyone wants to play the physical game.

139

JARED

CONVERSATION EIGHT

Irene: Jared, knowing what you know, if you were to return to the earth in physical form, what would you do differently?

Jared: I hear that everyone, as they're being born, tries to remember the totality of life by holding on to what they know is true and attempting to fit it into the limitations inherent in human form. The circuitry of the human body doesn't yet have the capacity to sustain the experience of oneness; it isn't capable of merging with someone and experiencing the connection that comes with unity. The physical body is always expanding and adapting to greater awareness with each birth, though, and that, I'm remembering, is evolution.

Irene: Still, given all that, if you could, how would you choose to be, or what would you choose to do differently?

Jared: I'd make love a priority. Knowing who I am, I wouldn't get caught up in the illusion of people's costumes; I'd see them for who they are and not who they're pretending to be. People pretend to be characters in order to play out certain patterns and discover their true nature.

Irene: And who *are* you? How do you define yourself?

Jared: I am love, part of a bigger whole, and yet I am wholeness itself. This is new to me, and yet it's not. This is what I'm remembering, not what I'm learning.

Irene: And what are you learning?

Jared: There's only discovery and remembering. I'm discovering who I am and remembering that I've always known. There's nothing new to learn, only more to expand into.

Irene: What are you currently discovering or remembering?

Jared: I'm remembering how powerful and expansive I am. I have the potential to be and to experience so much at one time! I can look through another's eyes. I can be in many different places at once. When I was focusing through a physical body, my perspective was narrow; I got caught up in my role as Jared, thinking I was only a personality in a physical body. Coming from that experience into this one is like being set free. I'm constantly being reminded of how big the playing field is and how powerful I am. This is the memory we all strive to keep intact when we're born on earth.

Irene: Do you have a name for where you are, and do others call it by the same name?

Jared: Everyone's experience is different, depending on the person's willingness to see. One labels the place according to one's experience.

Irene: Here on earth, we all seem to agree that we're living on the earth, although we're living in different countries, states, cities, and neighborhoods. How do you label where you are?

Jared: I like the word *heaven.* It expresses the freedom and bliss I experience. Some beings here hold a narrower perspective and suffer self-imposed punishment. The two factors that contribute to their experience are their willingness—or unwillingness—to receive love, and the strength of their beliefs before transitioning. When they tire of their self-imposed pain and ask for help, assistance is provided immediately.

Irene: What I'm hearing you say is that, when we transition from our physical bodies, we choose heaven or hell, not as places, but as states of being that we ourselves create, just as we do here on earth.

Jared: People have a choice about what to experience, based on their own beliefs and expectations.

Irene: On a different note, I'm wondering if my dog Scooter and I will be together after we transition. Do you know where animals go when they transition?

Jared: They change form like we do. No one goes anywhere; everything just changes, and they do, too. We all change into a less-dense form, but there's no *lesser* expression. All life has the same capacity; it's a matter of what each being is choosing to express at any given time. The love the two of you create and share makes heaven right now. Expressing love creates heaven. As you continue loving one another, you'll continue creating heaven in physical form or in spirited form. This is what I'm remembering.

Jared

Conversation Nine

Six weeks elapsed between Conversation Eight and Conversation Nine.

Jared: I've been working extensively on my life here.

Irene: What specifically have you been working on?

Jared: I've been experimenting with ways of loving myself and loving others, both here and in the physical world. I'm discovering what it means to love. When I was limited by my Jared personality, love was relational. I loved people based on the roles they played in my life. I loved my mother in a certain way and my friend in another, compartmentalized according to my expectations of their roles. Loving in physical form was often an effort and a strain; I tried to love others despite their behaviors. I'm discovering that it's not about loving them; it's about allowing love to flow through me.

Irene: What I'm hearing you describe is the distinction between love as an emotion and love as a quality of the Authentic Self, which is a state of consciousness beyond the small self and beyond ego that is characterized by love, peace, and compassion. At the level of Authentic Self, you are a presence for love. You emanate love. It's vibratory and has nothing to do with anything outside yourself.

Jared: That's a great description.

Irene: (Pause) What else have you discovered?

Jared: Everyone is an expression of God, and every moment is unfolding in divine perfection.

Irene: And so it is. When I'm not seeing life that way, I've discovered how to bring myself back to that place of equanimity.

Jared: How?

Irene: I get back to a state of love and peace by identifying the judgments I've placed on the situation—things like, *this is terrible,* or, *this shouldn't be happening.* After identifying these, I practice compassionate self-forgiveness: *I forgive myself for judging what's happening as terrible; I forgive myself for judging that this shouldn't be happening.*

Have you ever noticed that making something *wrong* causes internal disturbance? Self-forgiveness is like a delete button. On an energetic level, it erases the judgment and calls it back, like a "do-over" in a friendly baseball game when you hit the ball in a direction you didn't want it to go. It's like saying, "I judged in error and I'm retracting it, because I really don't know." When we judge, we're pretending to know God's will. Judgment is condemnation. Forgiveness is redemption. Compassion is the outcome.

Jared: How do you know if you've accessed forgiveness?

Irene: It feels like a weight has been lifted or like I've been washed clean. There's a shift in consciousness that's discernable. While the concept of self-forgiveness is in the mind, the experience of self-forgiveness is in the heart. Self-forgiveness is an expression of self-compassion, and it moves me into my heart. Remember when you were a baby and you could do no wrong, or when you were *with* a baby who could do no wrong?

Jared: Sure.

Irene: That's what I'm talking about. And I think that's how God sees us, because God doesn't judge us. Sometimes, as I'm practicing self-forgiveness and holding an intention to move into my heart, I think of myself as that baby—or I think of my children as babies—and my heart expands. My priority is acceptance—of myself, of others, and of what is. The best thing I can do to contribute to the planet is to resolve my own issues as quickly as possible, accessing the highest level of consciousness available to me. When I practice self-forgiveness, I'm cultivating an attitude of self-compassion. If my feelings are hurt, for example, I realize that I took something personally or I misinterpreted something. And so, I forgive myself for having bought into the idea that, when I don't hear from my son on a regular basis, it means I'm not important to him. I forgive myself for having bought into the belief that I'm not important.

Jared: (Pause) Your kids are lucky, Irene.

Irene: Thank you, Jared.

Jared: My mother's not yet here in Spirit, but when she arrives and drops the role of being my mother, I'll be able to love her through the Oneness, which doesn't require compartmentalized love.

Irene: How would your love for her change?

Jared: The love that's shared here is based on our capacity to love and be loved, without limits or qualifiers or roles or expectations. I've been remembering to go beyond the self-imposed limitations I created as Physical Jared. My belief that I wasn't good enough, for example, limited my ability to love and be loved, because I identified myself as someone undeserving of love. My expression of love was also limited by my roles. I would have liked to have shown greater physical affection for my friend Rick, for example, but I felt inhibited by cultural norms. When I meet a friend here, I don't need to identify them in a particular way and base my love on that definition. I feel love pour through me and into them, and I feel love pour through them and into me.

Irene: Jared, knowing what you know now, how would you love differently if you were here on earth, given the physical constraints of a physical body?

Jared: That's a great question, Irene. I'd remember that our capacity to love is an ongoing process. It's not about *getting* more love—it's about *allowing* more love. If I were on earth today, I'd live a more virtuous life; I'd choose patience, compassion, and acceptance, first and foremost with myself. I'd practice loving myself by respecting my choices. I'd throw perfectionism out the window and allow myself to make mistakes.

When we love ourselves fully, love flows through us to others. If we're undernourished from having ignored our own needs, it's a strain to nourish others. I now understand the self-love movement on the planet. Self-love creates the foundation that allows us to love *more.*

Unloving behaviors are passed down generationally from parents to children because parents can only love their children as much as they love themselves. Those places where they've restricted the flow of love to themselves are automatically passed on to their children, who get the message early on that parts of *them* are unlovable. These places are mirror reflections of the places the parents themselves consider unlovable. I saw this in my life review in relationship to my own mother and father. My job, then, is to find these places within myself that I consider unlovable—*and love them.*

Irene: May I offer something for your consideration?

Jared: Sure.

Irene: It's my experience that the only reason we consider those places unlovable is that we've judged them—as bad, wrong, shameful, unacceptable, or undesirable. Healing doesn't come as a result of loving those parts *in spite of* their unlovability. Healing comes from releasing the judgment that they were ever *unlovable.* And we do that by forgiving ourselves for the judgment we placed, for the belief we bought into, or for the misinterpretation we made. Want to give it a whirl from the perspective of Physical

Jared?

Jared: Sure. I forgive myself for having bought into the belief that any part of me was ever unlovable.

Irene: Anything else?

Jared: I forgive myself for having bought into the misinterpretation that I had to be different in order to be loved. (Pause) Thanks for the reminder, Aunt Irene.

Irene: You're so welcome. (Pause) Whenever I release what no longer serves me, it creates a space that I fill with loving truth that reflects who I am now. I invite you to fill the space you've created with your own truth.

Jared: I Am Love.

Irene: And so it is.

Jared: (Pause) All of life is perfectly orchestrated for us. By accepting it without judgment and allowing it, we learn to love ourselves more deeply. That's where it always leads.

Irene: I like that direction.

Jared: Each generation has the opportunity to heal more and more places where love has been restricted. *That's* evolution. Sometimes, these unhealed places go on for generations until someone wakes up and starts to change. Unresolved patterns cling to us whether we're in physical bodies or not, because they're ours to heal. We sponsored them. By choosing our specific parents, we chose to be responsible for healing the particular patterns that came with them.

JARED

CONVERSATION TEN

Irene: How did suppressing your feelings affect your physical body?

Jared: I mentioned previously that my parents were uncomfortable with certain emotions—disappointment, frustration, sadness, grief, and anger—so, as Physical Jared, I judged these as bad and didn't allow myself to fully express them. Energy moves through the body when we express emotions. Judging them as bad stopped the flow, and instead of being released, the energy of these emotions stagnated in my body, like water trapped in a clogged drain. I spent more and more energy trying to keep these emotions at bay, yet they continued to build up. This stagnant energy was gumming up the works and eventually expressed itself as pain and illness. It's the flow of emotion that keeps the life force moving smoothly through our bodies. Emotion is energy in motion.

Tremendous amounts of energy were freed up when I was released from my physical form. I not only had more energy to carry my baggage—the wounds I brought with me that needed love in order to be healed—but there were also beings here with tremendous amounts of energy who were more than willing to help.

Some people choose to hold onto their baggage because they think it's who they are. I saw this in physical form when I would meet people who identified themselves with their aches, pains, and traumas. They would immediately tell me about their medical condition or their childhood abuse. They claimed their baggage and made it their identity. This doesn't necessarily change right away when they leave their physical bodies, because it's who they think they are. Some, on the other hand, are willing to receive immediate assistance; they're tired of carrying their baggage alone, and they recognize that, while it belongs to them, it isn't who they are. (Laughing) There are also plenty of baggage handlers who are willing to assist.

Irene: What advice, if any, would you give someone preparing to transition?

Jared: The process of letting go of the body is happening non-stop all over the planet. It's an integral part of the physical journey. Remember that.

Irene: I've so enjoyed our conversations, Jared. Even though I could continue indefinitely, I have to conclude for now. Is there anything you'd like to say in closing?

Jared: What a blessing it is for me to give voice to what's not readily heard, and in so doing, to bring the power of Spirit into physical form. As I spoke, you may have conceived of me as the Physical Jared you knew, but I'm so much more. My hope is that you'll recognize that you, too, are much more. My heart, in all its fullness, embraces you. We've got a date to meet in the Oneness.

BEBA

My Mom

1929 – 2003

Some of the most memorable conversations with my mom took place over games of gin rummy. I remember a game six years ago while we lazed around on my mother's king-size bed. She laid down a seven of hearts.

"When I was a little girl," she said, "my mother told me that, when we die, that's the end."

Nobody else would have noticed the way the muscles in her right hand tightened or the way she bit the inside of her lower lip. But I did. I knew my mother.

"That was *her* perspective, *her* belief," I said, putting my cards down. "If the thought makes you fearful, choose another."

She drew a card. "Gin," she said.

BEBA

CONVERSATION ONE

Irene: Beba, what did you experience when you released your last breath on earth?

Beba: I'd been sleeping. I awoke, disoriented, and I couldn't place where I was. The colors were different, defined and radiant, so I thought I was dreaming—but it was so *real*. I felt self-conscious and embarrassed when I realized family members were present; I was accustomed to being in control of my surroundings, and I had no memory of how I got where I was.

Irene: And where were you?

Beba: I was at my funeral, overwhelmed by the love coming from everyone and wondering whether I deserved it. I felt someone kiss me on the cheek. It was my mother. I looked into her eyes and felt like a little girl again. She told me what had happened, and I remembered a scene with family members standing around my body.

Irene: The scene you're remembering was probably the day before your funeral. Steve (my brother), Deni (my niece), and I were at the mortuary, and at one point, we were all gathered around your body.

I was there to dress your body for the burial. I thought this was something only morticians did, but when my brother Joe presented me with the option, I instinctively agreed. I hadn't seen you in a few weeks, and I wanted to see you one last time to have closure. I'd heard closure was a good thing to have.

I was sitting in the lobby, nervously biting on my cuticles, when a mortuary employee approached. He asked if I was Irene, and when I nodded, he introduced himself as Eli. He told me to "come right this way," and I followed him down a long corridor, your flannel nightgown, a pair of cotton socks, and a bottle of tuberose-scented moisturizing lotion in hand.

We stopped in front of a door about midway down the hall. He told me that your body was on a gurney inside the room, and asked if I needed any assistance. When I said *no*, he turned the knob and opened the door. The gurney was in the center of the room. I had to assume it was your body, because it was hidden beneath a white sheet. Eli said, "Take as long as you need." I heard him turn and walk away, but my eyes were glued on the gurney. I entered the room and closed the door behind me.

I stood quietly for a moment or two before cautiously moving toward your body. With each successive, slow-moving step, I seemed to lose a decade of hard-won maturity. By the time I reached the gurney, I felt all of ten years old. *You could sit up at any moment,* I thought, *and that would scare the bejesus out of me.* Growing up with three prankster-loving brothers makes a girl sensitive to that kind of thing.

I stood frozen for what seemed like several minutes. An image of the Three Stooges came to mind as I *slowly* . . . inch by inch . . . began walking backwards to the door, my eyes riveted on the white sheet. "Ooookaaay, all-righty then," I said, as I grappled for the doorknob. I turned it and walked briskly down the hallway to the lobby, giggling all the way.

This habit of giggling whenever I was nervous had gotten me into trouble more than once. I remember sitting at my desk in my fifth grade classroom when the announcement, "President Kennedy has been shot," came over the loudspeaker. It sent me into full-out laughter. I can still see the disbelieving, critical stares of my classmates in my mind's eye.

I composed myself as best I could, and when I reached the lobby, I asked Deni if she would lend a hand. She was up and out of her chair without a moment's hesitation.

We returned to the room and walked up to the gurney. Deni stood on one side and I on the other. I confessed to her that I was afraid you were going to sit up. "Let's pull the sheet back on the count of three," she said. I attributed her ease to the fact that she didn't have siblings.

I was surprised to see how peaceful your face looked. It was obvious that you weren't there anymore. Your body was there, but you weren't—and it was okay.

I'd never touched a dead body. I thought it would be creepy, but it wasn't. Your body was cold, and your limbs were heavy. Deni and I chatted as we applied the tuberose-scented lotion to your body, something you'd done on a daily basis for as long as I could remember. We were both so comfortable; you would have thought we were preparing a Thanksgiving turkey for the oven and not your body for the burial.

When we finished, I asked Deni to step outside so I could have a private moment. As the door closed behind her, I let out a long sigh. I felt complete. I said a blessing and told you that your spirit was free to soar. I told you to travel safely. The last thing I said was, "I love you."

That was it. Steve returned to the room with Deni, and that's when we all stood around your body.

Beba: Seeing my lifeless body made my transition real, as well. That's when it registered that my physical life was over.

Irene: Wait a minute. You said you awoke at your funeral with your transitioned mother telling you what had happened, and as she did, you remembered a scene with family that had taken place the day before?

Beba: I didn't just remember. The memory took me there.

Irene: You went from being at your funeral to going back in time to an experience that happened *prior* to your funeral?

Beba: Yes. The funeral was like a dream. Seeing my lifeless body *before* the funeral provided closure. Time doesn't march in one direction here. My thoughts control the direction in which I go, whether into the past or into a possible future. In *that* moment, I traveled back to a time before the funeral.

Irene: Then what happened?

Beba: It would be more appropriate to ask, "Where did you think next?"

Irene: Where *did* you think next?

Beba: I was drawn to the love I felt coming from my physical family. Of course, they were also feeling grief, guilt, regret—and, I'm happy to say—joy. I looked beyond their tears, into their hearts, and I saw the place I occupied in each of their lives. I saw what I'd given to them and what I'd withheld. I also realized it hadn't been all about *me*. There were times I'd been critical of myself, beating myself up because I thought I wasn't enough. But it hadn't been about me; it had also been about their inability to receive me. All those times I'd judged myself inadequate, I'd denied myself the love I so deserved.

I wanted to show everyone how grateful I was for the love they'd given me, to say, "Wipe your tears."

"This is how people let go," my mother reminded me. And I remembered.

Experiencing their sadness was difficult for me; I'd never felt people's sadness so directly. It was *their* sadness, yet I wasn't feeling it vicariously; I was experiencing it as mine.

Irene: Where did your thoughts take you next?

Beba: I had thoughts of my dad, and there he was.

Irene: Did your thoughts take you to him or bring him to you?

Beba: He appeared right where I was. I didn't go anywhere.

Irene: What happens if you think of *me* right now?

Beba: It depends on how I think of you. If I have an intentional thought to connect with you as you are now, I become part of your current environment. If I have an intentional thought to connect with you when you were a little girl, I set the scene, and you become a part of that scene. But I'm not traveling over distance to where you are, and you're not traveling over distance to where I am. It's all done through thought. If, for example, I have an intention to connect with you when you were twelve—in order to work something out or to simply enjoy being with you—I can think of you in any environment that facilitates my intention: the home we lived in, for example, or the family car. Everything already exists. It's our intention that gives us access to it.

Irene: Am I hearing you say that if you wanted to connect with me as I am in this moment, you'd have an intention to connect and imagine yourself in my current location?

Beba: I wouldn't have to imagine. All I would have to do is think of you, and wherever you are would come into focus. Your presence would create the scene, and I'd become a part of that scene, whether in your car, the kitchen, or your office. It's not hard. It's as easy as remembering your best friend sitting in their living room, except this doesn't require memory. If I'd never seen your home, I'd still see whatever room you're in, because your physical environment is the background and a part of you—and I become a part of *it*. If you were reading a magazine in your bedroom and I ended up in the kitchen, I wouldn't have a very good visit with you. I go where you are.

Irene: I remember Jerry saying that he can visit physical loved ones only when he's invited because it's a function of free will. In other words, you can only visit me when I invite you, *right?*

Beba: (Laughing) That's true. As your mother, I felt I had the right to enter your space without asking first. Now I visit *only* when invited, *only* when you're receptive to me. If you hear a song and think of me, that's an invitation for me to share that moment with you. If I sense you need comfort, I know—by knowing you and feeling you—whether my presence would be helpful or not. If it would be helpful, *that's* my invitation. So it's true that I visit only when you're open and receptive to my presence, but I don't need a formal invitation. You don't have to say, "Beba, I invite you to join me this Sunday morning." I sense your receptivity to me in your energetic field and that's the invitation.

When I receive a call for guidance from a physical family member, I respond by holding a loving space for them. It's not up to me to whisper what they should or shouldn't do; I just hold them in a loving embrace and allow their own wisdom to guide them.

I enjoy watching my family at play. I haven't missed a family event since I've been out of physical form. (Laughing) I was the life of the party at your wedding. What would a party be without me?

BEBA

CONVERSATION TWO

Irene: You mentioned earlier that you thought of your dad, and there he was. What specifically did you think?

Beba: I wasn't aware of a specific thought. When he appeared, I realized he matched a comfortable image from my childhood. My father had always been reserved—uptight, you might say—and I was the opposite—emotional and unpredictable. He liked steady and dependable, and I liked being spontaneous and stirring things up. Our personalities clashed when I reached puberty, so the comfortable image was from a time when I was much younger.

Irene: You participated in a variety of programs in order to heal the negative patterns you'd adopted from your parents. I assume it had a qualitative impact when you reunited with your parents in Spirit.

Beba: Oh, yes. It was work that had to be done. I picked up here where I left off there with *all* my relationships, including my relationship with myself. Healing is taking place whether we're in physical or spirited form. Life is always moving to unite us. Our work is to heal the places within that keep us feeling separate.

Irene: How does healing in spirited form differ from healing in physical form?

Beba: It's easier in Spirit. When I'm reflecting on my life and assessing my ability to love and be loved, I'm doing it in an atmosphere of unconditional love and acceptance. Shortcomings are simply places where I'm withholding love, and while I see them, my focus is on the attributes required to strengthen and heal them.

Unconditional love was always available on earth, which is something I realized in my life review, but I wasn't always able to receive it. I was so busy judging how life *should* have been that I didn't allow it to be the way it was. My judgments blocked the flow of love that life had for me. With my attention often focused on problems instead of solutions, I was busy judging my wounds instead of applying the love needed to heal them. I was busy regretting my shortcomings instead of focusing on my strengths.

Irene: I appreciate your insight. (Pause) As Physical Beba, you shared a concern that there would be *nothing* when you transitioned, which was a belief you adopted from your mother. Since Jerry said that we initially experience whatever we believe we'll experience, I wondered whether you initially experienced nothingness.

Beba: No, I didn't. I was sleeping more during the last days of my physical life, and during that time, I caught brief glimpses of the other side. Every time I awakened from one of these glimpses, my fear of the nothingness diminished further and I felt more at peace with life—and death. I know now that these kinds of experiences are common and help people to prepare for spirited life. Resistance to the unknown can make transitioning more challenging than it needs to be.

Irene: What did you believe at that point?

Beba: I knew there must be *something* after death; so many people in my life had passed on, and I wondered where they'd gone. I never gave much thought to where *I* was going as much as I did to where everyone else had gone. I wondered where I'd see them and what it would look like. I pictured each one having their own little house where I'd visit them. By the way, this isn't far from the truth; people *do* create environments similar to houses and they personalize them with memorabilia from their last physical life—a favorite wall hanging, for example, or a colorful vase. They remember the item and, with focused thought, recreate a spirited version.

I never imagined people as being so much more than when I knew them on earth. When I thought of my father, for example, I thought he'd always have the same strict and serious personality of my father; I never imagined him beyond that. This was true for everyone who'd transitioned before me: I thought of them only as I'd known them. I assumed, for instance, that my aunt— the one who owned that tacky furniture—would have the same tacky décor when I saw her again. I was surprised when I saw how light, airy, and modern it was.

Irene: That's interesting. I just realized that I think of you only in terms of how I knew you as my mother.

Beba: And you get what you expect. I come through right now as you expect me to come through, saying things in ways that remind you of me. But I'm *so much more.*

Irene: Tell me about the *so much more.*

Beba: I've expressed through many personalities in many lifetimes on earth. I've experienced poverty and disease. I was a leper. I was covered in gold and jewels as the daughter of a great king. I was *your* daughter. All of these personalities brought forward different aspects of my spiritual body. There are similarities in all of them, because that's what makes me the unique expression that I am.

Irene: What are some of the similarities?

Beba: One constant in all my personalities has been the energy of non-conformity. I shake up the norm. (Laughing) Non-conformity has gotten me killed a couple of times. Irreverence is not for the faint of heart.

Irene: Will you choose another constant when this one is complete?

Beba: I suppose I could choose another, but I'm having too much fun with this one. It's a powerful catalyst for change, and I'm getting better and better at it.

Irene: Beba, given what you know now, how would you choose to live differently if you were in physical form on earth today?

Beba: I'd leave room for people to change and be different from how I knew them, because they're so much more. When I was on earth, I saw people in one of two ways: I either saw them as they wanted me to see them or I saw what I wanted to see. If I were on earth today, I'd look beyond people's presentations. (Laughing) Most people play three different characters: the person they present to the world; the person they are when they're by themselves—which, by the way, could be someone who's depressed but is the life of the party when in the public eye; and the third, the one they themselves may not even know, their true nature, the one who observes the other two, the one closest to the soul—the knower. I'd remind myself that there's more to each person than meets my eye.

BEBA

CONVERSATION THREE

Irene: Where did your thoughts take you when you were no longer thinking about the funeral?

Beba: I was taken on a wonderful tour of my new surroundings.

Irene: Who took you?

Beba: Someone I hadn't known during my lifetime as Physical Beba. She looked like someone from a fairy-tale—golden hair and a loving presence. She said she was a spirited friend of mine who'd been in physical form thousands of physical years before. Rather than reincarnate, she'd chosen to remain a spiritual helper, and said she was one of mine. She didn't *look* familiar but she *felt* familiar; her presence was comforting, and while I recognized the feeling of comfort, I couldn't associate it with any one particular moment on earth. As I thought that, I heard her in my thoughts, reminding me that she'd been there for me during times when I'd needed love, help, and an extra boost of comfort.

Irene: What did your new surroundings look like?

Beba: Just as I'd imagined, I started in what looked like a neighborhood. (Laughing) Imagine that! There were paths leading to individual dwellings. People smiled and waved as they emerged from their dwellings and onto the path to meet me. I immediately recognized friends and family from my most recent life—some from my childhood and some from my adult life—but it took longer to recognize and place others. As I greeted each one, I remembered the specific lifetime we'd shared. I was told there would be a gathering—a welcome home party—and they would all be there.

During my life review, I began to see how rich and full my physical life had been. So many people had participated in my life—people I'd hardly known! I saw how afraid I'd been and how fear had kept me from connecting with and learning about them. I categorized people. I labeled them and judged them. I thought, *Why get to know* him? *He's just the person behind the meat counter.* Or, *She's just a receptionist doing her job; I don't need to give* her *the time of day.* I saw these people regularly and knew their faces, but I never bothered to learn their names because of my judgments.

Irene: I can relate to what you're saying. A few years back, I became aware that I had a limiting belief about my interactions with service providers. I believed that getting my needs met was the sole purpose of the interaction. It was all about *me.*

Once I became aware of how limiting this was, I committed to making the *quality* of my interactions as important as producing whatever other result I was after—making an appointment to see a doctor, for example, or resolving an error on a bill. I committed to leaving service providers in better shape than I'd found them. I did this first and foremost by being in touch with my own divine nature. It worked so well that, before long, I was looking for opportunities to make a positive difference in *all* my interactions by acknowledging and appreciating others. Now I'm committed to win-win interactions; if it's not win-win, it's no win at all.

Beba: I love that. (Pause) I was afraid of being hurt and rejected, so I kept people away and didn't let them into my life. I kept myself separate by thinking I was a little better than they were, a little smarter and wiser; but underneath the pretense of supe- riority was the fear that I was inferior and inadequate—a misconception, of course, but such misconceptions can be challenging to heal because we assume they're true. Here in this unconditionally loving space, all that *isn't* love stands out. In an environment like this, it's easy to recognize anything unloving. I've been healing my feelings of inadequacy because they stand out in the same way lies stand out amidst truth. I've stopped believing the lies, and I've started believing the truth, going *with* the flow instead of against it.

Irene: So these patterns of keeping people away and the misconceptions about your worth initially transitioned with you.

Beba: Yes, of course. As Physical Beba, I thought they were part of my personality. After transitioning, I could easily see them for what they were—unhealed misconceptions—and I began working to heal them. Most of these misconceptions originated when I was a little girl. Here in Spirit, I can re-experience a situation that prompted a misconception and gain understanding, because I have access to the perspectives of all the participants. As I re-experience any given situation, the love that was available is intensified, and I *feel* it. So if I'm reliving an argument with my father, for instance, I not only experience *his* perspective, I also experience the love that was present—the love I didn't originally allow myself to feel. When I focus on the love in any situation, the fear rises to the top—like fat rises to the top of chicken stock—ready to be skimmed away.

Irene: How interesting. I'm doing similar self-healing work. The belief that *I* was inadequate was a misinterpretation I, too, made when I was a girl. I've been working with an incident that happened when I was eleven. Would you like to hear about it?

Beba: Yes, please.

Irene: It was the weekend before my brother Joe's Bar Mitzvah. I didn't know it at the time, but you were struggling with depression. You'd been in bed for days. You sent me shopping with Dad's secretary to get something to wear to the event. I don't remember what store we went to, but I found something I liked. When I returned home, I walked into your bedroom and pulled my new outfit from the bag: a blue pleated skirt and a matching white sweater with blue trim around the zippered front.

I felt proud. I was excited to show it to you. I said, "Look what I got!"

But you threw the skirt on the floor, shouting, "What's *wrong* with you? You can't wear *that!*"

I just stood there. You shook your pillow and hit it a couple of times, then you started tossing and turning to get comfortable.

I picked up the skirt. *What is wrong with me?* I thought. *How could I have been so off base as to think this was beautiful?*

At the bar mitzvah, I avoided eye contact and hid out in the bathroom.

I spent a lifetime avoiding social events. When there was no other option but to attend, I didn't just question the appropriateness of my attire: I questioned whether *I* was appropriate. And I never was.

Healing this issue was a process that literally spanned three decades. It began with learning to acknowledge, own, and express my feelings; but it wasn't until this past year that the issue was completely resolved.

Beba: I'd like to hear more.

Irene: We did an exercise in one of my Spiritual Psychology classes in which we were encouraged to connect with our younger selves. What came forward was the eleven-year-old me, Ireenie. I used a Gestalt technique and invited Ireenie to speak, giving her permission to fully express her feelings. She wasn't accustomed to doing this; she'd learned early in life that saying what she felt resulted in unpleasant consequences. I assured her that she could say anything she wanted. She was pissed at you. I told her to speak to you as if you were there. I encouraged her to let it out. And she did.

She didn't just speak to you, she screamed, "I hate you!" She said that if you'd taken her shopping, she never would have bought that stupid outfit. She wanted to know why you were always in bed and why you couldn't get up long enough to take her yourself. She compared you to her friend Janet's mom, who took good care of Janet. Ireenie said you were a good-for-nothing mom. She cried. She wanted to know why you never wanted her. She thought you didn't want her because there was something wrong with her.

During the exercise, I listened with heartfelt compassion to Ireenie; I was grateful that she was getting it out. When she spoke of you not wanting her, I couldn't help but wonder, *Did you ever want her? Did you ever want* me? I flashed on that time when I was sixteen and you told me, in the midst of an argument, that you'd tried using a hanger to abort your pregnancy with me.

Beba: (Pause) I'm so very sorry. (Pause) I was a young new mother. Your father was having an affair. I felt trapped. I didn't know what else to do.

Irene: (Pause) Having been a single mother myself at nineteen, I remember how trapped, desperate, and hopeless *I* often felt.

(Pause) I don't remember whether I ever told you, but I was raped at gunpoint when I was twenty-four. It resulted in a pregnancy that I aborted. My son David was five at the time.

Beba: Oh, my darling, it's every mother's dream to protect her children from pain, something that's difficult to do when she's consumed by her own pain. *I* was. You did share this with me, and I felt such anguish and guilt that, instead of opening my heart and reaching out to you, my own unresolved feelings overwhelmed me. I was angry that I couldn't protect you. I understood what it was like to live with a decision to end a life, because even though my attempt to abort the pregnancy had failed, I'd made the decision. With all of these emotions swirling around, it was difficult to be the mother you needed me to be.

(Pause) I wondered what this event would have looked like had I not been so immersed in pain. So, here in Spirit, I chose to change and relive the moment you told me that you'd been raped. In the new scenario, I allowed my love for you to be stronger than my pain. I embraced you when you cried. When your crying subsided, we talked about the challenge of being a woman—not just as mother to daughter, but also as woman-to-woman and friend-to-friend. I shared my own experiences with you. I told you, for example, of times in my own life when I'd agreed to have sex when I hadn't really wanted to, and how I felt like I was being raped. This was my way of helping us heal.

(Pause) I was able to get a glimpse of what my life would have been like without the fear, and it was freeing.

Irene: As a mother myself, I can certainly relate to wanting to protect my children and keep them safe. I've had my share of moments during which I, too, responded with my own unresolved pain rather than with love. I, too, have lived with a mother's guilt that I could have and should have done better. Now I know that I was always doing the best I knew how to do and I'm filled with compassion instead of self-condemnation.

Beba: (Pause) Tell me more about your healing process with Ireenie.

Irene: After Ireenie had gotten all her anger out, I thought about everything she'd said from my adult perspective. I realized that she blamed you, she blamed God, and she even blamed herself. She knew nothing about taking responsibility. What she didn't know at the time and what I've come to understand as an adult, is that, until one takes responsibility, one is powerless to change.

Taking responsibility includes owning judgments, and her judgments were clear: *There's something wrong with me. I'm no good. I can't do anything right. I can't trust myself. I'm a social moron. My mom doesn't love me. Janet has a good mom. Good moms take care of their daughters and take them shopping. I have a stinky mom. This shouldn't be happening. Things should be different. God must have screwed up.*

Beba: That took courage.

Irene: It didn't feel like courage; it just felt like the next step in my healing process. But thank you for the acknowledgment.

I saw that none of those things were true, yet I recognized how the eleven-year-old me would have thought so, given who and where she was at the time. So I began to compassionately forgive myself for the judgments I'd placed on myself, on you, and on God.

I forgave myself for having bought into the misconception that there was something wrong with me. I forgave myself for judging myself as no good. I forgave myself for buying into the belief that I couldn't do anything right. I forgave myself for judging myself as a social moron. I forgave myself for buying into the misinterpretation that you didn't love me. I forgave myself for judging you as a stinky mom. I forgave myself for judging that this shouldn't have happened or that things should have been different. I forgave myself for buying into the misperception that God had screwed up.

If I'm not in a position to judge anyone, there's never anything to forgive anyone for, because in order to forgive someone, I first have to judge them as wrong. But what if there *is* no *wrong*? What if people are just doing the best they know how to do? What if something that looks like an injustice in this lifetime is karma from a previous lifetime, working itself out? Holding this lifetime within a larger context helps me to let go of how I think things *should* be so that I can accept what *is*.

From this perspective, I'm the only person I ever have to forgive, for placing judgment—on myself, on another, on a situation, on life, or on God—in the first place. I didn't have to forgive you, Beba, because you didn't do anything wrong. You were doing the best you knew how to do. I had to forgive myself for having bought into the misinterpretation that I was worthless, that you didn't love me, that God had screwed up, and that it was all *your* fault. I blamed you for everything that I judged as wrong in my life.

Compassionately forgiving myself created space for the old beliefs to be replaced by new ones: *I am lovable and loving, always doing the best I know how to do—and so is everyone else. I am smart and tenacious. I am a divine expression of the beneficent universe. I choose to learn and grow from every experience. I had the ideal mom, given what I came to heal and what I came to learn. God is everywhere and in everything. This is a beneficent universe.*

(Pause) I had always thought this shopping "trauma" never should have happened. I thought it was a mistake and that I would have turned out better if I had been spared the experience. Surely, I would have been the person I desired if only this hadn't happened . . . wouldn't I? I'd always believed this to be true, but I discovered it was simply an assumption. Without this assumption, regret couldn't exist.

We automatically assume that whatever we regret—the event that did or didn't happen, or the thing we did or didn't do—would have turned out better than what actually happened. But how can we know that? What if there are no mistakes? What if every event that happens, no matter how it looks, holds a beneficent intention for our highest good? What if nothing happens by coincidence, and everything is unfolding in divine perfection?

Beba: You are so courageous and so wise, Irene. As Physical Beba, instead of healing the wounds on the inside, I maintained certain behaviors on the outside: shopping, eating, and watching television. These were ways I distracted myself from the emptiness I was feeling. Had I recognized that I had the power to heal the wounds of un-lovability with self-forgiveness, acceptance, and love, I would have made *that* my life's priority. The more we're able to bring love to the places that hurt, the more we're able to love ourselves and others and to receive the love that's always available. Had I gotten to the core of this misconception and healed it, I would have come into relationships providing love instead of seeking it.

Beba

Conversation Four

Irene: I'd like to share another experience with you that I've resolved and healed.

Beba: I'd like to hear about it.

Irene: I was working on resolving an issue, and as part of a Spiritual Psychology self-counseling session, I revisited an experience I had when I was seven. We'd recently moved into the house on Purvis Street. It was the middle of the night, and I awoke to the sound of loud, angry voices. You and Dad were arguing. I heard a thump on your carpeted bedroom floor. My thoughts raced. Was it the Italian hand-blown glass ashtray that weighed a ton or the glass clown that was even heavier? Before I could figure it out, you ran into the hall bathroom. I saw you from my bed. The door slammed. Dad was on all fours after you. I'd never seen him crawling on the floor like that. He hadn't had time to put on his orthopedic shoes, and as you well know, he couldn't walk without them.

He pounded the door, screaming at you to open it.

I ran to my closet and slid the door closed. Huddled in the corner like an earthquake duck-and-cover victim, I reached up and yanked my winter coat over my head. I begged God to please send someone to save me, to please send an angel.

When I awoke the next morning, I was in a fetal position and my pajamas were drenched in urine.

Beba: How terrifying that must have been.

Irene: It was. Over the years, I'd worked with this incident using a variety of therapeutic modalities, but I knew I hadn't gotten to the heart of it. So, as part of my master's coursework, I used the Gestalt technique of inviting seven-year-old Ireenie to speak.

Ireenie asked me why God had abandoned her. She thought it was because she was bad. She said she'd asked God to send an angel, but no one had come. Ireenie was afraid that Dad was going to kill you, and then maybe come and kill *her.* I was flabbergasted.

I imagined holding Ireenie close, stroking her hair, and humming a lullaby to her. I embraced her for several minutes until she felt safe. I let her know that I had forgotten just how terrifying the experience had been. I asked her if she was willing to talk about it. She said, "sure."

I told her that it was impossible for God to abandon her, because she and God were not separate. I suggested that all she had to do when she wanted to find God was go inside and find the love and joy. *"That's* God," I said. "God is inside you. So, can you see how it would be impossible for God to ever abandon you?"

Ireenie was amazed that God likes to play hide-and-seek. She giggled and said God was silly.

Ireenie believed that the reason no one had come to help was because she was bad. She thought maybe it was *her* fault that you were fighting. She thought she should have been able to fix the problem and make it better.

I thanked Ireenie for sharing this with me. "It wasn't your fault and you weren't bad," I said. I explained that your fight with Dad had nothing to do with her, that she didn't cause the problems in your relationship and wasn't responsible for them.

And then I lowered my voice to a whisper and told her I wanted to share a secret. "I want you to always remember this, *okay?"* And she told me she would. I said, "God doesn't see you as bad because God doesn't judge you." She smiled and said she would never forget; she told me that she had a really good memory and was the best in her class at remembering her times tables. "Being loving and kind is your nature," I told her. "It's impossible to *be* bad. But if you choose to *believe* you're bad, and you act badly, the kind and generous universe will let you experience that for as long as you want."

She wanted to know why the kind and generous universe hadn't sent her an angel.

It was a good question. I told Ireenie I didn't know why, but I *did* know I wouldn't be who I am today if that angel had appeared.

"My life would have been totally different," I said. "And I trust that somehow it was for my highest good and the highest good of everyone involved. Maybe I won't know why it happened the way it did until I review my life. I'm sure looking forward to finding out!"

I told her how much I love her.

I forgave myself for having bought into the misinterpretation that God had abandoned me. I forgave myself for believing that I was ever bad, unlovable, inadequate, or unworthy. I released the belief that I had somehow caused the problems between you and Dad. I let go of the judgment that things shouldn't have happened the way they did. I forgave myself for buying into the illusion that I was separate from God.

I chose new beliefs: *You and Dad were doing the best you knew how to do, given your unhealed wounds. I am lovable, adequate, and worthy. I am powerful. I am capable. I am free to express anger. I have a right to speak up and be heard. I'm responsible for my experience, and you and Dad are responsible for yours. I surrender to and trust in a divine plan that beneficently unfolds in each moment, regardless of appearances. I am one with God.*

Before I ended this dialogue with Ireenie, I asked her if there was anything else she wanted or needed. She said she wanted to ride a Ferris wheel! I laughed and promised that the next time I was in California, I'd take her to the Santa Monica Pier.

Beba: Did you do it?

Irene: Yes, of course. It was a memorable experience. I went to the pier on a Saturday afternoon during a two-hour lunch break from school. The air smelled fresh and fishy. The sun was warm on my skin. People on the rides laughed and screamed with joy. I felt like a kid. I was so filled with life, I thought I might explode! I'd forgotten that feeling of aliveness, of being present to the magic in the air, not knowing what new discovery would come my way but confident that it would, because every moment is brand-spanking new, and I am more than just witness to it: I am an inextricable part of it.

I purchased my ticket and stood in line for the Ferris wheel. It was a long line, and when I got to the front, I thought, *Why take up a whole gondola?* I approached the woman managing the ride and told her I was willing to ride with others. She walked over to three women who'd just been seated and asked one of them if it would be all right to include me. The woman leaned over to look at me and slowly shook her head *no*. I didn't take it personally. I knew it was in divine order. I wanted to reassure her, to say that I wasn't supposed to ride with them, and that it was okay.

And then a voice behind me said, "You can ride with us."

I turned to see the smiling face of a woman with short blond hair who looked to be in her mid-thirties. She was holding the hand of a six or seven-year-old girl who had shoulder-length brown hair and exquisite blue eyes. The woman introduced herself as Nancy and introduced the little girl as her goddaughter Ruby.

"Ruby," she said, "is riding the Ferris wheel *for the very first time.*"

Imagine that! It was as if the universe had conspired to have things happen exactly as they had—and exactly as they had not—so that Ireenie and Ruby could ride the Ferris wheel together.

We climbed into the gondola in a state of graceful innocence. When our gondola reached the top, I looked out over the Pacific Ocean and felt joyously free and eternally grateful. I felt whole and complete, reunited with Ireenie and one with God. I delighted in knowing I could nurture and support Ireenie in the way she wanted and needed. I trusted my Self. I trusted Spirit. I trusted Life.

Beba: That's beautiful, Irene. I celebrate every healing moment with you. (Pause) As you heal a wound—like the one you just described—it contributes to my healing the wounds I had as your mother. Your acceptance of me helps me accept myself. Your love for me helps me love myself. Wounds are places that have been denied love. My wounds as your mother became *your* wounds; these were places in you that I couldn't love because I couldn't love them in myself.

My work here is to keep remembering that I *am* love, and any part of me that doesn't feel the love is an aspect that needs healing, an old belief that needs revising. *Being* love: that's what I do here.

Irene: Thank you for having been my mother, Beba. I love you.

BEBA AND JERRY

CONVERSATION FIVE

Irene: Tell me more about your life review.

Beba: As I greeted each person during the reunion, I transformed into the person I'd been when I first met them on earth. I went from being ten years old to thirty-five and back to sixteen, depending on who I was with. This was the informal life review.

For the formal review, I was led into an elegant, yet comfortable room. I sat in an overstuffed chair, put my head back and closed my eyes. I started living my life again as Beba from the first moment in the womb. I was aware of what my mother was feeling. I heard her heartbeat and the whir of blood circulating through her body. I heard my parents' voices.

Irene: You were aware of being in the womb?

Beba: I wasn't *in* the womb. I was focusing my attention *through* my physical presence in the womb, but not on a constant, moment-to-moment basis. If, for example, my parents were experiencing strong emotions—fear, anger, love, or joy—it got my attention. The fetus was my link to the physical world I was about to enter. (Pause) Jerry has something to say.

Jerry: It's an honor to share the floor with Beba. (Pause) Development of a physical body begins at conception. The soul of the fetus is in charge of the body's development and constantly monitors the womb without occupying it.

Irene: The soul is focused on its developing physical body from *outside* the womb?

Jerry: Yes. And the amount of attention the soul focuses on the womb is determined by what's going on in the physical environment.

Irene: Why doesn't the soul reside within the womb?

Jerry: The womb would be too confining for the soul.

(Pause) The baby's soul is in constant communication with physical family members. Strong emotions, whether loving or fearful, signal the soul to pay attention. If the parents are angry and arguing, for instance, it's an opportunity for the soul to gain insight into the family dynamics as well as an opportunity for the soul to participate.

Irene: How does the baby's soul participate?

Jerry: One way is by providing unconditional love for everyone involved, which can serve to remind the arguing parents of how blessed they are to be having a child. Fear is diminished in the presence of love. Darkness is diminished in the presence of light.

The soul also monitors the biology of the physical body in the womb. If the body's nutritional needs aren't being met, for instance, the soul may influence the mother to change her diet; something she's been accustomed to eating may no longer sit well with her, or she may suddenly have an urge to eat a particular food.

Parents can hold an intention to become pregnant for years and it may never happen. It's the intention of the incoming soul to create a body during conception that makes it happen.

Irene: The parents' intention creates space for the intention of the incoming soul.

Jerry: Yes.

The soul always chooses the body that will best serve its agenda. This includes choices about gender, strengths, limitations, skin color, brain development, and general appearance. These are choices the soul makes in cooperation with family members.

The soul focuses more and more attention on the fetus as it develops, influencing the family about things like the birthing method and the name that will be chosen. The soul is in charge of its body and its life at all times. It's important that family members remain open to receiving guidance from the soul, as it has access to an "optimal life" template.

Irene: That's what you referred to in Conversation Nine, when you were talking about the process we go through in choosing our next life. You said, "You see your life lived to full capacity—a perfect life—all strengths and gifts fully expressed. This registers as a knowing that you take with you when it's time to incarnate, much like you take a shopping list to the grocery store so you can take full advantage of the trip. It's a preview of your best life, one that fully utilizes your God-Self, and it's imprinted in your knowing."

Jerry: Yes. An optimal life for the soul is one that meets the needs and requirements of that soul and its family—which may include miscarriage or abortion. In such situations, the entire family learns and grows from the event. Life cannot be killed. A woman who miscarries or aborts may feel guilty or ashamed, presuming the baby's life is gone or that she did something wrong. The incoming soul, having chosen its journey and having fully participated in the decision-making process, withdraws its attention from the fetus. With or without a physical body, the soul of the fetus remains an active part of the family, helping the woman to heal.

Releasing victim consciousness would change the world. Every soul is autonomous. Everyone who chooses to be born has a purpose and specific goals they intend to accomplish. The soul is conscious of the purpose for this physical journey, is clear about what it intends to accomplish, and shares this wisdom with its parents.

Irene: There are no victims. We choose particular experiences for our soul's growth. So when a mother chooses abortion, it's a decision based on mutual agreement with the soul of the child.

Jerry: Yes.

Irene: When I think of a child, an infant, a baby, or a fetus, I sometimes forget that their soul isn't in infancy; it's infinite and timeless. The soul is the soul regardless of the physical form it's choosing to focus through.

Jerry: Yes. And the agreement isn't mutually exclusive between the mother and the incoming soul; it's an agreement that involves the entire soul family. A decision like this touches many people, benefiting them all.

Beba and Jerry
Conversation Six

Irene: Can you elaborate on the soul family?

Jerry: The soul family extends beyond biological connections. It's a common spiritual bond in which experiences work together to expand the group as a whole. It's like planning a family vacation and taking the needs of each family member into account.

Irene: I understand that everyone involved in an event has agreed to participate and that everything that happens is of God. It's difficult, though, to wrap my head around a random mass murder—in a school or a mall, for example.

Jerry: This is an extreme event. And yes, everyone involved agreed to be involved. The shooter is outwardly expressing the inner pain and frustration of the many. The way to see the individual gifts from a mass killing would be to follow those involved beyond their pain and grief. If news organizations would take one or two families directly affected by a shooting, give them a year or two or three to grieve and be with the pain, and then see what blossoms from the experience, you'd see that these events created many opportunities: to reach out to others, to make changes, to forgive, to heal, and to strengthen one's ability to love and be loved. It's through these kinds of events that people become vulnerable and open themselves to the generosity and compassion of others. Events like these break through people's armored defenses; worn down by grief and loss, they no longer have the energy to defend themselves. Some people require this in order to receive the nourishment that will allow them to grow.

Beba: In events like these, there's always a great outpouring of prayers. Those who don't normally pray—pray. Those who don't normally reach out and give to strangers—reach out and give. People come together with a common purpose of comfort and support. And the ultimate gift is forgiveness. Forgiveness changes worlds, inner as well as outer.

Jerry: The setting for such an event, a school or a mall, for example, is a metaphor. Malls represent consumerism. Within the consciousness of consumerism is a longing for what you don't have. This is a great myth, because everyone has exactly what is needed at every given moment.

A myth that's often reinforced in the school system is that you're not enough. Students are viewed as empty containers that need to be filled rather than as filled containers that need tapping into. They're already whole and complete. They're already wise.

Irene: I've always appreciated the etymology of the word *educate.* It comes from the Latin, *educare,* and means *to draw out.* Education in its true sense is about drawing out what's already there. The educational system—public as well as private—often functions in direct contrast to how education was intended. Is it any wonder there's so much frustration on the part of students, teachers, parents, and administrators?

Jerry: The educational system is designed to fill the child's head with information and to reward them when they can spit it out the way it went in. Education *could* be about drawing out the child's unique expression, potential, and gifts. Change the educational system and you change the world.

Irene: I agree. It took a masters program in Spiritual Psychology at the University of Santa Monica before I experienced an educational institution with a course of study that reflected the true meaning of *education.*

Spiritual Psychology reclaims and integrates the spiritual dimension, which is essential to an authentic psychological inquiry. Evolving in consciousness includes surrendering anything that disturbs one's peace. If I want to evolve spiritually, I have to be willing to release judgments like, *this shouldn't have happened; he's wrong; she's a jerk; he shouldn't have behaved that way; this is terrible; he's to blame; I should have known better; I would have been better off if this hadn't happened; life is hard; death is scary,* etcetera. Judgment is always at the root of disturbance.

Jerry: There are people who live many lifetimes before coming to the consciousness of which you're speaking, Irene.

(Pause) The path to self-forgiveness sometimes comes through forgiving others. It's *all* self-forgiveness. There is only Self. If you forgive another, you're also forgiving yourself.

Irene: Ultimately that's true, but I think it's an important distinction in the interim, because the things we judge remain unresolved. I can't forgive my mother for being a "bad" mother. I can't forgive her as long as she's my "bad" mother, because I'm in judgment. I have to forgive myself for placing the judgment on her in the first place. And so, *I forgive myself for judging my mother as bad. I forgive myself for having bought into the misinterpretation that she wasn't doing her best.*

Prior to the masters program, the way I forgave was often just a more subtle form of judgment. Let's use the example of forgiving my mother. In the past, I would have judged my mother as bad, and then I would have forgiven her out of the goodness of my heart. But I'd still be in judgment that she was a bad mother.

On the other hand, if I release the judgment, then she didn't do anything wrong and doesn't require my forgiveness. She was always doing the best she knew how to do. If I can forgive myself for having placed the judgment on her—that she should have done it differently, or better, or like my friend Janet's mom—then healing can begin. I can own what's mine and work with it. It's a graceful and elegant model. That's not to say that I don't take action when appropriate. The difference is in my motivation.

Instead of being motivated by righteousness, I'm motivated by compassion. An example might be useful.

Jerry: Sure.

Irene: The scene is any discount department store. A child is seated in the shopping cart, crying and yelling. Their parent responds by threatening, belittling, pinching, hitting—you get the picture. Years ago, I'd judge such a parent as incompetent, unloving, lousy, mean, bad, wrong—take your pick. I'd also judge the child as a victim and feel sorry for them. If I chose to intervene, what was motivating me was self-righteousness: I was right, and they were wrong; I was superior, and they were inferior. Not only did this *not* improve the situation, it made it worse, because my negative judgment was added to the already challenging mix.

Take the same situation, now. I'm no longer judging the parent. I know they're doing the best they know how to do in that moment, given their beliefs, state of mind, level of physical well-being, upbringing, level of awareness, etcetera. I know there are no victims. The child, for purposes of spiritual growth, has chosen this parent. And the parent, for purposes of spiritual growth, has chosen this child. I feel the parent's frustration. I feel the child's pain. And I know they love each other and are doing the best they know how to do. If I choose to intervene, compassion is what moves me. Standing nearby, I allow my heart to open up to them and I send a blessing—which oftentimes will shift the interaction. Sometimes I gently interrupt by adding loving energy. "Oh," I say softly in passing, "it can be so challenging to be a parent; be gentle with yourself." I'm not right, because there's nothing to be right about, and they're not wrong, because there's nothing to be wrong about. We're all just doing the best we know how to do. Regardless of the action I choose to take, coming from a place of compassion makes a world of difference. Some days are easier than others. I'm committed to being compassionate with myself and embracing all parts of myself without judgment.

Beba

Conversation Seven

Irene: I'd like to hear more about your life review.

Beba: Throughout the life review, I was keenly aware of myself and others: their thoughts and my thoughts; their feelings and my feelings; their beliefs and my beliefs; their influence on me and my influence on them. It was beautifully choreographed. We were all dancing together, sometimes gracefully and sometimes stepping on each other's toes, but always affecting one another. I had affected others without so much as a glance, and they had affected me with their moods, attitudes, and thoughts.

During the life review, I became aware of how important I am. I'd always imagined doing great things in the world, not realizing that doing simple activities with love *is* great. I never felt like I was doing enough, and yet I'd had the opportunity to influence and contribute to the world, day-to-day and moment-by-moment, by choosing a positive, loving attitude.

Irene: Applying love to the parts that hurt and healing them is the most important work I do. Loving myself fully is the greatest gift I can give the world, and I can do this by replacing negative self-talk—that terrorizing inner voice—with compassionate self-talk. Being at peace with myself is my contribution to world peace.

Beba: You are so wise. By loving yourself, you're nourishing yourself, which gives you the ability to nourish others.

Irene: (Weeping) Well, I *am* my mother's daughter, after all.

Beba: You and I had an agreement that I wouldn't be able to love you in a way you could receive. My inability to express love came from my upbringing and was part of my contract with my parents and with my Soul Self. Agreements and contracts are never one-way: the way of the soul is fair and efficient and always in service to the whole; when something serves one, it also serves the other; when one is served, all are served.

You learned to receive love despite your belief that you lacked love as a child. This belief—that love wasn't readily available through me—required you to find it within. You left home with a perceived emptiness that you longed to fill, an emptiness that motivated you on your path of self-love, enlightenment, and expansion. Just as someone who's starved seeks food, you were hungry for love, and you sought it and found it within yourself. You came *in* hungry.

Irene: How divinely guided.

Beba: It was—it is. During my life review, I recognized how perfect my own childhood had been. I'd chosen my parents, just as a seed chooses the perfect spot on which to land and grow. I'd chosen everything that was present and challenging in my environment, as well as everything that was absent from it. I knew instinctually how to extract the love I needed from my family's dysfunction. Love is always available, no matter how harsh the environment.

As a child, I was always seeking love from my father, and yet it was rarely given in the way I wanted. I expected it to look and feel a certain way, and when it didn't, I rejected it as *not love.* But in my life review, in the absence of my judgments, I saw and felt my father's love. And it was constant. I came into the world with an unfulfilled place inside me that I tried to fill with my father's love, but it wasn't a fit. That place required *my* love, not his. I blamed him for that emptiness for many years.

The healing began when I stopped blaming him for not giving me what I thought I needed and acknowledged the ways in which he *did* love me. Once I let him off the hook, I had to take responsibility for my own experience—for the emptiness and inner pain—and begin loving those places within myself. Not only was I the one who'd believed I was unlovable, I was the one who'd believed he was the cause. I was the one needing forgiveness for the misunderstanding! I spent so many years believing the lies I'd made up. My father could only love me as much as he was capable of loving me. Period. His pain prevented him from loving any differently. It wasn't me and it wasn't anything I did or didn't do. It was what he knew.

Irene: Yes, of course. As children, we misconstrue what's happening. We don't have the cognitive ability to think, *My dad has places within himself that are unhealed, so he's unable to love those places within me.* Instead, we make it mean something negative about ourselves: we're inadequate, flawed, unlovable, unworthy, not smart enough, pretty enough, good enough, talented enough— the list goes on and on. We want so much to be loved, that we adopt the traits of our caregivers, as if to say, "See? I'm like you. *Now,* will you love me?" Or we do the opposite and we rebel. But we're not to blame. And neither are our parents. We pass down, from one generation to the next, those places that haven't been healed, those places that are in need of self-love. (Pause) I have a question for Jerry.

Jerry: I'm here.

Irene: Beba and I had a soul-level agreement that I wouldn't be able to receive her love and that this would ultimately lead to loving myself. Given that parents love the best they can, and they can only love their children to the degree they love themselves, did I *perceive* that love wasn't present in my relationship with my mom, or was it simply not present? Beba said it wasn't that her father didn't love her, it was just that his love didn't look and feel the way she wanted it to.

Jerry: Beba wasn't able to give you what you needed because she was lacking in the same way you were lacking. You chose each other based on similar wounds you were here to heal. It was also agreed that you'd both heal these wounds. Remember: love is never lacking. If there's a place inside you that's in need of love and the same place is in someone else, then neither one of you can provide it for the other.

Getting back to Beba's father: yes, he loved her, but the places inside himself that he didn't love were passed down to her. She was born with those same wounds. That's why she picked him as her father. That's why you picked Beba as your mother. The places in need of love matched. The wounds matched.

Beba: I also loved you in the ways you needed love. I made sure you were fed and clothed. We had fun together. We shared the same sense of humor and could always make each other laugh.

During my life review, I saw all the places in me that were tended by my father's love, and all the wounds that were healed by his love. You will see it in your life, too, my darling.

BEBA

CONVERSATION EIGHT

Irene: How did you access your life as Physical Beba for the life review?

Beba: I was guided to close my eyes, and the rest just came without any effort. I didn't have to count backwards or consciously relax or do anything special. I just closed my eyes and my life review began. It was like a dream, except I was fully conscious.

Irene: Was it challenging?

Beba: If someone had told me that I would be experiencing my entire life, including how I had affected everyone and everything, I would have panicked, thinking of the times I spoke in anger and was hurtful; but an indescribable love was present throughout the review, surrounding me and flowing through me. Even though I felt the harshness of my words and the pain of another, I had tremendous compassion for myself. Imbedded in these feelings was a two-fold understanding: *where* the pain that provoked the harshness originated and *why* people responded the way they did.

In some instances, the pain within *me* that had provoked the harshness and unkind words was also in *them,* and it created an opportunity for them to get in touch with their own pain. My pain was reminding them of theirs. It was all lovingly orchestrated. Choosing love is ideal, but I saw the benefit of every choice I'd made throughout my life. And each of my choices eventually had a beneficial effect on all those involved—if they chose to benefit.

Irene: What do you mean by *if they chose to benefit?*

Beba: Let's use us as an example. If I were to say something to you that you experienced as painful, would you react by focusing on *me*—becoming angry with me and blaming me—or would you take responsibility for your upset and get in touch with your own painful reaction, asking yourself what it was in my comment that had triggered you? If you were to stay focused on me instead of on yourself, that wouldn't be so beneficial. Healing starts from within.

Irene: As your daughter, I focused on *you* instead of on myself. I blamed you because I thought you didn't love me. I didn't take responsibility for what was happening inside myself. Whatever I didn't like in me, I projected onto you and judged you for it. I couldn't see that *I* was selfish, so I projected it onto you and blamed *you* for being selfish. *If only I had a mother who wasn't so selfish*, I thought, *I would have turned out better.*

I've learned that whatever I judge in someone else is also within *me*. Now, instead of blaming others, I have an intention to own what I see. The world is my projection. The world is my mirror. The same is true for owning the positive traits I see in others. When I acknowledge Oprah as a powerful woman making a difference in the world, I also have to own that in myself. It works both ways.

By forgiving myself for judging you, I'm left with owning and healing the judgment within myself, which results in compassion and acceptance for both of us. I realize that you've always done the best you knew how to do. How could I fault you? It's a Godsend to know that the only person I ever have to forgive is myself.

(Pause) On a different note, I wonder what age I'll be when I transition and what circumstances will surround the event. Were you surprised by the circumstances surrounding your own transition?

Beba: Yes and no. The part of me that says *yes* is the part that was afraid and didn't want to know. The part of me that says *no* is the part that was preparing me through hints and messages that the time was approaching. I didn't share these hints and messages with you because it would have made it too real. I thought I was saving you from your fear, but I was really attempting to protect myself.

Irene: What kinds of hints and messages did you receive?

Beba: My spunk was dampened. I lost some of my fight. I slept more. I received other people's suggestions more willingly and allowed them to help me—something I didn't normally do. My dreams became more vivid and the images began to meld into my waking time. I'd see family members who'd passed, and while it was comforting as it was happening, I'd get scared when I realized my eyes were open and I hadn't been dreaming. I was afraid of what others would think if I told them, afraid of the implication that I might be hallucinating or losing my mind.

Irene: I hear you. I know how challenging it can be to own my own fears, and sometimes I still project them onto others. Most of the time, though, when I'm worried about what people will think of me, I turn it around and ask myself what *I* think. I remind myself that what they think of me is none of my business.

BEBA

CONVERSATION NINE

Irene: What happened after your formal life review?

Beba: My spiritual helper showed me how to create my own space by using my desires as the basis for the design. She used her power of manifestation, because my abilities were rusty.

Irene: If you were to create that living space for yourself now, how would you go about it?

Beba: I'd picture what I want and where I want it, and through my intentional focus and confidence, it would appear.

Irene: When you say you'd picture it *where* you want it, I have a hard time picturing how you'd choose the *where* in infinite space.

Beba: (Laughing) When I say *where,* I mean the coffee table in front of the couch.

Irene: (Laughing) What does your personal space look like?

Beba: I first want to say that I change it a lot, depending on my mood. It's easy to do. I'm currently into pastels: a powder blue couch and peach-colored walls. If I want a different style of furniture, I simply change it by imagining what I want. If I tire of the colors on my walls, I simply change them as well.

Irene: What about the *where* in a larger context, like a neighborhood?

Beba: *That* where is a little different, because there really is no *where.* I may choose to create an environment around me that looks like I'm near the ocean, for example, but rather than my home being near the ocean, the ocean is part of my home, part of my creation. We don't have to choose locations based on whom we want to be near, because we're always just a thought away. Some of us like to duplicate the earth environment, though, so we create neighbors. If I wanted my home to be near my friend Lila and it wasn't already, one of us would need to recreate our home. Recreating a piece of furniture takes more energy and focus than changing the colors of the walls, but it's certainly easier than physically hauling the furniture from a store.

Irene: Where does your energy come from?

Beba: The same place *your* energy comes from.

Irene: And where's that?

Beba: It's infinite, always present and available.

Irene: What's the difference between how you and I access energy?

Beba: We both access energy in the same way. The difference is that you're operating within physical laws and I'm not. I focus on my desire and the energy responds by creating it. There aren't any malls to walk through or phone calls to make. There's always an immediate response to my desire, followed by the manifestation of it. The response is the energy that comes forward. When I focus that energy, manifestation happens.

BEBA

CONVERSATION TEN

Irene: What activities do you enjoy?

Beba: I love walking through open fields and along beaches. It's wonderful to walk without a destination and without concern for whether I'll have enough energy to walk back, because I don't have to walk back, and energy is infinite. I don't have to think about what time it is. I just walk. The scenery changes according to my mood; I might find myself near the ocean because, given my thoughts, that's what's most nourishing.

Irene: Can you help your loved ones on earth?

Beba: When they let me. The biggest help is to love them as they are, and without judgment. Just love them. I sometimes whisper in *your* ear when you feel confused or at night before you fall asleep.

Irene: What do you whisper?

Beba: I tell you how beautiful you are and that you deserve everything. I tell you to love yourself and to forgive yourself. I tell you to remember me, not as sick or old, or during those times you perceived I *didn't* love you, but to remember the times I *did*—because that's all that matters. I kiss you on your cheek. I see you in your dreams.

Irene: How do you see me in my dreams?

Beba: I see and feel you when you free yourself from your physical body through sleep. We've had conversations over tea. I've held you during stressful times.

Irene: That's beautiful, Beba. Thank you.

(Pause) Beba, what's your understanding of God?

Beba: My understanding is that there *is* no such thing, and yet it's everything. The Divine resides inside of me, expanding as I allow it to expand, without limits or boundaries. This power exists in each of us. We diminish or strengthen it by the love we give and receive. *That's* God.

BEBA

CONVERSATION ELEVEN

Irene: Any words of advice?

Beba: Don't believe everything you read or everything people tell you. Question things. Life goes by quickly. Take advantage of each moment. Breathe deeply and express yourself. Connect with your own creativity. Be eccentric. Dance. Enjoy.

Irene: Was there something specific you read or something someone told you about the afterlife that was untrue?

Beba: I'd read about heaven, and frankly, I thought it was going to be boring. And here it is, not the least bit boring; there's always something to do. I thought everyone would be sent to one place or another—some people would be here and some in hell and some in between—and I'd never see them. That's not true, either. But my original reason for saying, "Don't believe everything you read or everything people tell you," was to remind you to listen to your heart. See if what you're reading feels true to you. If someone tells you something, check in with yourself and see how it resonates with you. That's something I didn't do. If someone told me something, I'd either say they were full of shit or I'd believe them whole-heartedly. I reacted to *who* was telling me rather than to *what* they were telling me.

Irene: Thanks. I appreciate your honesty. And as for the term you so often used in physical life—*full of shit*—consider yourself quoted verbatim. (Laughing) Now it'll be in print. By the way, I'm looking forward to playing cards with you—and winning.

Beba: (Laughing) When hell freezes over. You'd better practice up.

Irene: (Pause) Beba, if you were on earth, how would you live differently given what you know?

Beba: I'd be more present with life by not being so involved with my own thoughts. My inner conversation was incessant. Someone would be talking with me and I'd be commenting to myself about their appearance or judging the way they expressed themselves. I'd be practicing what I was going to say when they finished, or I'd be off into my own story while they were talking. More often than not, I just wasn't present with the person in front of me. So, in answer to your question, I'd live fully present to life, focusing on what I could *give* someone instead of what I could *get* from them. I'd take time to compliment others and to acknowledge their qualities.

Irene: What do you love most about the Spirit world?

Beba: Freedom. There are no limitations here. I can be and do anything. There are no time constraints, because there's no time. I always feel good; there's never an ache or pain or indigestion or congestion. Don't get me wrong—I enjoy experiencing a physical body; it's a rich experience and nourishing to my soul. I have treasures I could only have gotten by being Beba and all the other people I've chosen to be. I'll incarnate again and again, and I'm grateful for the opportunity. But right now, I'm happy where I am. The thought of going through a physical life doesn't appeal to me. You know how there comes a time when you're on vacation, when you don't ever want to think about going back to your day-to-day life, and there's also a time when you've had enough and you're itching to get back?

Irene: I do.

Beba: I'm still in the I-don't-ever-want-to-think-about-going-back phase.

Irene: (Laughing) I get it. (Pause) What was most surprising to you about shifting your focus from physical life to spirited life?

Beba: That I didn't have any regrets or remorse about my life as Physical Beba. I had a lot of regret *during* my life as Physical Beba: after visiting with someone, for example, I'd reflect on the visit and think, *I wish I had said this,* or *I shouldn't have said that.* Feelings of regret and remorse diminished my enjoyment of life.

As Spirited Beba, I can be eating my chocolate ice cream and looking at all the flavors I could have had, but the thought that I could have had a different flavor doesn't diminish my enjoyment of the chocolate I'm eating.

Irene: What is your priority?

Beba: My prioriy is to experience love under all circumstances.

Irene: That's my priority, too.

BEBA

CONVERSATION TWELVE

Irene: Hi, Beba! What have you been up to?

Beba: I've been challenging lots of people to cards, and I've played with some of the great ones. I'm having such a wonderful time. There's so much fun and laughter here, and I've met up with lots of people who don't take life seriously. Life's not meant to be taken seriously. I see people arriving here who expect seriousness, but they lighten up right away when they experience the freedom and the fun of interacting with others.

I can't help but laugh at the contrast between the lightness here, which is our natural state, and the seriousness and sadness of people on earth. I bring this lightness with me when I visit physical friends and family, reminding everyone of the joy, laughter, and play that children come to earth remembering. It takes a while for children to put on their serious adult personas and forget their joy. I still like to laugh and remind people how much they can benefit from seeing the humorous side of things. I've tickled many family members just by passing through them and letting them feel, for a brief moment, the lightness I feel now.

I also like to dance. I have a "partner in charm," by the way. We like to be charming together and we both share an appreciation for the absurd. We sometimes dress with great decorum and behave very prim and proper, for example, but neither one of us will be wearing shoes.

Irene: You always enjoyed shocking people when you were in physical form.

Beba: And I still do. Surprising people wakes them up; the unexpected makes people more present in the moment.

Irene: Beba, what do you look like?

Beba: I pretty much look like I did during the last few years of my physical life but I have more vitality because my body isn't taxing me anymore. I have the vitality of my twenties, but in my "older woman" body. I also enjoy smoking cigars—the little ones, not the big ones. There's so much playfulness here! (Laughing) Sometimes I like to wear a visor and smoke a little cigar while I play cards, pretending it's a serious game with serious stakes. Play permeates this environment. It's all choice. No one tells you what to do.

When people first come here, they make adjustments depending on their state of being when they transition. I often see people taking "the big sleep" while their non-physical bodies are worked on, which helps them adjust to this new environment. They're also assisted in letting go of issues that are weighing them down. It's all about lightness here, about being light-hearted, and about lightness of spirit. When someone passes from their physical body after having experienced trauma—either *to* them or *by* them— there's a necessary period of adjustment to sever those cords that would weigh them down here. It's fascinating to watch the healing that takes place while the non-physical form is unconscious. As they experience waves of love and clearing. the colors of their bodies change right before our eyes. Once they wake up and start feeling where they are, they don't want to go back to sleep. They attend the reunion with loved ones and begin feeling right at home. Since there's no physical form here, sleep isn't required. Children in physical form never want to go to sleep, because they sense they'll miss something. It's not until their physical bodies literally *fall* into sleep that they stop.

Irene: Beba, are there any animals where you are?

Beba: Not where *I* am, although there are people around me who want the presence of their pets and call them forth with their love. (Pause) You may think Physical Fido is just a dog, but it may be your wisest spirit guide using a canine form to be close to you as a vehicle for unconditional love. Sometimes it's easier to provide it that way.

Irene: Thanks, Beba. I've enjoyed our conversations.

Beba: I've enjoyed them, too. They're helping me teach what I'm learning.

Irene: They've been of great value to me, and I trust they will be to others.

Beba: I know. (Laughing) I want to give them a slice of spiritual pie!

BILL

1953 – 1988

Bill and I met while volunteering at a personal growth seminar. He was dashing and debonair, yet unpretentious and unassuming. Bill enjoyed music, dance, and avant-garde art and film. He had a dry sense of humor and enjoyed a cigar every now-and-then. He was a gentle and loving husband and father.

Bill found it difficult to share his feelings and allow love into his life. He committed suicide, but not before blessing the world with his beautiful presence and with two extraordinary sons.

BILL

CONVERSATION ONE

Irene: Bill, what did you experience when you released your last breath on earth?

Bill: I was laughing. I looked at my body and laughed that I ever could have taken myself so seriously. I realized I was laughing and wondered how I could be laughing. *Isn't laughter for bodies?* I thought. I stopped. I realized that laughter comes from the soul.

Who is looking at the body that I thought was me? I wondered. I had killed Bill, but I was still alive. I still *felt* like me—like Bill— but lighter. I wondered where the heaviness had gone. Had it stayed in my physical body? I looked at my face and I could see the pain I'd just been through. My mouth and eyes were open. That's when I started laughing. I realized that I wasn't my physical body.

I went from feeling consumed by emotional pain in physical form to feeling a sense of relief in this new form. I became the observer. I'm not saying that I was free of pain, because I took it with me. But the despair and hopelessness were gone. If you were to imagine the pain of having a car door slam shut on your hand and the ensuing relief the moment your hand was removed from the door, you'd have a sense of the relief I'm talking about.

I reached out and caressed my body's cheek. It was still warm.

Irene: You could feel the warmth?

Bill: I could feel the energy of my body's cheek and it registered as heat.

Irene: Were you focusing through a form?

Bill: Yes. It was similar to the one I'd just left, but I felt younger and more alive. (Laughing) I felt more alive than when I'd *been* alive!

A stranger approached and saw my body. I felt their shock, confusion and fear, but from my new perspective, I also connected with the part of them that's unchanging—the joy, elation, and love. That's what you look for in people when you speak of seeing the God in them. It's like the Rumi poem about the field: "Out beyond ideas of wrong-doing and right-doing, there is a field. I'll meet you there. When the soul lies down in that grass, the world is too full to talk about. Ideas, language, even the phrase 'each other' doesn't make any sense." When I say I connected with the essence of this person, I'm referring to a place beyond personality, individuality, or separation. I wondered if I'd been this connected in physical life, and if so, *why had I felt so alone?*

BILL AND JERRY

CONVERSATION TWO

Irene: Was there a penalty for taking your life?

Bill: If, by penalty, you mean was I punished, the answer is *no*. There's no such thing as punishment. Who would we punish? Who would do the punishing? You're the only one who can punish yourself, and when you do, you affect everyone.

We all choose to end our physical lives; it's just a matter of when and how. There's no such thing as ending life too soon or too late. Life is filled with endings and beginnings, and they're all in harmony. (Pause) Jerry wants to say something.

Jerry: You choose *all* the changes in your life, including the death of your physical body. Death through "natural" causes is still your choice.

Irene: Why the "quotes" around *natural?*

Jerry: There are people whose deaths aren't considered suicide, yet they've dedicated themselves to resisting life and ignoring their bodies' needs for nutrition, hydration, and exercise, actively sabotaging the organs of their bodies by smoking, drinking and abusing drugs. These choices are contrary to the health and well-being of the body. When these people take their final breath in physical form, no one calls it suicide; they call it lung cancer or alcoholism or drug addiction. These aren't "natural," yet we call it dying of "natural" causes. These are prolonged suicides. The ways people choose to end their lives are as varied as the individuals. Some are more deliberate than others.

Irene: Why is there so much condemnation and shame associated with suicide, particularly in religion?

Jerry: The original reason was to discourage people from choosing this option, and it was done in much the same way a parent threatens to punish a child for running into the street instead of explaining *why* running into the street is a harmful, self-defeating act. If religious institutions were more educational in nature, people could be educated in the truth about suicide. Suicide isn't *wrong*. It's an option. And that option could be put side-by-side with many other options.

To create another body and grow that body to maturation takes a lot of time and energy—time and energy that could be spent in the present body, healing the root causes of loneliness, isolation, and despair that brought the person to the decision of suicide. And then, from that point of healing, the person could carry on with their soul's mission, perhaps gaining insight and wisdom to help others through the process of choosing differently. This would create a productive life, which is the goal of everyone who chooses a physical life.

Irene: Jared said he'd planned a short physical life. How can we become more aware of what we've chosen for ourselves?

Jerry: How aware we are of prior soul agreements depends on the depth of consciousness we maintain in physical form. A person who consistently cultivates a spiritual connection through prayer and meditation has a deeper connection to their soul's agenda.

Most people who plan a short physical life tend to pack a lot in. They're more conscious of the time they have and want to make the most of it. While a short physical life greatly impacts family and friends, it is a choice that's made in service to all. It may seem like a greater loss when someone transitions at a young age, but that's only from a narrow, physical perspective; it's actually a great gain for all concerned. While the individual who has transitioned is free and, for the most part, finding peace, it is often anything *but* peaceful for those left behind: with their lives stirred up and in a state of flux, they have an opportunity to reevaluate, change and grow.

BILL

CONVERSATION THREE

Irene: Bill, what were your thoughts prior to committing suicide?

Bill: I felt like a burden to my family. I wanted to support them financially and still have the time and energy to enjoy their company, but the financial struggle was too great. I wanted to be everything to them. I wanted to provide everything *for* them. I had such high ideals and yet I never felt like I was enough. I was supposed to be the one supporting *them,* but I was often the one in need. Every attempt I made to succeed financially seemed to end in failure. I couldn't shoulder my responsibilities anymore. I felt like I was doing the opposite of what I was supposed to do: instead of boosting my family up, I thought I was dragging them down. I felt hopeless and despairing. I did my best to put on a strong face, but I just got so tired. The strong-capable-and-everything's-okay façade got to be such a heavy load; it felt like I'd been carrying a hundred-pound weight for years. I was exhausted. It wasn't like I had a concrete plan for *where* I was going to set down the hundred-pound weight; it was more like, "I've got to drop this—*now!*" I couldn't take it anymore.

I didn't think I could express what I was feeling, because in *my* mind, my feelings equaled *weakling, deadbeat, failure,* and if I'd shown *that* to my family, I'd have been my father, my kids would've become *me,* and my wife would have turned into my mother. So I thought they'd be better off without me.

I wanted relief, and suicide provided that. I thought of suicide as a release from this façade I was presenting to the world. It would finally be over and I could take a break. I didn't give a lot of thought to what would happen *after* I ended my life, but I knew that God had to be accepting enough and understanding enough for me to be *me*. I knew that, if my life were to continue—even if it were to continue exactly as it had in physical life—I could at least be myself in front of God.

BILL AND JERRY

CONVERSATION FOUR

Irene: You mentioned that there was a stranger near your physical body and that you connected with the part of them that's unchanging.

Bill: I saw this person's body as a fluidly moving, golden-white light. As this light expanded, I realized it was responding to feelings—theirs and mine—and I laughed again as I realized that *that's* what we are: light in motion. If we all realized we're light in motion, we'd put more emphasis on what we feel and less on how we look. We'd be more aware of how our feelings affect others because we'd see it.

Irene: I wonder how we specifically affect one another emotionally. If two people are interacting—let's call them Steve and Shannon for the sake of this example—and Steve is feeling angry while Shannon feels joyous, how will Steve's anger affect Shannon's joy and Shannon's joy affect Steve's anger? Is it a matter of who's feeling the emotion with greater intensity? Will Shannon feel more anger and less joy, or will Steve feel more joy and less anger? I suppose it also has to do with how vested each person is in holding onto a position, a point of view.

Bill: I'll let Jerry speak about that.

Jerry: I'd be happy to. In terms of your question, the emotion that's closest to your true nature—love and all its attributes— is strongest. In terms of your example, the anger in Steve will resonate with any anger in Shannon, and the joy in Shannon will resonate with the joy in Steve. So it really depends on how much joy is present in Steve and how much anger is present in Shannon. If Shannon has a lot of anger, her joy will be diminished and her anger will grow stronger. In turn, if Steve has a lot of joy, his anger will diminish and his joy will grow stronger. But as far as which emotion is stronger, it's always the emotion that's closest to our true nature, which is love.

You're correct, Irene, when you say that it also depends on how vested each person is in holding on to their feelings. Sometimes when people are fighting, it's a question of holding on to a position. Steve may think that the only way he's going to "win" is to appear more powerful, which will prove he's right. Expressing anger may be his way of accomplishing this.

To continue with your example, if Steve and Shannon share a loving relationship, Shannon will be more patient with Steve, and Steve will not only be more receptive to Shannon, he'll be concerned with how his anger is affecting her. If Steve and Shannon share a more competitive relationship, Steve may want someone to be angry *with,* like the adage, "misery loves company." And finally, if taking responsibility for her feelings is foreign to Shannon, she may get angry with Steve for bringing her down—and blame him.

Being conscious means taking responsibility. Responsibility isn't burden or obligation. Responsibility is the ability to respond. The willingness to take responsibility allows you to consider options and choices absent of blame. Choices produce consequences. Do you have the willingness to choose differently and produce new consequences? If you want different results, make different choices. A conscious person takes responsibility for their feelings, their choices and for what life brings them—without blaming others.

BILL

CONVERSATION FIVE

Irene: Bill, can you tell me more about this fluid, golden-white light and how it responded to feelings?

Bill: It was light in motion. There were sluggish areas where the light was darker and moving more slowly.

Irene: Do you know why?

Bill: Feelings are energy in motion. When feelings aren't experienced—when they're suppressed by a judgmental thought, for example—the energy slows.

Irene: So if I'm feeling sad and I think, *It's silly to feel this way,* or *Sadness is a sign of weakness,* or *I should be feeling happy*—the flow of energy in my body is slowed?

Bill: Yes. Judgment slows the flow of energy. When this becomes habitual, stagnation occurs. If you have a thought that what you're feeling is inappropriate, wrong, or not aligned with your beliefs, you won't allow yourself to feel what you're feeling, and you'll divert the energy from *feeling* to *thinking*.

Life itself is a flow, and inhibiting feelings inhibits the flow of life. If you feel angry but think, *It's not spiritual to feel angry,* or *I'll be like my dad if I feel angry,* or have any other judgmental thought, then, instead of moving *through* you, the energy hits a judgmental wall and gets stuck in your body. I learned at a young age that expressing myself emotionally was a sign of weakness, so I suppressed my feelings. Over the course of my life, the energy in my body became stagnant, and eventually I felt hopeless.

Irene: It sounds like part of your conditioning as a child included pairing the expression of feelings with weakness, so expressing emotions meant you were weak. We're all conditioned according to our spiritual agendas. Do you know what your agenda was as Physical Bill?

Bill: My agenda was to trust the wisdom of my feelings and express myself fully.

Irene: Amazing.

Bill: Some background about a prior life might be helpful.

Irene: I'd like to hear about it.

Bill: I was an influential philosopher in ancient Rome. Appalled by the barbarism, cruelty and injustices of that system, I rebelled against the ruling party and was killed for speaking out.

I came in as Bill, not trusting my feelings, my opinions, or my perspectives. I carried an unconscious fear that I'd be killed for expressing myself. You spoke of the association I had made as a child: expressing emotions equaled weakness. This was a reflection of an even deeper association: self-expression equals death. How ironic, or maybe not, that death came as a result of not being true to myself—and by my own hand.

Irene: You created what you feared most.

Bill: Yes. And as I think about it now, even the way I committed suicide—by taking poison—was a reflection of that ancient Roman culture.

Irene: It's intriguing to see how your childhood experiences fit into your lifetime as Bill, and how your lifetime as Bill fit into the greater picture of your soul. (Pause) Did your life in ancient Rome immediately precede your life as Bill?

Bill: No. Healing isn't sequential from one lifetime to another. Between my life as Bill and my life in ancient Rome, I was an orphan in England, a socialite in Paris circa 1800, and an aviator in World War II. In each of these lifetimes, I created circumstances that challenged my self-expression.

Irene: How so?

Bill: As an orphan, I was placed in a state-run institution where self-expression was discouraged. As a socialite during the 1800s, what little power I had was monitored and controlled; and during my life as a Japanese kamikaze pilot, I was trained from a young age to sacrifice myself for my country, so individuality had no place in my life.

We may experience a wound over many lifetimes before we're ready and willing to heal. In my case, the wound had its origin in my life as a Roman philosopher, so during my life review, I was counseled to revisit that lifetime for greater understanding. As a result, I was able to find compassion for all those involved, including myself. My death in that lifetime was the result of self expression. The experience was so profound and the wound so deep, it's requiring many lifetimes to heal. It's no different in physical life. In order to heal something in the present, you often have to heal it in childhood, where it originated.

The circumstances we create are also contingent on the availability of soul family members. Complementary agendas are necessary so that everyone's needs can be met. Our biological family and friends in this lifetime—whether loving or antagonistic—comprise our soul family and are the characters in our play. Roles are interchangeable: your son Josh could be your mother in another life, or your brother David might be your wife. A lot of planning goes into each lifetime.

Irene: So, the circumstances you chose for Physical Bill supported what you were here to heal. In this case, making the association, "expressing emotions equals weakness" was necessary in order to remind you of your spiritual agenda and what you were here to heal.

Bill: That's correct.

Irene: If, as an adult, you'd been able to identify the

misconception and replace it with a more accurate belief, such as, "allowing feelings is self-honoring," you might not have committed suicide.

Bill: If I'd been aware that I had the power to trace my beliefs to their origin and change them, perhaps I would have. Maybe then I wouldn't have ended my life as a result of feeling hopelessly alone. I would have seen that the association, "expressing emotions equals weakness" was made by a frightened child. (Pause) From *my* perspective, the act of suicide was an act of power—the only power I thought I had.

Once I refocused my energy from physical to spirited life, I saw that holding back emotions slows the body's energy. I also recognized that who I am is separate from what I believe. I'm blessed to bring this awareness to others.

From a spiritual perspective, life is continuous. The change from physical to non-physical isn't that big a deal. Not accomplishing what you set out to do—in the context of infinity—isn't that big a deal. If the agenda isn't completed as one personality, it'll be completed as another. You come back into Spirit, regroup, revitalize, and choose another set of circumstances to help you heal the wounds created in other lifetimes.

Irene: As my friend Ron would say, "There is no failure, only repeated opportunity."

BILL

CONVERSATION SIX

Irene: What happened after your experience with the stranger who found your body?

Bill: I was drawn toward a warm, bright light. As I moved toward *it,* it moved toward me. My awareness of physical reality disappeared.

Radiant beings with fluid bodies were welcoming me. They felt loving and familiar. I sensed they'd been waiting for me and that this welcome was more personal than the standard greeting given to everyone who passes from physical to Spirit. I knew they knew me and loved me, and without any apprehension or hesitation, I trusted them. That was something! I'd never experienced this depth of love as Physical Bill. I'd even doubted my mother's love.

I realize now that doubting someone's love was a function of my own self-doubt, which had a lot to do with the limiting beliefs I held about loving and being loved. These limiting beliefs were all based in fear: fear of not being enough, fear of not being lovable, and fear of not getting my needs met.

These spirited beings who were greeting me were unlimited in their capacity to love—at least that's what it felt like to me. I could've stood in their presence for the rest of eternity. I was hungry for this kind of love that, as Physical Bill, I hadn't received—not because it hadn't been available, but because I thought I wasn't deserving of it.

Irene: What I'm hearing you say is that, when we judge ourselves as undeserving, the judgment we place on ourselves gets in the way of receiving the love that's naturally and always available to us.

Bill: Yes.

Irene: And the universe is loving and responsive. If you *believe* you're unlovable, you get to experience it. If you *think* you're inadequate—you're right. If you *believe* you're unworthy, then so it is in your reality. It's like I shared with Jerry: we're already Lovable, Adequate, and Worthy. (Laughing) It's the LAW. (Pause) I was coaching a woman recently who asked, "If that's the case, why bother doing good deeds?"

"You do good deeds," I responded, "because it's your heart's desire, because love is who you are, and because it's your nature to be loving, kind, generous, peaceful, and joyful."

We're often motivated to do good deeds to disprove our worst fears: that we're inherently bad and we deserve to be punished. We love our neighbor, not because we're in touch with our true nature, but because we've been conditioned to think that if we don't, we won't get into "heaven." We're looking outside ourselves for how to behave rather than allowing it to come from within.

Bill: I was starving myself, believing that I was unlovable, inadequate, and unworthy. These judgments reinforced my feelings of separation and isolation and stagnated my body's natural energy flow. Living is about nourishing our true nature, not denying it.

Irene: Bill, what's the most important thing we can know about ourselves?

Bill: The most important thing to know, without a doubt, is that we are lovable—just the way we are.

BILL

CONVERSATION SEVEN

Irene: You spoke of being greeted with a great depth of love.

Bill: Yes. Experiencing this love was healing and energizing. I realized how cramped the energy in my physical body had been due to the strain of holding on to feelings that I could have released—if only I'd known how. It was as if I'd been walking around for years with clenched fists that suddenly relaxed and opened, and it was only because of the sudden contrast that I recognized my fists had been clenched at all.

The strain of physical life was gone, and I was present to the natural flow of my non-physical form. I recognized the distinction between who I am and the beliefs I held. Releasing my physical body—as well as some of the self-defeating beliefs I'd held—left me feeling lighter, refreshed and renewed. I was one with everything and filled with joy.

In this state of oneness, I felt great compassion for myself and for the decision I'd made to end my physical life. What a contrast between the oneness I was feeling and the separation I had experienced as Physical Bill. Undernourished and choked off from the flow of love, it's no wonder I committed suicide.

Irene: Ending your physical life seemed like the only way to end your suffering.

Bill: Right. I didn't know how to end my suffering any other way. I didn't feel part of my family or community; I was always on the outside, looking in. From *my* perspective, as someone isolated and cut of from the nourishment of love, life had already ended.

Irene: What would you say to someone who is in great emotional pain and perhaps contemplating suicide?

Bill: Pray. Pray for divine intervention. Even a sip of water would be enough for such a thirsty person.

If someone had tried talking me out of suicide by telling me that I had a lot to live for, it would have been useless. I wouldn't have believed it. Had I believed in the power of prayer, I could have used it to create an opening, and Spirit could have helped me make necessary changes. My sense of self-worth might have been strengthened, and then, *maybe,* I would have believed my physical life was worth living.

Since transitioning, I've witnessed changes in people who pray and opportunities that have resulted. When asking for Spirit's assistance, it's important to remain open and receptive to the different ways assistance can occur. The help may not come in the way you think it should. Pay attention. Open your heart, your mind, and your imagination.

In the long run, there is no running from your pain. You can try to numb yourself with slow, self-sabotaging methods—excessive eating, drinking, and drugs—or you can end it through suicide. But in the end, these methods don't heal anything.

While I'm reminded here in Spirit that I'm much more than my wounds, being here doesn't heal the wounds I ran away from. I can gain understanding about how and why the wounds were created, but when I choose another physical body in another physical life, the same wounds will be front and center. Spirited life rejuvenates me, gives me greater perspective and strengthens my power to love myself *with* the wounds; but I have wounds that can only be worked out in physical form. I'll strive to remember and bring this fresh perspective back into a new physical life, but I'll still be subject to the veil of forgetfulness. We choose the physical circumstances that will remind us of what needs to be healed. Everything is orchestrated to provide us with what we need.

During my life review, I saw that I'd had countless opportunities to heal the wounds, but because I'd been so afraid of change, I hadn't even entertained them as possibilities. If I'd acted on the opportunities, I could have taken Physical Bill to his full potential. Instead, I'm now focused on creating another physical life and having to do it over again.

Irene: Isn't reincarnation a choice rather than a requirement?

Bill: It *is* a choice. I could remain in Spirit for eternity and never experience physical life again, but I want to go where the action is. I want to experience life through a physical body. Hopefully, I'll have the courage and conviction to embrace my own wisdom and take advantage of the opportunities to expand myself.

Irene: Why were you so afraid of change?

Bill: The belief that I was a failure was deeply ingrained in my thinking. I interpreted everything that happened as proof that it was true. When you have a hammer, everything looks like a nail. When you think and feel you're a failure, everything that happens is interpreted as proof that you're right. I couldn't take one more failure.

Irene: If there were one thing you could say to people, what would it be?

Bill: Know that you affect each other with your thoughts, your feelings, your words, and your actions. Be aware of what you believe about yourself. It can enhance and empower you, or it can detract from and disempower you.

BILL

CONVERSATION EIGHT

Irene: I'd like to talk about young people who commit suicide. As a parent, I can't imagine anything more painful.

Bill: It's painful anytime a child's death precedes their parent's; when it's the result of suicide, there are added components.

The parent-child relationship is unique. Parents are instinctually responsible for their children and are hard-wired to protect them from harm. It's instinctual for a parent—and especially for a mother—to put their child's life ahead of their own. While everyone who survives the suicide of a loved one thinks about what they might have done to prevent it, this response is stronger in parents.

People often hide feelings of inadequacy by putting on an act of superiority, and this is especially true for parents. Parenting, by its very nature, includes being responsible for someone who is dependent. Parents of a child who commits suicide think they could have or should have been able to prevent it. They review their relationship, picking it apart to find ways they may have contributed to their child's decision.

Parents aren't responsible for their children's choices. Children come with their own spiritual agendas and choose their parents based on full disclosure of their parents' limitations. Parents provide their children with a color palette, if you will. Sometimes the palette is large and the children have many choices, and sometimes the palette is small and choices are limited. What children do with these colors is *their* choice, based on what they bring into this lifetime. That's why siblings who grow up in the same

220

environment can have such different experiences and ultimately such different lives. They've chosen different ways of combining the colors in the palette, based on their individual needs.

Parents teach best by example, so their first responsibility is to themselves and to their own healing. By doing their own inner work, they're not only better able to meet the needs of their children, but to model what it is to be a healthy human being, living in harmony with life. The more that parents are able to love and accept themselves, the more they're able to love and accept their children.

Children aren't victims, and it's a misconception to think they aren't powerful. Victimization is a disempowering concept that is based on false beliefs.

Irene: Yes, Jerry and I talked about that. What are some of the false beliefs to which *you're* referring?

Bill: Beliefs like, *Outer circumstances are more powerful than I am; My mother died of cancer and so will I; I'm unworthy, so I don't deserve to be happy; I'm unlovable, so I'll never have a good relationship*—things like that.

Irene: What are some of the misinterpretations people make about children and power?

Bill: Most people don't consider that, not only do we choose our parents and all the circumstances into which we're born, we also come into physical life with innate wisdom.

What primarily distinguishes an adult from a child is current physical lifetime experience. Adults appear more experienced as a result of having chosen the parental role and having lived more physical years in the current lifetime. A child, however, may have lived more lifetimes with greater consciousness and be more in touch with their own innate wisdom.

We access wisdom by living consciously. Taking responsibility for our circumstances, choices and reactions is a life examined, a conscious life. If parents recognized the inherent wisdom of their children, they might not feel responsible for their children's choices. What may look like an injustice is a well-orchestrated plan for the benefit of all concerned.

Irene: I'm reminded of Louise Hay, who experienced physical and emotional abuse as a child. As an adult, she looked for ways to change and heal so she wouldn't continue repeating the same patterns of abuse. Her quest led her to a Science of Mind lecture, where she learned that, in order to change her life, she'd have to change her thoughts. I wonder if she would be influencing millions of people today as a pioneer in the field of spirit-mind-body if she hadn't had those early childhood experiences.

Bill: The soul chooses life experiences for purposes of growth and expansion.

Irene: That's why it's impossible to judge a situation without access to a greater perspective. (Pause) How would you characterize a healthy parent?

Bill: A healthy parent is one who does their inner work. If they feel inadequate, for example, they would heal it rather than hide their feelings and try to overcompensate. I thought I had to be strong for my children rather than true to myself. They wanted me to be happy, but I didn't see that. I missed a lot of joy in relating to them by trying so hard to be something I wasn't. I kept telling myself that I was doing it for *them,* that I was modeling what it looks like to be a good provider and a strong person. What I was really modeling was inauthenticity. I had so many judgments about how a good parent *should* be that I couldn't hear my own inner wisdom.

The more inner work we do to release the misconceptions and judgments we've made, the more we're able to access our loving and joyous Selves, and the happier we are. And what great role models we are for our children when we're truly ourselves. After all, isn't that what we want for each other?

BILL

CONVERSATION NINE

Irene: How did your suicide affect your children?

Bill: Once I transitioned into Spirit form, I felt the emotions of my loved ones as if they were mine. I recognized that what my children were feeling was part of their growth, so I didn't try and steer them away from their feelings. My only intervention was to love them.

From a physical perspective, it's tempting to envision healing as making someone feel "better," or "differently." Thinking I could somehow have convinced them *not* to feel shame, guilt, or anger—that it was unproductive or that they had nothing to be ashamed, guilty, or angry about—would have interfered with their process. Their feelings are an expression of divine intelligence. They were and are learning that what they think of themselves is far more important than what others think of them. My love and ongoing support is helping them access this wisdom.

I saw how my actions affected them, yet I also saw how *my* life choices fit into *their* life choices. My suicide provided an opportunity for my family and friends to grow. It's important for everyone to know that it was *my* choice to end my life. Everyone in my life knew, on some level, that this was an option for me. They also knew what they stood to gain from the experience in terms of growing in love and wisdom. It's up to them to remember. The more they remember what there is to gain, the deeper they'll grow in wisdom. The feelings that have surfaced as a result of this experience are designed to guide them to the wounds within themselves that need healing. These are wounds that have nothing to do with my choice to end my physical life.

Irene: Have you been challenged by your children's process?

Bill: No, because I know they're okay. I know they're safe. They can't get hurt. Nothing "bad" can happen to them, because they're the ones creating their lives. They're always loved and divinely guided.

Irene: What about your wife?

Bill: She felt guilty. I merged with her while she slept so she could understand my perspective and why I'd made the decision to end my life. As she grew in understanding, she grew stronger in her own sense of Self. She had a tendency to feel responsible for others, which she has since healed. My kids continue to grow stronger in their sense of Self by honoring their own wisdom, just as my wife continues to grow stronger by knowing she's responsible only for her own choices and not for the choices of others. In both cases, the power of Self was strengthened through my suicide.

Irene: What prompts people to choose one particular method of suicide over another?

Bill: In most cases, there isn't a lot of rational thought. There are quick and assured methods, and there are methods that allow for intervention or changing one's mind.

BILL AND JERRY

CONVERSATION TEN

Irene: Were you confused when you transitioned?

Bill: No. I knew what I'd done, and I knew why. I was still present to the emotional pain that had led to my decision, but I felt hopeful.

As Physical Bill, I didn't think there was anything else I could do. I was in despair. I couldn't see any other possibility. I thought I was my body. I thought I was what I believed. I thought I was what I felt.

Putting an end to my physical life shifted my perspective and I no longer felt trapped. I still had my limiting beliefs—they didn't vanish—but I saw and knew that I was *more.* The feelings of separation disappeared. I found myself in a space of unconditional love in which I understood that my feelings of separation in physical life had been generated by my thoughts and beliefs.

Irene: You no longer felt powerless when you realized the distinction between who you are and what you believe.

Bill: Indeed. I'd always felt cut-off and alone, no matter how many people were around or how much love they expressed. It was like a constant and unquenchable thirst that was so intense, I couldn't think about anything else. The deep-seated issues that had prevented me from receiving love took a back seat to the symptom.

(Pause) After I transitioned, the thoughts and prayers of physical loved ones got through to me. I was able to receive their love in the same way a dry sponge absorbs water.

Irene: What about people who transition who don't have physical loved ones thinking of them or praying for them?

Bill: If they don't have physical friends and family, they have spirited friends and family. No one is ever alone.

Irene: What would you say to someone who has had a loved one commit suicide and thinks that, if only they had said *this* or done *that,* they could have prevented it?

Bill: A person contemplating suicide feels isolated, alone, and afraid. They've constructed what they think is a protective enclosure, but it's actually a confinement that reinforces their feelings of isolation. They have to be willing to create an opening within that enclosure for family and friends to enter. You can't help someone who doesn't want to be helped.

Irene: I've often heard it said that you can't help someone who doesn't want to be helped, but it's never been as clear as it is now. I look forward to sharing this information with my friend Denise. She was scheduled to have dinner with her brother Dan, but she had to cancel at the last minute. Dan committed suicide. Denise felt guilty. She thought that, if only she hadn't cancelled, Dan would still be alive.

Bill: Even if she'd had dinner with him, Dan still would have had to be willing to create an opening in order for her to have made a difference. If he'd been willing to create an opening, some-one—in this case, Denise—would have stepped in. And even if *she* hadn't, someone else would have. Something as simple as a smile or a kind word from someone would have made the differ-ence. Everything is orchestrated. If Dan had needed someone's assistance to guide him in a new direction, someone would have been there. There is always a response to our needs. Had he been open to such a change, there would have been no way Denise could have cancelled. The universe would have responded to the opening. We are not in this alone. And remember: no person is responsible for the actions of another.

Irene: My friend Archie discovered the body of his friend Judy after she committed suicide. Where's the win in that?

Bill: Why people choose what they choose can be very complex. Everything's agreed upon. There is a rhyme and reason for every event in which we participate. (Pause) Jerry has something he wants to say.

Jerry: A God-filled day! Yes, it's an agreement between the two people—in this case between Archie and Judy—and I agree with Bill that it's very complex and as unique as the person choosing.

One consequence may be that the person finding the body is now "forced" into counseling or therapy, thinking they're going because of the trauma. In the course of the therapy, however, other issues surface, and healing takes place that had nothing to do with the original issue. This is one way in which the soul keeps a person's life on track. The soul is always furthering its own agenda.

The answer to why we choose what we choose is that our choices create opportunities for expansion and a deeper, more meaningful relationship with life. "Why did this happen to me?" It creates opportunities. "Why did she choose that?" It creates opportunities. The more shocking the event, the more it wakes you up, and the bigger the opportunity for change.

Discovering Judy's body was an act of compassion on Archie's part. On one level, he may have been in shock or afraid, yet on another level, he knew this was a possibility and was prepared to be of assistance. When you're the first one on the scene with someone who's chosen to end their life, you're helping them transition. It may have seemed to Archie that Judy wasn't there, but she was present through her spirited body.

Irene: Can you be more specific as to how Archie was of assistance to Judy?

Jerry: Someone who's made the decision to commit suicide feels distraught and isolated. Self-absorbed in their despair, their only thought is, *How can I end this pain?* Archie assisted Judy in experiencing the physical reality of her act. She felt Archie's emotional response, which broke her illusion of isolation, reminding her that we are connected, and we do, indeed, affect others.

BILL

CONVERSATION ELEVEN

Irene: You left off in a previous conversation by saying that you were able to access great compassion for yourself and for the decision you'd made to end your physical life. What happened then?

Bill: I was introduced to a being, *the counselor,* who explained that it was his* job to work with individuals whose last experience in physical form had included trauma and deep emotional pain. He said he was there to ameliorate the pain that had fueled my decision to terminate my physical life before I had originally agreed.

Irene: I'm hearing you say that you ended your physical life before you had originally agreed, yet you mentioned previously that no one dies too soon or too late.

Bill: Let me use an analogy. You, Irene, have every intention of completing the masters program you're in, as do most people who begin the program. While the option exists for students to stop, quit, or choose an alternate route, no one begins the program with that intention. It's no different with marriage: when two people vow to spend their lives together, they intend to do so even though they know that divorce is an option. *My* original intention was to go through physical life to an old age. We feel an initial enthusiasm—whether it's for a degree, a relationship, or a

---

*Gender isn't necessary beyond the physical experience. It is an option.

physical life—yet we can't foresee the challenges we'll face along the way or how we'll respond to feelings that surface. There's intelligence behind every challenge, and each one is designed to provide opportunities to heal wounds and expand into greater expression.

The judgment I held—that expressing feelings was a sign of weakness—prevented me from expressing my feelings. Needing something or someone outside myself meant I was weak. I would have described myself as strong and independent, but what I was really saying was that I didn't need anyone. Being unable to receive love meant I was self-sufficient. I made *not* receiving love into a virtue.

What I'm learning is that feelings are energetic and they guide us to our innate wisdom. Withholding the expression of feelings restricts the flow of energy. This is contrary to life, because it's the nature of life to flow. Just as there's intelligence in the flow of life, there's intelligence in the flow of feelings, and it's this intelligence that's guiding us to ever greater expression and expansion.

We choose these avenues—school, relationships, life—to expand ourselves. It's in the journey of expansion that the places of contraction reveal themselves for the purpose of making us aware of our wounds so that we can heal them. Each time a wound is revealed, we have a choice: we can go within and release the judgment or misconception that generated the wound, or we can distract ourselves with food, sex, TV, shopping, gambling, drugs, video games, or the Internet. These activities aren't wrong; sometimes we just aren't ready to heal. Sometimes we have to leave school, the relationship, or even physical life. Life will still continue to present us with opportunities.

Irene: There is no failure, only repeated opportunity.

BILL

CONVERSATION TWELVE

Irene: What happened when you met the counselor?

Bill: Imagine sitting across from someone who knows your heart, your thoughts, and your intentions, and who loves you unconditionally. He was focused and attentive, and I was his only concern. He said he was going to take me on a journey that would include my physical life as Bill, as well as moments from other lifetimes that were directly related.

The journey began with the planning of my physical life as Bill. I was in the company of the counselor and two others, and we were telepathically communicating about the plan for my life. They reminded me of unresolved issues from other lifetimes and how they'd figure in to what I intended to accomplish. My inner strength and conviction were strong before beginning my physical journey.

Then I re-experienced my entire physical life, seeing and feeling the moments that either strengthened or weakened my original intention.

Irene: And what was your original intention?

Bill: My original intention was to heal self-doubt by yielding to the wisdom of my soul. I intended to fully express the skills and gifts I'd cultivated throughout lifetimes and to stand strong in being Bill. I intended to express my unique perspective without allowing the opinions of others to distract or dissuade me.

My life force was strengthened when I made choices that supported my original intention. When I worried about what others thought of me and I made decisions based on their opinions, my life force weakened. During this journey, for each disempowering choice I had made, I was taken on a side excursion that enabled me to trace the self-doubt back to its origin, which often meant a different lifetime.

Irene: And what was the origin of your self-doubt?

Bill: False beliefs about my Self and denial of my power as Spirit. (Pause) There was no room for judgment or regret during this exploration. By the time we finished, I had a greater understanding of myself. Each of my decisions made perfect sense in the context of all my experiences.

Irene: Fascinating.

Bill: That's not all. As if that weren't amazing enough, I was then shown the life I would have lived if I had made empowering choices in place of the disempowering ones. I saw myself taking my last breath at age eighty-six, after having lived a fulfilled life, surrounded by family members who loved me. This vision was filled with hope. By seeing these alternative choices, I realized I had always had the power to live my life to its fullest potential. I had always had the freedom to choose.

Irene: So your life review was a little different from the standard review, in that you were able to see an alternative life had you made choices in alignment with your original intention.

Bill: Just as different kinds of nutritional supplements support different conditions, *this* specific supplement best supported *my* condition. Those of us who have pain and shame associated with our transition need to be reminded of how powerful we are. We need to be reminded that we had the inner strength to follow-through on our intentions.

Irene: It reminds me of Dorothy's journey in *The Wizard of Oz* when she realizes that she's had the inner power to fulfill her intentions all along.

BILL

CONVERSATION THIRTEEN

Irene: What happened after your life review?

Bill: I was filled with appreciation for life. It was in this state that I found myself at a party, surrounded by transitioned friends and family. I felt like I'd accomplished great deeds, just by living the life I'd lived.

This was a celebration, but it was also an extension of the orientation, because talking with friends and family reminded me of all the opportunities available here in Spirit. People authentically and joyously shared how they were participating in their spirited lives, what they were accomplishing, and how much they were enjoying themselves. Unlike parties I had attended as Physical Bill, no one here had anything to hide, nor was anyone pretending to be someone they weren't.

I was shown people's living arrangements, and I began planning how I would choose to reside here. I was amazed by the freedom. Someone reminded me that freedom is also available in physical form, but we limit ourselves through fears, doubts, and erroneous beliefs.

I had more questions, so the counselor and I had an in-depth conversation. I realized that I had grown, and I saw that my life as Physical Bill had been powerful and productive. As a result, I was able to understand the process of life and the wisdom of Spirit with greater depth. I learned that, no matter how long or short a physical life is, we're always expanding. Even a life lived unconsciously and unexamined will expand a person. There is no such thing as a wasted lifetime.

Irene: Did you attend your memorial?

Bill: Yes. It felt important for me to attend the service as a rite of passage. I also used it as an opportunity to connect with family and friends and comfort them. I was aware of a lot of judgments—not from my immediate family, but from friends and extended family. Some people were angry with me; they didn't understand my decision and judged me as selfish. It's useful for people to know that their thoughts are very loud to those of us in Spirit. I'm not suggesting that people monitor their thoughts; I'm suggesting that they be more conscious of their judgments and work to heal them.

Irene: Bill, this has been such a heart-warming and eye-opening dialogue. Thank you for your willingness to share yourself and your experience for the highest good of all concerned. I am grateful for our friendship and I look forward to seeing you when I transition. Blessings, my friend.

Bill: Thank you. I've loved being recognized and heard. I appreciate these conversations and the contribution they've made to my life. Your questions encouraged me to go deeper into my own wisdom. Some of the things I shared were realizations that emerged in me as I communicated them. I've also grown from hearing your perspective on spirituality and life. Connecting with Jana has deepened my understanding of what it is to work closely with someone as part of a team, and it has strengthened my ability to connect and communicate with the physical realm.

As with all heartfelt conversations, I feel expanded and in touch with a greater sense of who I am.

VINCE

1927 – 2003

Vince had just turned seventy when I met him. He was an artist, poet, and author, open and curious about physical life and beyond. He was also something of a philosopher, and I enjoyed many a stimulating conversation over a cup of coffee at his kitchen table. Talking with Vince was always an adventure because I never knew where the conversation would lead.

He was as colorful a character as I'd ever met. I'm fairly certain he owned false teeth, but I can't say that I ever saw him wear them. Vince enjoyed chewing tobacco, and every-now-and-then, he'd walk over to the kitchen door where he'd spit into a jar that he kept specifically for that purpose. He made the worst coffee I'd ever tasted and never had cream in the fridge, but the conversation was always exceptionally refreshing.

VINCE

CONVERSATION ONE

Irene: Vince, what did you experience when you released your last breath on earth?

Vince: It was as if I pushed myself out of my body. In the final days, my spirit or my soul or my life force—I don't know what to call it—was lying right above me.

Irene: How would you describe it?

Vince: Have you ever seen pictures of a jellyfish? It looked like a jellyfish made of light. It was a pulsating, translucent glob, and it hovered over my body.

Irene: Did you have any thoughts or feelings about it? Was it comforting? Unnerving?

Vince: I was amazed. I didn't know what it was. I just knew it was there above me and that somehow it was connected to me. When I was ready to release myself from my physical body, I pushed myself away with one last exhalation and I heard a noise— a popping sound—that I interpreted as some kind of separation. I realized I was free from my physical body and didn't need to be around it anymore. Once this severance took place, I was free to move around the room.

Irene: What was most surprising to you about the process of transitioning?

Vince: I was surprised at how familiar it felt to be out of my physical body, as if I'd awakened from a dream. Seeing my physical body asleep made this just-awakened feeling all the more real. Everything around me was resplendent.

My physical friend, Ben, was present in the room, and I realized we were feeling each other's feelings. I was feeling his sadness blend with my elation, and he was feeling my elation blend with his sadness. I felt more connected to him than I ever had. I knew feelings were contagious, but I never knew we had the capacity to feel so deeply. I wondered if we affect each other this deeply in physical form and we're just unaware of it. I knew the answer was *yes*. I felt someone's presence.

Irene: Who was it?

Vince: It was my grandmother. I remembered being a child and going to her with questions about life. She'd answer my questions with other questions, always encouraging me to think for myself and come to my own conclusions. I sensed the same thing was happening again. She hadn't told me the answer to my question, I just knew the answer while in her presence. I realized that it was the quality of her presence—then and now—that had led me to the answers I sought.

Irene: She created the space for you to access your own wisdom by being fully present and holding a loving space for you. She knew you had all the necessary resources within you to find your own answers.

Vince: Yes. And then it occurred to me that appreciating each other's qualities is part of our responsibility in physical form; it's the only way we're going to get the best out of one other. I applied this realization to my friend Ben by focusing on the qualities I love about him. I could feel him expand and become more assured by what had just taken place. He thought, *Vince is okay and in a better place.* He became more joyful and less fearful about my release.

I also realized that we often have a personal agenda when we connect with others. I could have thought, *Ben, I don't want you to be afraid; I want you to feel the joy of my release and be happy for me.* Instead, I focused on the qualities I love about Ben, and he came to that conclusion on his own. I didn't originally have that in mind, like, *I want him to feel better so I'll focus on his qualities.* I was simply expressing my love for him, and with that love, the shift took place.

Irene: If you could tell people on earth one thing, what would it be?

Vince: Love each person for who they are, and let love work its miracles. Love has its own agenda. It's not up to us to decide what's best for anyone.

VINCE

CONVERSATION TWO

Irene: What happened after you became aware of your grandmother's presence?

Vince: I gained insight as I saw myself through her eyes. I'd been inquisitive as a child, and as a result of her early encouragement, I remained that way throughout my life. She'd always taken the time to be present with me, and as a result, I learned that I was worthwhile and deserving of attention. What an enormous contribution to my self-confidence and self-expression! I recognized how much she had influenced me and how much we influence each other by showing up and being fully present.

Irene: What a loving and powerful relationship you shared.

Vince: It influenced the course of my life.

Irene: What happened next?

Vince: That was the beginning of my life review.

Irene: What form were you focusing through?

Vince: I didn't become aware of my form until later. It looked similar to the physical body I'd left behind, but it was energetic. When I moved my hand, for example, it left a visible trail. If I moved my hand back and forth, it lost form easily, but when I stopped the movement—*whoosh*—it would regain its form. While I recognized that light could pass through it, I also recognized that I *was* the light.

I felt tired. I wanted to close my eyes and fall asleep, and with that thought, I lost sight of my grandmother and peacefully drifted away.

When I became conscious again, I realized that Creation had responded to my need for a comfortable place to sleep: I'd been lying on a surface made specifically for my body. A custom fit! Most of my needs in the physical world had been met by someone else's creation. When I'd sit down, for example, I'd attempt to conform to a chair someone else had made. When I have a need to sit in a chair here in Spirit, it's a custom fit that comes through me and for me.

Irene: Fascinating. So you awoke . . .

Vince: I awoke refreshed, like I'd been asleep for centuries. I reflected on my physical body, my transition, and my physical friends, and with that thought, a man wearing a robe appeared. He introduced himself as an old friend and explained that he'd been a spiritual assistant to me throughout all my physical incarnations on earth. He said that, during his last incarnation, he'd walked with me during the time of Buddha. One lifetime with Buddha had been enough to catapult him out of more physical experiences.

Irene: Why had it been enough to catapult him from physical experience and not you?

Vince: I wasn't finished with physical life. I'm curious, and human nature is a universe in itself; the best way to explore it is in human form.

Irene: Don't we all want to achieve the level of consciousness of a Buddha or a Christ?

Vince: You aren't required to pass some test or jump through hoops in order to *be* that consciousness. You already are. Your human experience only appears to be less evolved. Physical life has a protocol and rules; it requires a certain "toning down" of consciousness. Buddha and Christ are living examples of how much consciousness your physical body is capable of embodying, supporting, and expressing. They're inspirational reminders of who you would be and what you could do if you chose to bring that consciousness into physical existence. But the earth isn't a series of tests we attempt to pass in order to achieve what Buddha or Christ did, nor is it a game we're trying to win. The purpose of life is to allow and accept ourselves as we are, without judgment, which is the only way to fully embody love. By loving and accepting ourselves, we're able to love and accept others, which strengthens the flow of love. "Irene" is a character you've chosen to focus your consciousness through. It's like playing *Clue:* you know you're not really Colonel Mustard or Professor Plum.

Irene: How about Mrs. Peacock?

Vince: (Laughing) No, not even Mrs. Peacock.

Irene: (Laughing) Okay, back to your friend wearing the robe.

Vince: I asked him his name and he said it was Jonifer. He had read my thoughts about my physical friends and asked if I wanted to visit them where they were gathered at a memorial for me. I thought, *I've been sleeping for what seems like centuries—isn't that over with?*

Jonifer laughed and said, "You're no longer limited by time. You have the power to visit any part of your life as if you were living it, now." He laughed again. "Now is the time, and now is the only time."

I remembered how directly I'd felt my physical friend's sadness and decided I didn't want to experience more. But then I thought, *Maybe they need me at the memorial.* As soon as I had that thought, I had a realization: *when I choose what's most loving for me, everyone benefits.* I locked eyes with Jonifer. He smiled, and I knew this was universal truth. I chose to honor myself and not attend my memorial.

It occurred to me that we were communicating without moving our lips. I smiled, celebrating the ease of our connection. I felt such a deep love for him and from him; I didn't know I was capable of such love! As we embraced, I knew the power of love was coming through me, through him, through us, and was all around. *If this is the mystery of life after death of the physical body, why do we fear it? Do we fear our power?* I felt jubilant. I wanted to get back into physical form and shout to everyone, "It's okay! You don't have to be afraid!"

Irene: I know that feeling. When I realized that my transitioned loved ones were still alive, I wanted to shout, "There *is* no death!" I danced around my house for days. (Pause) Go on . . .

Vince: I joined Jonifer on what I would have called a stroll, but this was a glide. Putting one foot in front of the other was effortless, like moving on an electric walkway, except there was no pressure on the bottoms of my feet. I noticed people sitting together, engaged in conversation. Jonifer and I stopped near two such people. They looked up at us and exchanged greetings.

As they focused on me, and I on them, I became aware of their voices welcoming me Home. One said that the adventure was just beginning and there was so much to do, see, and experience. I felt the love in his words and his eyes. He said that, for him, it was like revisiting his hometown after a lengthy absence, because everything was familiar and new at the same time. I felt his excitement and exhilaration and realized that the feelings weren't coming from me; they were coming *through* me—from *him*. I'm now familiar with the difference between feelings *I* generate and those that come through me from someone else's sharing.

Individuals were surrounded by different scenery; everyone had their own landscape in which they were playing, walking, or just sitting. Two people were sitting near a stream, for example, and there were wildflowers, trees, birds, and butterflies—the whole nine yards—but there was a point at which the colors became watery and the scene began to fade. The two people were creating that particular scene, which was serving them without needing to stretch beyond their needs. I asked Jonifer if I could do this and create any scene I wanted.

"What would you like?" he asked.

"I want to be in a studio with floor-to-ceiling windows, over-looking Florence pre-World War II," and before I could finish the details of the scene, I found myself with Jonifer, in that scene.

"Does this answer your question?" he asked, and we both laughed.

Jonifer told me that I could make this studio a part of my home base if I wanted. He said there were master artists with whom I could meet, converse, and study. The elation I felt was indescribable.

"We have more to do," Jonifer said. And the glide continued.

VINCE

CONVERSATION THREE

Irene: What happened next on your tour with Jonifer?

Vince: I was informed that I would be experiencing the life I'd just lived. As Physical Vince, the thought of all the painful memories would have scared me, but in *this* atmosphere, in *this* form, in the presence of *this* friend, I welcomed the adventure.

I was simultaneously surrounded by and part of what looked like a 3-D theater. The scenes weren't on screens, though, nor were they separate from me like they'd be in a movie theater. Instead, they were under me, above me, and somehow coming *from* me because I was part of each scene.

I re-experienced my life as Physical Vince, starting as a cell in my mother's womb. I had a deep connection with my mother and father through this cell, and I was aware of their thoughts and feelings at the time I was conceived. When my mother discovered she was pregnant with me, our connection grew even stronger. I was aware of the influence I had on them and the influence they had on me. I felt their excitement, but I also felt their fear—about what kind of parents they'd be and how they'd provide for me—so I provided reassurance by focusing on them and on their power as co-creators of this situation. I reminded them of the infinite abundance and wisdom available.

Irene: When you say you had a deep connection with your mother and father through this cell, was this cell *you*?

Vince: My connection with the cell took place from a distance, because my fetal body hadn't developed enough to sustain my life force.

Irene: Where did this life force exist if it wasn't in the fetal body?

Vince: To put it simply, my life force was in the non-physical dimension, where it was focused on creating my physical form.

Irene: Is the life force the same as the soul?

Vince: Yes and no. The soul is the source of the life force.

Irene: Can you elaborate?

Vince: Is sunlight the same as the sun?

Irene: Yes and no. Okay, I get it. So you were connected to your fetal body from the non-physical dimension.

Vince: Yes. And it wasn't until I was moments away from birth that I committed to this lifetime. I was aware throughout the gestation that I could have chosen to abort my mission. I was also conscious of what I wanted to do in physical form as Vince. Just prior to being born, I was told that the best time for changing my mind was within the first few days after birth. Even though it would have been painful for my parents, my ability to help in their healing would have been great.

Irene: Why might you have changed your mind?

Vince: (Laughing) Cold feet. The prospect of forgetting the oneness was as appealing as the thought of shoveling snow off the driveway on a wintry morning when the temperature's below freezing and the sun hasn't risen.

Irene: How would you have accomplished helping your parents if you'd chosen to abort your mission?

Vince: I would have put my attention on them and expanded my energy field to include them in the reality of oneness—a reality they'd forgotten. You know you've forgotten the reality of oneness when you blame yourself or another, which is a common occurrence when parents experience the sudden loss of their child.

Irene: I heard you say that you were told that the best time for changing your mind was within the first few days after birth. Who told you?

Vince: There were spirited beings—consultants—assisting

with the planning of my physical lifetime; they were guiding me and answering my questions. I had asked, "What if I change my mind?" That's when I received their answer.

Irene: You left off with feeling a deep connection with your mother and father.

Vince: Yes. And in colorful detail, I relived every second of my life. It was a rich experience, and even though each moment was filled with emotion—either mine or someone else's—it was an objective review. There were times as Physical Vince, for example, when I'd felt pleasure at someone else's expense. In the review, I simultaneously felt my pleasure—or what I thought was pleasure—and their painful reaction. But I remained objective all the while, reliving the emotions, but not creating new ones.

Irene: Did you primarily feel empathy and compassion for yourself and others?

Vince: I observed and analyzed. I felt every emotion without judgment. I noted how the emotion felt and how it affected everyone and everything around me, as well as how the reactions of others affected *my* emotions. I felt their feelings as if I'd lived their lives. Emotions are alive and constantly changing; like colors in motion, they blend together to form new ones. If you cheer up a friend, for example, you're adding your joy—in the form of optimism and encouragement—to their sadness; and while their sadness may not transform into joy, it'll probably lighten. Experiencing emotions during the life review—without reacting to them, judging them, or generating new ones—was gratifying.

As I witnessed how each person had influenced and changed me, I was reminded of the importance of every person in my life. Moments I had judged as insignificant and taken for granted—someone saying something that had gotten me back on track or inspired me—I now observed as significant. So many people had been like angels in my life, empowering me. And while certain interactions had weakened and *dis*empowered me, I realized that people weren't intentionally trying to harm me; they were simply responding to their own beliefs about themselves—feeling threatened by my power, for example, instead of embracing their own.

Irene: You mentioned that some people had kept you on track. How so?

Vince: To be on track as Physical Vince meant seeing the magic in the mundane and successfully communicating that magic through my art. As an artist, I set out to make visible the unseen beauty that's often taken for granted in physical life.

People had often encouraged me, both blatantly with words and subtly, though their unspoken responses to something I'd created. As Physical Vince, I could have been standing right next to such a person and missed their reaction. In the life review, I not only saw their reaction, I felt it and recognized how it had encouraged me. Every character had their place in my life, and I in theirs; I watched, delighted and amazed by this divine orchestration. Even something seemingly insignificant—like passing someone on the street—held meaning in my life.

Irene: How so?

Vince: One such encounter occurred when my creative energy was at a peak. I was walking down the street, appreciating life, imagining my next painting and the vivid colors I would use. I passed someone whose life force was very low—someone who was feeling despair—and I saw how my energy had intersected with theirs and uplifted them. I'd been oblivious to these kinds of interactions as Physical Vince. I also saw the opposite—the times when *I'd* been the one in despair—and how it had affected the people around me or how the despair had shifted as a result of a brief encounter. Some encounters had been like seeds planted in the ground, and while I may not have seen an immediate change, I saw the effects later. There are no insignificant moments. Everything that happens is significant and has meaning and effect.

VINCE

CONVERSATION FOUR

Irene: When you completed your life review, had you been able to find the loving wisdom in every interaction?

Vince: Each interaction was like a puzzle piece, which, when assembled, was the completed puzzle of my life as Vince. Sometimes I knew where a piece fit, and other times I needed surrounding pieces before I could make sense of it.

When I was in my early twenties, for example, I was turned down for a position at an art school. It wasn't until I saw this in relation to other pieces—in this case to other events—that I saw the wisdom behind what had happened. Had I gotten the job, I wouldn't have met the people or had the experiences that ultimately made me the artist I was.

Irene: Is there a point of completion with the puzzles?

Vince: No, it's an endless journey. I enjoy studying my lifetimes and noting the inherent patterns. Life is exciting. I'm glad there isn't an end to this.

Irene: What inherent patterns have you discovered?

Vince: Independence and trust, for example. While I'd always prided myself on being independent, I discovered that the motivation behind my independence was a lack of trust in others. I didn't often make room for people in my life, and when I did, it was on *my* terms. I was frequently provided with opportunities to experience interconnectedness with others—something my soul wanted for me—but, more often than not, I chose to remain alone. I'm seeing progress in this arena, though, because I experienced the deepest levels of intimacy in many lifetimes as Physical Vince.

Irene: If you could be in physical form right now, how would you choose to live differently?

Vince: I wouldn't do anything differently. Under the circumstances and with the awareness I had at the time, I think I made the most of my life. It was a rich experience, and I'm grateful for my perspective. Yes, there were moments I glossed over and took for granted, but it would be foolish of me to have regrets or wish I'd done it differently. As I view my lifetime using the puzzle analogy, each piece was necessary in order for me to be who I am today. I'll have many more opportunities to live physical life while retaining the wisdom that's mine as a spirited being. And even though physical form shades much of the light that I have access to as a spirited being, I know that I *am* this light—and when I forget, friends and family will remind me. We're never alone. We're so important to one another. That's something I want everyone to know.

If I were to compare my life review to a play, I was in the audience observing the performances while also being every character in the play. It was the most thorough character study any actor would ever need in order to play a role. I was aware of the experiences that made me who I was in any given moment and simultaneously aware of the experiences that made others who they were. What each person said and did made sense, given their experiences prior to a particular moment in time. I experienced each moment with this kind of depth. I felt skilled and adept in being able to pull off such a feat. It was an easy and familiar process.

Irene: How did fear affect your life as Physical Vince?

Vince: I had a lot of judgments about myself; I was afraid people wouldn't like me or like my art, so I kept them at arm's length. During my life review, I saw how my fears had created barriers that prevented love from coming into my life.

When I visit my physical family and friends now, I like to tune-in to how many layers of self-imposed "protection" they have around their bodies. If you'll remember, I mentioned that, when I transitioned, I focused my love on my physical friend Ben, acknowledging his qualities. Now I do that with all my physical friends and family. When I'm in their presence, I allow my love for them to reach through their self-imposed layers of protection.

Irene: What happened when you completed your life review?

Vince: I had leisure time and was free to do whatever I chose.

Irene: Aren't you always free to do whatever you choose?

Vince: Of course, but it was suggested that I review my physical life while those in physical form were still in the grieving process, while I was fresh in their minds and while physical reality was still active in me. The more focused I am in my spirited body, the more physical reality seems like a dream.

VINCE

CONVERSATION FIVE

Irene: Vince, do you have routines like we have in the physical realm?

Vince: Yes. Routines describe a process. For example, in order to maximize your expression of physical health, you create routines and processes that support your intention: brushing your teeth and choosing nutritional foods. If your intention is to be financially abundant, you create routines unique to *that* intention: saving, investing, and tithing. I, too, have intentions, and the choices I make, as well as the routines I create, support those intentions.

I have an intention, for example, to learn more about how artists use creative energy to express themselves in a variety of mediums: music, writing, acting, painting, drawing, sculpting, and so forth. How do artists use creative energy? How does creative energy use *them?* Do they express creative energy freely, or does it stagnate inside of them as a result of self-doubt or self-loathing? Many artists die penniless, questioning their worth, even though their works—now considered priceless—hang in museums. These artists based their worth on what others thought of them because they thought so little of themselves.

I'm also learning new ways to see and feel color by using colors that stimulate specific emotional responses. Each color has a specific vibration and light frequency. Here in Spirit, colors go through me and I *feel* the difference between orange and blue—something not possible in the physical realm where, when light hits dense matter (your physical body), it meets with resistance. In the non-physical realm, blue and orange are more than just visually distinct. I want to capture and convey this when I'm in physical form again.

The senses here aren't the same as on the physical plane. If there were such a thing as a Depth of Experience Scale from 1–100, the potential on earth would be 1–25, and the potential here would be 26–100. We in the Spirit realm are capable of experiencing 26–100, but not 1–25. I'm not able to smell fragrances like I did on earth, but I don't miss it. I'm not able to hear sounds like I did on earth, but what I *am* able to experience, I can't convey to you. My intention is to absorb this realm so deeply that, when I'm in physical form again, I can be the poet or the artist who moves your soul to remember this spiritual vision. This is what I want to take back with me.

Irene: Others have spoken differently about the senses. Your description makes the most sense to me—no pun intended. (Pause) I've enjoyed connecting with you, Vince. Is there anything else you'd like to add?

Vince: I'd like to say this to your readers: when you believe your transitioned loved ones have ceased to exist, you close the door on the unseen and deny yourselves access to their continued existence in spirited form. I invite you to speak to your transitioned loved ones and listen for their reply—with *all* your senses. Be open. You may experience their response through nature, a song on the radio, a thought, or something you see or smell.

I'm grateful for this book and for my place in it. It's an honor to have my presence acknowledged in both worlds.

ZAYDEH

1900 – 1965

Zaydeh was my beloved grandfather. I remember him singing, "Yes, we have no bananas, we have no bananas today..." as we passed fruit vendors on our way to Chapultepec Park in Mexico City. I was five.

I also have vivid memories of sitting down to eat lunch with him. Before the meal was served, he'd raise his shot glass in the air and exclaim, "Le Chaim!" which in Yiddish means, "To Life!" Zaydeh always enjoyed a single shot of tequila before the main meal, and every now-and-then, I enjoy a shot of tequila in his honor. "To Life, Zaydeh!"

He died suddenly of a heart attack when I was ten. I laughed uncontrollably at his funeral.

ZAYDEH

CONVERSATION ONE

Irene: Zaydeh, what did you experience when you released your last breath on earth?

Zaydeh: As my body released me, I looked around the room and noticed how colorful the members of my physical family were. They weren't just people as I'd seen them hours before; they were like Joseph, with coats of many colors.

Irene: Can you elaborate?

Zaydeh: Each person was projecting different colors, some bright and others subdued. Each one seemed to have a dominating color that was uniquely theirs. These colors shifted and changed as family members interacted with one other. I felt like a child, mesmerized by what I was seeing.

Irene: If I recall the biblical story, Joseph's brothers were jealous of him because their father had given Joseph a coat of many colors.

Zaydeh: I love studying religious literature and traditions and finding the essence within the allegories and metaphors. It's my understanding that Joseph was a spiritual teacher and master, revered by his father and envied by his brothers. The robe was a gift from his father, and had a multitude of colors that represented Joseph's spiritual mastery. Most people have one dominating color that represents their level of consciousness; Joseph had more than one dominating color because of his expansive consciousness.

(Pause) As I looked around the room, I was amazed at how colorful human bodies are. As my physical family reacted and responded to my passing, the colors shifted and changed. And then, just by focusing on family members, I discovered I could feel their feelings—a mixture of sadness and relief. I could feel what they were feeling!

I noticed my physical body and laughed, thinking, *I'm glad I don't have to spend any more time being that old, shriveled-up prune!* Yes, I'd been feeling older and weaker in previous weeks, but I hadn't felt as bad as that body looked. I never thought I was *that* old!

Irene: What did you feel as your body released you?

Zaydeh: Relief. If you held your breath until you couldn't hold it a second longer, and then released it, you'd feel a sense of relief similar to what I experienced. I felt a warm sensation, as if someone were putting their hand on the middle of my back, between my shoulder blades. This warmth was comforting and assuring, and I could feel it all the way down to my feet, which led me to look down and see that I still had feet—and a body!

And then, just by thinking about turning around, I turned around, and there was my grandmother, the way I remembered her. I felt like a little boy, and with that thought, she wrapped her arms around me and I *became* that little boy, enveloped in love. We merged as one, embraced in a love I hadn't felt in a long time. Part of me remembered this love, and as I remembered, the love grew, and she became more than my grandmother. The light within her expanded and she became formless. The room with my physical body and physical family faded away, and I became formless, too, aware only of this love.

(Pause) I found myself in form again when I became aware of other forms around me.

Irene: What kind of form did you find yourself in?

Zaydeh: (Laughing) A vital version of the old prune.

Loved ones, some from childhood and others from my adult life, welcomed me. I felt like the center of everyone's attention, the prodigal son returning home. This was a place I never wanted to leave. *If this is heaven,* I thought, *I hope it's eternal.*

I was guided to my memorial service, where physical family members were present. I realized how narrow my perspective had been because it was reflected in their memories of me as a husband and father. Their memories mirrored the limitations I'd placed on myself: limitations about emotional expression, financial abundance, and about my potential, in general. Fear had held me back from physically expressing my love for family and friends; I didn't express emotions beyond what I thought was expected of me as a man. I didn't take risks in business, either. I considered it my obligation to take care of my family, so I was cautious in my business dealings. I preferred stability to risk-taking.

Family members were referring to me as the character I'd played, but I now knew myself as so much more. I wanted to stand up, be seen, and shout, "It's only a play! These are temporary roles! There's more to life than what you're experiencing!"

Irene: How frustrating that must have been!

Zaydeh: Yes, it was—and still is. It's not simply a lack of receptivity on the part of physical family members, though. I've had to relearn how to connect with the physical world through a non-physical body. As I've developed this skill, physical loved ones have become more responsive to me. I know I've gotten through, though, because I've seen and felt changes in them.

Irene: How did you develop this skill?

Zaydeh: By learning to communicate with them through their thoughts and feelings. It's an underutilized skill that all physical beings have, by the way. Simply passing into Spirit doesn't magically give us abilities; we're remembering and strengthening what's already present. These abilities can be developed while still in physical form.

Irene: What would you suggest?

Zaydeh: When I connect to the physical world, I notice that people say one thing but feel something different. I suggest you listen to what others are saying *beyond* their words. Don't just listen with your ears; listen with your heart.

Irene: I call that *heart-centered listening*. I set an intention to listen, not only to what is said—the content—but also to *how* something is said: the energy upon which the communication rides.

Zaydeh: Exactly. Connecting with that person's heart also strengthens your ability to read their thoughts.

Irene: That happens a lot with Charlie and me. I'll be thinking about something, and Charlie will voice it. Yesterday, for example, I was thinking about a movie we'd seen, and Charlie turned to me, commenting on how that particular movie had impacted him.

Zaydeh: The two of you have dropped your filters and your baggage and you've strengthened your heart connection; it's the most effective way to communicate.

Irene: Zaydeh, tell me more about your life review.

Zaydeh: It began with an urge to revisit situations from my physical life that had greatly affected me. We leave energetic imprints everywhere we go in the physical realm. When we're impacted by an experience, the energetic imprint serves to "bookmark" the event. By revisiting and exploring the experience, either immediately afterward or later in physical or non-physical life, we have an opportunity to learn more about ourselves. I was guided to explore these moments as part of my life review.

Irene: Can you tell me more about these energetic imprints? If an event that occurred when you were six years old had an impact on you that needed further exploration, then . . .

Zaydeh: Then I'd be exploring it as if I were six, in my six-year-old body, but with the wisdom of having lived my entire physical life—and more. Along with my own perspective, an even wider perspective is available in the wholeness of Spirit, so I would be looking through the lens of many lifetimes, as well as having access to the perspectives of everyone involved in that event. It's my understanding that the life review is tailored for each of us to meet our need for greater understanding.

ZAYDEH

CONVERSATION TWO

Irene: What was most surprising about your transition?

Zaydeh: I was surprised to see how solidly I still existed. My preconception was that I'd be a gossamer figure and just flit around. Beyond that, I wasn't sure. My beliefs were based on religious dogma, but they weren't very clear. I thought I'd have to go through a series of tests about religious knowledge to determine whether I was worthy of moving on to a heavenly state—and I was worried that maybe I should have studied more. After I released my physical body, though, I felt stronger, more confident, and more present than I'd ever felt.

Irene: So there were no tests, no *pass* or *fail*.

Zaydeh: (Laughing) I passed the test by passing out of my body!

Irene: Was there anything about the process that was upsetting?

Zaydeh: No. Nothing.

Irene: Were you in physical pain prior to transitioning?

Zaydeh: No, I wasn't in physical pain. I felt my physical body weakening and I wasn't strong enough to inhale. I went to sleep before transitioning, and that helped me release my physical body.

Zaydeh

Conversation Three

Irene: From what you shared in our first conversation, I gather you can change form or even choose to be formless.

Zaydeh: Yes. While form follows thought, form couldn't contain the amount of love present when I merged with my grandmother. Boundaries dissolved and I lost myself in love. The urge to connect with whatever you love and with love itself is also present on earth; there are times when you're so connected, you *feel* formless.

Irene: Zaydeh, what do you look like now?

Zaydeh: I look like I did when I was in my twenties, which was a time when I felt full of life.

Irene: You transitioned forty-five years ago. Why choose that particular form?

Zaydeh: You called on Zaydeh, so here I am. My form changes depending on who I'm interacting with. As I associate with friends, my mind creates a body that they're most familiar with or one that I'm most familiar with when I'm with them.

You do something similar by emphasizing certain characteristics with different people. When you meet a friend for lunch, for instance, you express yourself in a way that's unique to that relationship, and different, perhaps, than the way in which you express yourself with your spouse. This is similar to what I do; it's just more evident here.

Irene: So you look like you did in your twenties, but your body is less dense?

ZAYDEH • CONVERSATION THREE

Zaydeh: Yes. If I were to appear to you, I'd take on a form that you'd recognize from the times on earth when we connected most deeply. The particular memory you have of me would contribute to creating my form.

Irene: What if you meet two people in the Spirit realm that you knew from different times in your physical life? Maybe you were a child with one and an adult with the other.

Zaydeh: Initially, each one would see me differently. Once our connection was established, the form would no longer matter, and I'd assume whatever form I desired. It's like what *you* do when you feel free to be yourself and dress any way you like.

Irene: Do you experience emotions?

Zaydeh: Yes.

Irene: How is the experience of emotions in non-physical reality similar to or different from the experience in physical reality?

Zaydeh: As Physical Zaydeh, I was afraid of my emotions. I monitored them and tried to control them. I judged them. I questioned why I was feeling a particular emotion, and then I justified or rationalized why I *shouldn't* be feeling it. I blamed others for it, or I judged it as wrong and kept it inside, where it would build until it had a life of its own, finally coming out in ways I hadn't intended. If I felt angry and frustrated with a customer, for instance, instead of working it out with them, I'd take it out on my wife. Here in Spirit, I see emotions for what they are: expressions of energy. I don't judge them. If I feel frustrated, I express it, and it's received with acceptance. No one takes it personally.

Irene: Under what circumstance might you experience frustration?

Zaydeh: I experience frustration when the physical people I love are struggling in some way and I can't get through to them, because they can't or won't acknowledge my presence. The

261

frustration isn't directed at them or at myself; it's just an expression of energy and, once expressed, I continue to love and accept. Without the constraints and challenges of a physical life, I simply experience, express, and release emotions.

Irene: Experiencing, expressing, and releasing—that's what young children do.

Zaydeh: That's right. They just get it out and go on. My favorite relationships as Physical Zaydeh were with people who accepted me. They didn't try to change me for the sake of their own comfort. I felt free to speak my mind, knowing they'd listen without judgment. That's what it's like here.

Irene: Unexpressed emotions contribute to illness.

Zaydeh: Absolutely. When I see physical family members suppressing their emotions, I want to stick a pin in them—like popping a balloon—to help them vent their emotions and feel what they're feeling.

Irene: When I spoke with Beba about how she experiences emotions in the Spirit realm, she said she feels elation for the most part, and sometimes fear when she forgets her true nature.

Zaydeh: Fear is the root of many emotional expressions. It's true that if one forgets their power, even here in this heavenly experience, one can experience fear. Fear can look like anger, resentment, blame, and hate toward self or others. But again, these emotions are like puffs of smoke that appear and float away. You're transparent here, so you can't hold on to emotions. And there's no reason to hold on to them, because no one's going to deem your behavior inappropriate or point a finger at you and tell you that you're wrong for feeling what you're feeling. Unconditional love is our foundation and our essence.

Zaydeh

Conversation Four

Irene: What part did religion play in your physical life?

Zaydeh: It was conceptual. Even though I participated in the rituals of my religion, most of them didn't move me. These were rituals designed to connect me with God, so when I didn't feel the connection, I thought there was something wrong with me or with the way I was doing things. I felt incompetent and undeserving. I realize now, through my non-physical experience, that connecting more deeply with my Self is the way to connect with God.

Irene: With this new perspective, what part would religion play in your spiritual practice if you were on earth today?

Zaydeh: If I were to participate in a religious practice, I'd remain flexible, keeping in mind that religious principles are based on someone else's perspectives and beliefs about life. Some principles provide valuable guidelines, such as, *Love God with all your heart.* If that were the only principle you followed, your life would transform. Deeper reflection would reveal that everything and everyone is God. Imagine loving everything and everyone in your life! That would be many lifetimes of work right there. That would be the only religion you'd need. One could build temples, churches, and synagogues for the purpose of strengthening that one truth.

Irene: It's not necessary to build temples, churches, and synagogues to strengthen love.

Zaydeh: That's true, Irene, yet they serve the purpose of bringing people together under one roof or one canopy to strengthen love. "Where two or more are gathered . . ."

Irene: Do you have any suggestions for people who are currently practicing one religion or another?

Zaydeh: I would tell people to question the beliefs within their religion. Contemplate each one, and as you do, see if it serves and expands you. Ask yourself whether it brings you closer to God, closer to love. Love is unifying.

Irene: I was changing TV channels the other day when I came across a fear-based minister, warning his congregation about how dangerous and threatening the gay population is to the moral fiber of America.

Zaydeh: That's an extreme example of a belief that separates rather than unifies. Sometimes hearing it out loud helps people see how hateful it is. Don't accept a belief just because it's under the umbrella of religion.

I've been learning about the original intention of religions, and they all began from pure heart and mind. Most religions were rooted in the wisdom spoken through a prophet, and love was its basis. Mistranslations have tainted the truth inherent in all religions. For every hand these truths have passed through, there's been an opportunity to misinterpret.

Original scriptures spoke of the Power being within us. They served to guide us by providing ways of tapping into this Power and bringing it through us and out into the world. Motivated by fear, those who wanted control convinced others that the only way to access this Power was through a representative. Religious organizations have taken something as pure and beautiful as "love thy neighbor as thyself" and instilled in it the fear that, if you don't, you'll be punished. Maybe you don't feel love for your neighbor, and you need to understand what's blocking the flow, like your judgments about them. This offers a golden opportunity to explore and heal. If you skip over this process of self-exploration and pretend to love someone because you're afraid you'll be punished if you don't, or because you're concerned with how you'll be perceived, then you're not being true to yourself *or* to your neighbor. When love isn't fully expressed, you're not fully expressing your Self.

I'm already influencing my family by reminding them of the prime motivation of religion so that they can see the original truth. At the root of all religions are methods and guidelines to help us walk the path of loving ourselves and loving each other.

Irene: (Pause) I know people who claim to follow God's word, yet they judge and condemn those who don't. Isn't acceptance a way of expressing God? And I realize, Zaydeh, that if I judge and condemn *them,* I'm guilty of the same thing.

Zaydeh: Yes. Acceptance is allowing. God is a creative force that expresses in infinite ways. It's virtuous to allow for all expressions. People who don't accept others don't accept themselves. They believe they're insufficient, so they put on a pretense of superiority. Many people responsible for interpreting and passing on the scriptures throughout the ages have been plagued by feelings of inferiority.

Every expression has a place in creation. My challenge in physical life has been to accept and trust the wisdom behind *all* choices. When others choose to express themselves differently than I do, I don't need to judge them because of my own discomfort.

Zaydeh

Conversation Five

Irene: I'd like to hear more about your life review.

Zaydeh: The life review was objective and methodical. Everyone's required to do it at some point, not because it's in a rule book, but because we want to look at our lives for the purpose of expanding and experiencing more love. Love feels *so* good that everyone wants more. At various times throughout non-physical life, I've chosen to visit the Hall of Records and look through my lifetimes.

Irene: Hall of Records?

Zaydeh: It's like a library with an entire section devoted to me! To put this in visual terms, each book represents a lifetime, and I'm able to experience every event and everyone in that lifetime.

Irene: What if you just wanted to experience a specific event during a lifetime?

Zaydeh: Most events are best understood in the context of a whole lifetime, and each lifetime is one event in a greater context of the whole of who you are. I can isolate and explore a specific theme throughout four or five lifetimes—poverty or abundance, for instance—and identify the attributes from these themes that either have been successfully integrated or that require further attention. We choose a theme based on the attributes we need to strengthen in ourselves. This strengthens the God within us, which is the soul's agenda.

Take *your* life, Irene. Certain attributes are strong enough now that you wouldn't need to create circumstances to test them. The attributes of trust and honesty are integral enough in your character that you wouldn't choose to shoplift today in order to experience the consequences.

The Hall of Records plays an important part in planning one's next life. I'm able to see and feel whatever was going on and to observe where I gave love and where I withheld it. When I come across a particular moment in my life when I withheld love, I have an opportunity to explore the origin of the fear that restricted the flow. I regret the moments when I didn't demonstrate what I now know to be true: love is who we are and what we're here to express. But it's not regret as you know it in the physical realm. It's lighter here. In the physical realm, regret and remorse are often accompanied by judgment. You fear that you're not enough, so you condemn yourselves. The energy you *could* be using to change is spent feeling guilty or wishing you had done things differently.

Love permeates everything in the Spirit realm. There's no judgment here, so the feelings of regret and remorse simply signal a need for change. The incidents that trigger regret and remorse are simply moments when we could have loved more. Once we recognize them, we have the opportunity to heal the aspects within ourselves responsible for withholding and denying the flow of love. If you could infuse regret and remorse with self-love, you'd feel what we feel here.

Irene: If love permeates the spiritual realm, and if the physical realm is Spirit made manifest, doesn't love permeate the physical realm, as well?

Zaydeh: Yes. Love constitutes everything. But you can restrict the flow of love by choosing limiting beliefs.

Irene: Beliefs like, *I'm not good enough; There's something inherently wrong with me; I should be ashamed; God has abandoned me; I deserve to be punished; There's no point to anything; I don't matter,* and so forth.

Zaydeh: Yes. If, you held these beliefs and walked into a room of people who were heart-centered and expressing their love, it would be uncomfortable for you to be there. You'd either shift to a more loving state or you'd leave. The non-physical world is like a room full of loving people, so it's easier to feel and express love because you're surrounded by it. It's challenging to hold on to anything that is unloving here.

Irene: You said previously that, as you review a particular moment from your physical life, feelings of regret and remorse simply lead to the realization that you could have loved more. But is that true? Could you have done things any differently? You can feel the regret and choose to love more *now*, but the past can't be changed—and wasn't it perfect exactly as it was?

Zaydeh: We can always do things differently now. The purpose of reviewing a life is to look at each moment with acceptance of where we were at the time, and learn a different way, so that when a similar moment presents itself, we'll choose differently. Remorse and regret provide the opportunity to recognize the fear, process it, and heal it, which clears the way for more love.

Irene: Healing is allowing love into the places that hurt.

Zaydeh: And love expresses itself as compassion, kindness, understanding, and patience. Healing begins when you apply these qualities to yourself. You are never robbed of a chance to love unless you rob yourself, by denying yourself the opportunity to love and be loved. Love is always available. It's always available in the spiritual realm, just as it is in the physical realm.

Since every experience is always available and always in the present here in heaven, you can re-experience a situation and express more love than you originally did. In fact, we are encouraged to seek opportunities to express more love. This is accomplished by healing the pain that originally interfered with the love. You can create heaven on earth by allowing love to flow where it was previously blocked. You feel the pain, acknowledge the fear that created it, and allow love to heal it. Fear disappears in the light of truth. There are no missed opportunities except those you choose to miss.

Irene: Thank you. (Pause) You were talking about your life review.

Zaydeh: I not only reviewed my last physical life, but other physical lives, too. I saw the virtues I'd strengthened, as well as those that still needed work. It was like a progress report that allowed me to look at every life I'd lived in order to assess what needed further healing.

Irene: Why did your life review include more than your physical life as Zaydeh?

Zaydeh: I was curious and thirsty for knowledge. I wanted to know as much as possible about my life in the context of all my lives.

ZAYDEH

CONVERSATION SIX

Irene: Do you have eyes, and do you see in the way you did on earth?

Zaydeh: I do more than just see with my eyes. They allow me to access the thoughts and feelings of others. When I look at someone, I know what they're thinking and feeling. It's the same as on earth. When you look at Charlie, you not only see him and observe his facial expressions and body language, but through your connection with him, your knowledge of him and your intuition, you can feel his feelings and hear his thoughts. It's easier in Spirit because there's no veil, no density.

Irene: What about listening?

Zaydeh: The difference between hearing in the physical realm and hearing here is like the difference between swimming with your clothes on and swimming in the nude. There's nothing between you and the water, nothing between you and what you're hearing. On the physical plane, your thoughts often distract you from what you're listening to. You could be sitting near a waterfall, listening to the way the water splashes off the rocks and feeling the breeze as it caresses your skin, but your thoughts interrupt the experience, and instead of fully embracing the sounds and sensations, you remember the last time you were here with your friend. You think back to the conversation you had and you begin to analyze what you said. Your thoughts fill the foreground, while the waterfall and the breeze fade to the background. That doesn't happen here.

Irene: What about touch?

Zaydeh: Touch provides a deeper connection. It's possible to feel every lifetime someone's lived—with their permission.

Irene: That's what I call being an open book.

Zaydeh: It's the same with all the senses, because there's nothing impeding the experience. There's no mental chatter.

Irene: What about the sense of smell?

Zaydeh: If you think you've smelled a gardenia on the physical plane, wait till you smell it here. It sends us into an ecstatic state to experience the creative joy that runs through a blossoming gardenia. While you experience this in physical form, you think it's *your* joy, and that limits it. You limit how much joy you're willing to receive. You limit how deeply you'll connect with someone or how deeply they can connect with you. You limit your experience of listening by not being fully present with what you're listening to. And you even limit what you see by what you're willing to see. Fear prevents you from completely feeling what your senses are providing. And yes, there are some physical components that impede the full experience, but your lack of willingness and openness impede it even more. The spiritual realm is a realm of freedom. There are no unconscious limitations. You have complete access to every expression available.

Irene: What do you mean by *unconscious limitations?*

Zaydeh: I'm referring to the unconscious fears that influence your life: fears that begin in childhood, passed down by your parents; fears that create beliefs about you and the world around you; fears that you're not even aware of—hence, they're unconscious. People may think it takes a lot of work to release their fears, but it takes a lot more work to keep them at bay. There's no need for that here, in this realm filled with love. As you mentioned, Irene, you're an open book when you're no longer focused in the physical realm. When you come into the spiritual realm, you can release everything you've been trying to hold down. And that frees up a lot of energy.

ZAYDEH

CONVERSATION SEVEN

Irene: When you look around, what do you see?

Zaydeh: It depends on how I focus. Everything in this realm can be seen, so I choose my focus according to what's appropriate for a particular experience. In order to channel my attention and energy into this project, for example, I tune into you and Jana and to the guidance that's pertinent. I could get very distracted otherwise. (Pause) Vision in physical form is limited, and that has its advantages.

Irene: (Pause) What if you wanted to see the ocean? Would you imagine it?

Zaydeh: Yes. I'd focus on feeling the ocean waves lapping at my feet, hearing the sounds of the seabirds and smelling the ocean air. That's why I have to focus on what would best fulfill my desire and intention; if I thought about the ocean right now, it would take me away from this session and I wouldn't be hearing your questions. This is easier to do than you may think, because you've been doing it here in Spirit for eternity.

Irene: What's your perception/understanding of God, and has this changed from the perception/understanding you held while in a physical body?

Zaydeh: It's changed greatly. Being in physical form, I had a very narrow vision of life. I saw myself as separate from everyone and everything. I've now learned that God and life are one and the same. If I have life inside me, then I have God inside me. Everything I experience as life is God. (Pause) There are infinite ways to express the Infinite. If you were to look at a colorful tapestry under magnification, you'd see colorful dots. Each dot would have a slight color variance separating it from the next dot, but that wouldn't change the fact that it's still one colorful tapestry.

ZAYDEH

CONVERSATION EIGHT

Zaydeh: The density of physical form can fool you into thinking that life is solid and relatively unchanging, but everything is fluid and constantly in motion. When you resist change because you fear the unknown, it impedes your ability to heal. Mental and emotional pain may be unpleasant, but at least they're familiar. Many people are afraid to embark on a healing journey because they don't trust where the journey is taking them. Healing and change go hand-in-hand.

In the Spirit realm, where there is no linear time, you see everything. Trust is strengthened because it's evident that change leads to a greater expression of you. And with greater expression comes a greater sense of love, peace, joy, wisdom and compassion—qualities many people pray for. Nothing is hidden here. Everything is revealed. Allowing and accepting serve to grease the wheels of change. It's easier to trust when you realize that change is ultimately benevolent.

Irene: I often wonder about people who are experiencing dramatic change as a result of extreme circumstances, and I question how that's good for them. But then I remind myself that I'm not seeing the whole picture. I'm not seeing who they can become as a result of the experience. I'm not seeing how their lives will be touched or whose lives they will touch in the process. I'm not leaving room for the Benevolence. As soon as I take my blinders off and stop judging the situation as "bad," I feel expansive. Possibilities arise that I hadn't considered.

Zaydeh: When people are challenged with great change, it's important that you hold the possibility of Benevolence working through their lives. You empower them by providing an opportunity to step out of the victim role. Trust in the wisdom inherent in any given situation. When someone does something that upsets you, remember: they are the Benevolence working in your life. If a situation unfolds in a way that challenges you, remember: this, too, is the Benevolence working in your life. Sometimes we need to be pushed into changing, and when we do, the force behind that push is . . . *what?*

Irene: Benevolence.

ZAYDEH

CONVERSATION NINE

Irene: Here on earth, most people have a routine and structure. Is it similar where you are?

Zaydeh: Yes, but the motivation is different. The motivation for routine in the physical realm is often to create the illusion that things aren't changing. That's how I lived as Physical Zaydeh. I continued down the same path in the same way, not wanting to stir things up. I didn't like to talk about my feelings with my wife and children, for example, for fear that they'd see me as weak. I was afraid I would lose my authority as head of household, so I withheld and withdrew. And I remained that way throughout my marriage.

Here in the non-physical realm, I like to organize my experiences around my ability to be of loving service. Flexibility is key. I am always willing to change my intention based on a greater need that may present itself. On earth, you may have the intention to go to the grocery store, but on the way you get a call from a friend who's crying and needs assistance. To serve the greater whole is to abandon your intention to go to the store, and instead, be with your friend.

Irene: Zaydeh, how would you choose to live if you were here on earth today?

Zaydeh: I'd love myself and love others wholeheartedly and without reservation. I'd have compassion for myself as one would have compassion for a small child who mistakes a shadow for a monster. And I'd like to think that I would have that same compassion for my fellow man.

ZAYDEH AND JERRY

CONVERSATION TEN

Irene: I have moments when I feel overwhelmed by what's happening on the planet: war, genocide, global warming . . .

Zaydeh: Jerry would like to respond.

Jerry: I hear you giving outside circumstances much more power than you're giving yourself. You're not feeling powerful enough to change outside circumstances and it frustrates you. But from a spiritual perspective, you're a part of all you see. The outer circumstances are reflecting what everyone on the planet is experiencing within themselves: war, deceit, and manipulation—they're all happening in each individual. It must be that way, or those things wouldn't be present.

Irene: Thanks for reminding me. Outer experience is a function of inner reality.

Jerry: Exactly. Look at how you're contributing to what you're seeing. If you see war, notice any inner conflict going on within you. If you see deceit, look at where you're lying to yourself. If you see manipulation, look at how you manipulate situations to get what you want. If you see terrorism, look at how you terrorize yourself with fearful inner dialogue.

Your power comes from following your heart. There are some people whose hearts tell them to change within so as to match what they want to see on the outside. If your heart tells you that global peace will be achieved through inner peace, find the peace within yourself. Look at how you contribute to what you're seeing, to pollution and to the experience of global warming. Focus your power within instead of without. Your power to love is greater than someone else's fear-motivated power.

There are others whose hearts tell them to act: to march, boycott, or write letters to their government. Follow what your heart tells you. There is power in it.

Irene: When it comes to global warming, though, how are we "warming up" within ourselves?

Jerry: When you feel inadequate and unlovable, it often results in behaviors of excess. You buy more things in an attempt to distract yourself from the pain you're feeling, or you eat excessively to fill the emptiness inside. It takes energy to manufacture, produce, and transport all of these, which contributes to global warming. When you heal within, it results in outer changes that contribute to the well-being of the planet.

Zaydeh

Conversation Eleven

Irene: Do you have any suggestions for someone who is about to transition?

Zaydeh: It depends on the life they've lived. Some people are more prepared to transition because they have faith in the next step. Someone who's demonstrated faith in life and flexibility in how they've lived wouldn't need much counsel from me.

Irene: What suggestions might you have for someone who's afraid?

Zaydeh: It depends on what they fear. If they're afraid of change, I suggest doing things a little differently each day. Try new foods. Drive a different route to work. Introduce yourself to someone new and strike up a conversation. Shake things up in your life in small ways. If you push your boundaries a bit, you'll start experiencing change in a more comfortable way and you'll find yourself growing in courage. You may even make a new friend or see some new scenery. After a while, you'll begin looking for opportunities to make even bigger changes. Maybe you'll find yourself changing careers or moving. Start small. That's my advice.

I also encourage you to make friends with your body. Your body understands change. It's constantly in a state of change, creating new cells and discarding old ones. At any given moment, there's always something in your body that's changing. Nothing stays the same. Make friends with your body; it will help you when it comes time to transition out of it.

Irene: How specifically will the body help?

Zaydeh: When it's time to change and move on, your body will cooperate easily and naturally with the process, responding objectively to the call of your soul. Some people slip into a coma, which can be their body's way of easing them into the Spirit realm. Working with your body through the transitioning process is like surrendering to the flow of a stream.

Irene: You said that your advice for someone who's afraid would depend on what they're afraid of, and you addressed fear of change. What about other fears?

Zaydeh: If someone's afraid that there's nothing beyond the death of the physical body, or that they'll meet with some terrible judgment, they'll be fighting their body and actually fighting the call of their soul. Trust that the flow will carry you to your next experience in non-physical form.

If a person believes that there's nothing beyond physical life because they're ruled by logic and reason, there's nothing I could say to them, because they're looking for proof, and there is none. Their unique expression, however, is needed just as much as the poet's, whose life is inspired by that which can't be proven. No one can convince anyone of anything. Change in perspective always comes from within. No matter what someone postulates—about life, the afterlife, metaphysics, or spirituality—it's the love and acceptance expressed during a communication between two people that will have the greatest influence. When your intention is love and acceptance, you're no longer trying to be right about your point of view.

Irene: A good friend of mine has a strong commitment to logic and reason, which often frustrates me.

Zaydeh: From a very young age, we look for ways to feel safe in the world, and one way to feel safe is to try and make sense of it. Your way, my dear, is to strengthen your faith in life by exploring the unknown. Others find safety in what they can see, touch, and understand. To them, the unknown is just that: unknown. It's labeled that way and, as far as they're concerned, it can stay that way. They think there's enough to explore in this world by exploring what can be known.

If, on the other hand, a person is *afraid* of the unknown, then there's room for discussion. When we're afraid, we feel cut off and alone. Fear isn't a natural state of the body, so when someone's feeling fear, they're open to reassurance and open to other points of view that can transform their fear into peace. Discussions with people who are willing to explore life beyond the physical can lead to more questions than answers. So why not explore together? When a child is afraid of the dark, the loving thing to do is to turn on the light, explore the room, and discover together that there's nothing hiding under the bed or in the closet.

Irene: Zaydeh, what might you say to someone who's fearful of being judged when they transition?

Zaydeh: (Laughing) I'd say, "You should be accustomed to it by now; you've been doing it for so long!"

Irene: Now, Zaydeh! What would you say to someone who's spent a lifetime judging themselves and others and is now projecting that characteristic onto God and fearing God's judgment?

Zaydeh: These are fear-based judgments, not wisdom-based judgments. They're not the same. When we judge by finding fault and blame or by making ourselves right and others wrong, fear is the driving force. That's fear-based judgment. When we judge by assessing, discerning, and evaluating—for the purpose of gaining understanding—that's wisdom-based judgment.

Judgment Day, as spoken of in the scriptures, was never meant to imply blame or condemnation. When you review your life, it's with the kind of judgment that's motivated by wisdom. You're assessing and evaluating your life for the purpose of expanding your capacity to love. Oh, and by the way, there's nothing anyone could ever do that would make them unlovable.

ZAYDEH

CONVERSATION TWELVE

Irene: If a person is in physical pain, does the pain stop as soon as they transition into the Spirit realm?

Zaydeh: Not always. You've heard of someone feeling sensations from a phantom limb, one that's been amputated? When you transition, something similar can happen. The physical body is an expression of the spirited body. If a condition exists in the physical body, it already exists in the spirited body. When someone releases the physical body, healing occurs in the spiritual body where the condition originated.

Healing here is easier. The energy is faster, so change happens quickly. In an atmosphere of love and acceptance, there's no need to hold on to the pain. Knowing why the pain was created makes it easier to heal. The source of physical pain is often mental or emotional.

Irene: I've tried a variety of ways to heal the chronic back pain I have. Any suggestions? I ask this for all people dealing with ongoing chronic pain.

Zaydeh: Healing is a journey, and one hopes the destination will be "healthy and pain-free." Sometimes, however, your soul has another path it wants you to travel before arriving at that destination. Because of the pain in your back, for example, you've met many people you wouldn't have met otherwise. You now have greater compassion for others who are experiencing chronic pain. Sometimes, when people aren't listening to the whisperings of their souls, the illness slows them down so they'll listen. Some people have beliefs that contribute to their experience of chronic pain and aren't willing to change them. Some people choose to travel their entire lifetime without reaching the destination of being pain-free while in physical form. This may have been a conscious choice on a soul level.

ZAYDEH

CONVERSATION THIRTEEN

Irene: Do you know if there's a penalty for people who take their lives?

Zaydeh: (Laughing) I'm amused by the phrase, "take their lives." People are more likely to "take their lives for granted." The penalty is evident: they aren't able to experience the depth and richness available to them in the physical realm.

Our power to choose can be conscious or unconscious, including the choice to end physical life. You can choose to deliberately take a step to end physical life, for example, but you can also make unconscious choices to end physical life—as a result of accidents, karmic contracts with others, diseases, overindulgence and lack of self-care. A person who unconsciously chooses to end physical life as a result of an accident, for example, would tell you—prior to the accident—that they wanted to live their physical life. How their life proceeds makes a different statement and tells a different story.

Your level of consciousness impacts your choices. If you have a rich spiritual life—a connection through prayer and meditation, for example—and you know that life continues after your physical experience, your choices will be less fearful and more conscious, and you'll be better able to hear messages from your soul. If you're unconscious, the soul's messages have to *sneak* in. When you're not even aware that there *is* a soul to which you can listen, your soul has to work primarily through your unconscious, creating circumstances and situations to wake you up to your spiritual life, which sometimes means ending the physical. The only way some people know they have a spiritual life is through the absence of a physical one.

Wake up to your spiritual selves while you're in physical form. I had a sense of this as Physical Zaydeh, but fear narrowed my perspective until the only way to widen that perspective was to leave my physical body. You can have a panoramic view of Spirit while still enjoying physical life. This is available to everyone.

Irene: What would assist us in waking up to this panoramic view?

Zaydeh: Trust that a greater Intelligence is at work in your life. You can build trust by observing your physical body and being present with how it functions without your conscious awareness: respiration, digestion and circulation all go on without your conscious awareness! This is the Intelligence working within you. This is the Intelligence working in harmony with you. This is the Intelligence that's always serving and benefiting you. You can observe this Intelligence at work all around you: grass grows, seasons change and the sun shines, all without any conscious effort on your part. Consider the miracle of a single leaf falling from a tree and turning into soil!

You can't see this Intelligence; you can only see the results. This is the same Intelligence that's guiding your life. You can observe this Intelligence at work when the phone rings and it's someone you've been thinking of, when your friend expresses just what you need to hear, or when money appears unexpectedly, just when you need it. It's easy to observe and appreciate the Intelligence during times like these.

During times when nothing seems to be happening, or when what *is* happening seems to be contrary to what you desire, you need to trust that this Intelligence is guiding your life. Remember, everything you see around you is Intelligence in motion. Intelligence is always active. There's never a pause. Why would you think it pauses in *your* life? It doesn't. The Intelligence in motion in your life is the same Intelligence that moves the earth around the sun. So, even when it doesn't seem like this Intelligence is guiding your life, trust that it always is. Isn't it a miracle that you have access to this Power? And isn't it comforting to know that this Power is working on your behalf, under any and all circumstances?

Irene: Absolutely. And so it is. Thank you, Zaydeh. I've so enjoyed our conversations. I've felt your unconditional love in every word, as well as in the silence in-between.

Zaydeh: Contributing to this book has been a blessing. It is a blessing that continues with every person who reads it, and for that, I am grateful. I think of the times we were together as grandfather and granddaughter with much fondness and appreciation. To be with you beyond those roles is something I never could have imagined as Physical Zaydeh. Little did I know that our connection would continue in such a powerful way.

Irene: Thank you, Zaydeh. I love you.

PAULA

1922 – 2006

I adored my Aunt Paula. She was a strong-willed woman, devoted to family. I guess that's why, after my own mother transitioned, I valued Aunt Paula's presence in my life all the more.

She lived in Mexico City, and I in the United States, so we connected more often by phone than in person. Her response to a call from me was always immediate and joyful:

"¡Hola, mi reina!" which means, "Hello, my queen!"

When I'm quiet, and I think about my Aunt Paula, I still hear her voice, clear as a bell: "¡Hola, mi reina!"

Maybe the only place relationship ever really exists is within each of us.

My Aunt Paula transitioned unexpectedly in her sleep.

PAULA

CONVERSATION ONE

Irene: Aunt Paula, what did you experience when you released your last breath on earth?

Paula: Getting out of my physical body was similar to the slow and gentle way I'd gotten out of bed each morning.

Irene: Were you consciously aware of the moment you were released from your physical body?

Paula: Yes. Sometimes, when a character in a cartoon or in a movie dies, you see their physical body remain in a horizontal position on the bed while a less-dense image of the character sits up, swings their legs over the edge of the bed, sets their feet on the floor and stands up, leaving their physical body behind. That's what I did. I stepped out of my physical body, and then I turned around to look at it. When I saw how peaceful it looked, I felt an immediate rush of joy. My weak body was no longer a burden.

My body and I had not been friends. In fact, I'd say our relationship had been adversarial. I was constantly at odds with it. It had been like a needy child, and I resented it for demanding so much of my time and attention. For as long as I could remember, I'd also been dissatisfied with my appearance, and as my body aged, my dissatisfaction grew.

As I looked at my physical body, I saw it from a perspective that hadn't been previously available to me. It was like looking at an annoying old friend I'd taken for granted. Even though I wasn't going to miss being with that old friend, I appreciated the experience we'd shared. I looked at my physical body and felt sad that this was goodbye, but I was quickly overcome by a sense of freedom. I realized that my physical life had been temporary, and I was everlasting. I felt invincible. Have you ever had a lucid dream—aware that you're dreaming while you're dreaming—and you know that you have the freedom to do whatever you want? That's the kind of freedom I felt. I knew I could go anywhere and do anything. I knew I was in my power and that this power was unchangeable. I knew I was the source and not the effect.

I was glad my passing had been quiet and undramatic. I didn't want my loved ones to be present and I was thankful they weren't. I'd spent a lifetime being strong and I wanted to be remembered that way.

Irene: It sounds like you didn't want anyone to see you in what you deemed a weak or vulnerable state.

Paula: That's right. I did, however, appreciate the attention I received after passing from my physical body. It was reassuring to see the difference I'd made in the lives of my loved ones and comforting to feel their love. I was aware of their appreciation because I could hear their thoughts and prayers. There was never a time I wasn't aware of everything.

Irene: Did you relinquish your physical body, or did your physical body relinquish you?

Paula: I relinquished my physical body. (Laughing) Finally, it accommodated my wishes and cooperated with me, although now I realize it had been cooperating all along. I felt like a victim as Physical Paula because I thought my body was the one in control. From this new perspective, however, I saw that the being I am now had always been in charge of my physical body. I was the power.

Irene: Are you saying that you were unaware of being more than your physical body when you were in physical form?

Paula: Yes. I felt victimized by it. I had to feed it, water it, groom it and rest it. It wasn't until I stepped away from it that I became conscious of my power as separate from that of my body's. The reality was that I'd been in control all along. My choices had directly affected my body, sometimes to its benefit, but usually to its detriment. It was obvious that I'd been in charge: I'd survived and it hadn't! Without me, my body was nothing. We're all born knowing we're distinct from our physical bodies; whether we're conscious of it or not doesn't change the fact. Stepping away from my physical body was like flipping a switch and standing in the warm, brilliant light of truth.

Irene: I'm surprised that you released your body with such grace and ease since your relationship with it had been so adversarial.

Paula: While it's true that I resented my body because of its demands on my time and attention, I didn't fear death. It's my understanding that fear of dying is what causes most people to struggle while transitioning. When someone mistakenly thinks they *are* their body, they're afraid of losing their identity. They're afraid they'll cease to exist. When one's existence is contingent on the existence of a physical body, it's easy to resent the body for wielding this kind of power and control. When their soul decides it's time to transition, the part that identifies with the physical body struggles, and this results in a lengthy and challenging transition.

Irene: I heard you say that, as Physical Paula, you were unaware of being more than your physical body. Didn't it follow that the death of your body meant an end to *you?*

Paula: Yes. But I wasn't afraid of dying. I didn't even fear non-existence. To tell you the truth, I really hadn't given it much thought. I didn't buy into hell and damnation and those kinds of things. I just felt stuck in my body, and when my body died, I figured I'd be unstuck and in peace. It was the adversarial relationship I had with my body that made me glad to die.

Irene: That's interesting. Thanks for explaining. (Pause) You said you turned to look at your physical body and appreciated how peaceful it looked.

Paula: Yes. It was the first time in my life I could remember being at peace with my body. Then I noticed how bright everything was. Even the formerly drab room was brighter and more defined. Colors I wouldn't normally have noticed were vibrant. I wondered why, as Physical Paula, I hadn't been able to see this way. I thought, *I wish I could share this with my family,* and then I thought of how sad everyone was going to be. I knew that, if they could have seen what I was seeing and felt what I was feeling, their sadness would have vanished.

PAULA

CONVERSATION TWO

Irene: You said you were noticing colors and how vibrant they were.

Paula: Yes, and I realized I wasn't alone; I was in the presence of spirited loved ones. My husband, for example, looked the same as the last time I'd seen him, but without the pallor. As our eyes met, I felt his love and appreciation. Another man was standing next to him, a man I recognized as my husband from another lifetime, and in that moment of recognition, I experienced an inner shift: I was no longer looking through Paula's eyes but through the eyes of who I'd been as this man's wife. I was overjoyed that both men seemed to be friends. I felt the love they had for one another, and at the same time I felt the love they had for me. If someone had asked my thoughts on an afterlife, I never would have described it like this. Being greeted by two men who'd been in love with me in two different lifetimes was heaven.

I noticed a young girl whom I recognized as my best friend from childhood; she looked just as she had when I'd known her. We ran toward each other to hug and, as we did, I became the young girl who'd known her during childhood. I felt giddy—like I'd felt as that young girl—and we both let out screams of delight amidst our giggles. How revitalizing to re-experience the exuberance of childhood! As my two husbands looked on, I could tell they were feeling what we were feeling. My girlfriend and I clasped hands, and she accompanied me to my memorial service.

I saw my physical family praying. *If they could see me now as a little girl, would they even recognize me?* Everyone was so serious. I couldn't help noticing that some of them were afraid. They were afraid of the unknown and afraid I wasn't okay. I appreciated their prayers, but I sensed that some were praying more for themselves than for me, because their prayers were helping *them* feel better. *I* couldn't have felt any better than I did.

I felt the love everyone had for me, but with so much to see and do, my girlfriend and I left. We went back to those special childhood places—places where we'd played—*our* places. We were communicating in silence because there was no need for words; I knew her thoughts and she knew mine, and we were showing each other shared memories. And then she squeezed my hand and communicated that there were more people who wanted to connect with me.

My mother appeared, her eyes shining with delight. She looked younger than when I'd last seen her. And even though my mother in physical form had struggled in her expression of love for me, love was now radiating from her in the way I'd always dreamed possible. As we embraced, I expressed my love and gratitude for her. I returned to the memorial, this time with my mother.

She shared how supportive she'd been of me and of my family even after she'd transitioned. While she hadn't been physically present throughout my children's lives, her love as their grand-mother had been ever-present. I felt how pleased she was with the family I'd created, and I received her acknowledgement for a job well done. I experienced her unconditional love and compassion, especially for some of the painful challenges I'd created in my life.

I found myself in the company of many spirited beings, not just from my life as Paula, but from other lifetimes, as well. Even when I didn't initially recognize someone, I recognized who I had been during the lifetime we'd shared. The love I felt was indescribable. As good a writer as you are, Irene, there's no way you could possibly put the love I felt into words.

I was surprised to see tables of food. People were enjoying eating, and when I sampled the food, I understood why. It was delicious! *What an amazing array of global cuisine,* I thought. I heard someone laugh and say, "It's fitting. You've lived in so many different cultures, we didn't want to leave any of You out!"

Paula

Conversation Three

Irene: What surprised you most about the reunion?

Paula: More than anything, I was surprised at how intact my transitioned loved ones were. I'd felt a quiet connection to some of them after they'd passed, but seeing them and feeling them over here—as alive and animated as they were—was a surprise.

Irene: Paula, many people believe they'll face judgment when they transition. Were you judged?

Paula: (Laughing) I judged myself throughout my entire physical life. By the time I passed into heaven, I was all judged out.

Irene: What happened after your reunion?

Paula: I continued with my life review, which had started with the reunion.

Irene: Where did your life review take place?

Paula: The setting I chose was a white cushioned chair in a beautiful garden. I didn't see the chair, walk to it, and sit down, though; it wasn't sequential. It was more like I imagined the chair, and there I was, sitting in it while my life as Physical Paula unfolded from the womb to my last breath. When the life review was complete, I began looking at the issues that had surfaced within the larger context of all my lifetimes.

It was easy to see where I'd withheld love. And the reason was always the same: fear. Judging myself and judging others had nourished my fear, causing it to grow stronger. The more judgments I'd had, the more separate and fearful I'd felt.

The first step I took toward healing was to trace the fear back to its origin, either in my life as Paula or in a different lifetime. I was like a gardener, tracing the roots of an invasive weed. This kind of self-exploration is objective and educational, and I love it. My physical life as Paula had served to deepen my consciousness, which enabled me to explore with great depth. Each lifetime lived—no matter how shallow it seems—provides greater understanding and a deeper connection with Self.

Irene: What's an example of something you understood with greater depth?

Paula: As Physical Paula, I thought I had to be a certain way in order to maintain the image others had of me. Family and friends saw me as strong, and not wanting to disappoint, I expressed myself in ways that fit their expectations. The energy would have been better spent being true to my Self and strengthening my connection to God.

As I continued reviewing, it became clear to me that I hadn't fully trusted life. Loving others had been easy for me because I perceived I was in control; it was allowing myself to be loved by others that had been a challenge. Being open and vulnerable to receiving love—whether through a hug, assistance, or a compliment—had been difficult for me.

I now understand that giving and receiving are two sides of the same coin. Receiving is a gift of giving when we make space to receive from others. My inability to receive had frequently left others feeling obligated because they had no way to satisfy their desire to give. It was an incomplete cycle that left me unfulfilled, as well. And how do you think I responded to feeling unfulfilled?

Irene: I give up.

Paula: I continued giving! In some ways, the more I gave, the more unfulfilled I felt because I hadn't allowed the circle of giving and receiving to complete itself. And it was exhausting.

(Pause) I'm an explorer on the ultimate adventure: the mystery of how I've evolved. I review my lives, seeing myself in role after role. I marvel, not only at the wisdom that guides me in choosing each role, but at how real each drama seems at the time. And the people participating with me, lifetime after lifetime, are essentially the same people playing different roles. The person who played my father in one lifetime, for instance, is my brother in another and my child in the next.

Being in Spirit is like being backstage and seeing everyone without their costumes. And guess what? From *this* perspective, the person playing the villain in any one of my lifetimes is really someone who loves me, and it's *because* they love me that they were willing to play that role. I encourage you to keep this in mind. That's not to say that someone in an abusive relationship should stay in that relationship; but know that the essence of the abuser is more than the costume they're wearing. Some people get so caught up in their roles that they forget who they really are.

As I mentioned, it was a lack of trust as Physical Paula that kept me from receiving. When I re-experience my lives with the love that permeates them and the wisdom that's threaded throughout, I realize there's nothing to fear. I enjoy this kind of exploration.

Irene: I see myself in you. I'm more comfortable giving than receiving. I, too, like to be in control. And I love self-healing work. When something disturbs my peace, I enjoy discovering and clearing the cause, whether it's a judgment, a misconception, or an irrational belief. Sometimes what's needed is to give voice to a part of myself that wants to be heard. I enjoy the results that come from inner healing: joy, satisfaction, greater compassion for myself and others, expanded well-being, a feeling of spaciousness, and an experience of oneness. And I love how life shows up with even greater ease and synchronicity as the result of releasing what wasn't mine to begin with. And because I've healed and therefore changed, people respond differently.

Paula: What a blessing for you to have the opportunity to heal while still in physical form. When you heal mental and emotional wounds, you create more opportunities for love to empower you.

PAULA

CONVERSATION FOUR

Irene: What's been the most challenging aspect of transitioning?

Paula: The most challenging aspect, by far, is that my physical loved ones are unaware of my presence. I'm aware of being real and seeing everything as so alive, and yet they refer to me as dead and think of me as absent. I feel more present now than I ever did in my physical body.

Irene: What's been the most joyful aspect of transitioning?

Paula: The depth of connection with others. When I laugh, for example, I never laugh alone; the feelings that stimulate laughter are shared by anyone around me, so the experience is doubled or tripled. I feel what's making *them* laugh at the same time I feel what's making *me* laugh.

I also enjoy discovering the deeper wisdom of my life: why I chose what I chose, and what could have happened if I'd chosen something else. I can even experience the wisdom behind the choices that others make. If someone's crying, for instance, I have access to a deeper understanding of why they're responding the way they are, and I can let them be. I don't get caught up in trying to fix them, change them, or make them feel better. I just observe and send them love. I now experience genuine compassion for others.

When I transitioned, the sadness I felt coming from my daughters was overwhelming. I understood, though, that their sadness wasn't all about me; they were simultaneously working out issues from other lifetimes. I still nurture them, but they're not consciously aware of me. I visit them while they're sleeping. I caress their foreheads and tell them how much I love them.

Irene: What are you enjoying most about being where you are?

Paula: The freedom. I'm free to go beyond who I was as Paula. I was constrained by certain boundaries in physical form, like an actor playing a role in a play and having to remain in character. Now, guided by what I choose to experience, I can be that character or any other; I'm boundless in expression. I shift perspective during interactions with others, and my appearance changes accordingly. If I'm relating to someone with whom I've shared a life—say we were male friends in that lifetime—I just slip effortlessly into the "costume" I wore when we were together during that lifetime, and I assume the male form I had at that time. Relating in familiar ways provides comfort and ease.

Irene: So you create the perspective that facilitates the greatest connection with whomever you're relating.

Paula: That's it. Having a physical form is like living in a house with many windows, yet restricted to looking out through only one; the best you can do is to describe the ever-changing scene from your one window. Every individual has their own window within this house and they're doing the same thing—describing the view from their window.

In non-physical form, you can look out of any window you choose and experience the view directly. You're no longer dependent on someone else's description.

Irene: What's an example of something you've experienced as a result of looking out any window you choose?

Paula: When I don't understand why someone has chosen a particular path, for instance, I look out their window—through their eyes—at how they see the world. If I want to understand Genghis Khan's intentions, for example, I can access his lifetime, look through his eyes, feel through his heart, think his thoughts—you get the picture. It's easier to access compassion when we look through the eyes and hearts of others. We understand why Hitler behaved the way he did (laughing) or why that person pulled out in front of us on the street. You can do something similar in physical form. The goal is to allow compassion to flow through your life unimpeded. How do you do this in *your* life, Irene?

Irene: I speak kindly to myself. I see myself in others. When I notice I'm judging, I practice compassionate self-forgiveness. I seek first to understand and then to be understood. And sometimes—and this is very useful—when I'm with a particularly challenging adult, I imagine them as a child or a teenager. That often helps my heart to open.

Paula: When I judged someone on earth—someone who'd committed murder, for example—it was because I'd forgotten that we're in the same house. Here in Spirit, I can look out from their window, see through their eyes, and understand their choices in the larger context of their soul's growth. As a result, my compassion deepens. I can relate in an empathetic way because I've experienced their perspective without judgment. I'm able to connect with their essence in a way that just wasn't possible as Physical Paula.

Paula

Conversation Five

Irene: What are you focusing on in the Spirit world?

Paula: I have so many choices. I love to socialize. I go to dinner parties, galas, and all kinds of social events. I also enjoy outdoor games. I play a game here that's similar to lawn bowling, although we focus less on playing the game and more on laughing and having fun.

I also love to commune with loved ones here. When I share a breath with someone, I can choose to experience everything they've experienced, seeing it through their eyes and hearing it through their ears. I'm not just watching their life as if I were watching a movie; I'm in the movie as their character, experiencing the scenes as they experience them. I love this. Sharing a breath is so full! I enjoy understanding *why* people choose what they choose; I plan on applying this knowledge in service to others in my next physical life. My heart's journey is to assist people in connecting with their inner power. I can show them that, not only are they much greater than what they experience, but all of their experiences have been beautifully orchestrated to reflect their inner reality.

Irene: Outer experience is a reflection of inner reality.

Paula: Yes. If you believe you're poor, you'll feel poor, and poverty will become your reality. If you expect the world to be against you, it will. If you think you're alone, you'll feel alone, and you'll find yourself alone. Reality accommodates your beliefs.

When we strengthen our heart connection, by manifesting our hearts' desires and by giving and receiving love, we deepen our connection to everyone and everything—which is God.

(Pause) I have, of course, been thoroughly studying my own life, and any questions I have are immediately answered.

Irene: How are your questions answered?

Paula: There are beings here who assist me in understanding why I made the choices I made; they provide me with a broad, compassionate perspective of how my experiences as Physical Paula fit into the wholeness of who I am. As a result, I'm able to recognize the gifts that resulted from my choices; I experience the wisdom behind my decisions—even the decisions that created pain for others. It's become clear to me that the experiences of one lifetime have affected every other lifetime, as well as everyone in those lifetimes. This is the perspective I have in the company of these beings.

Irene: Can you share an example?

Paula: I was shown a lifetime during which I was a young mother forced to sell one of my children—my daughter. Needless to say, it was painful. I never knew what happened to her during my lifetime as her mother, The perspective made available to me here in Spirit, however, was that the daughter I'd sold had chosen me as her mother with full knowledge that I would abandon her. From *her* perspective, I sold her for money. From *my* perspective, I was acting in her best interest because I couldn't provide for her. I was able to observe this experience from a wide, compassionate perspective and witness the profound gifts that resulted. She was sold as a slave to a royal family and, because of the abandonment, she became fiercely independent. Determined not to be uneducated like her mother, she found ways to educate herself. She was headstrong and tenacious. The prince fell in love with her and she became part of the royal family. I saw the influence she had on the people of that kingdom.

I, on the other hand, had chosen that lifetime in order to give birth to my daughter and provide an environment in which she could position herself to become that princess. The ingredients for this included abandonment and her fierce desire *not* to be like her mother, which meant hating me. I was willing to be hated by my daughter as a lesson in unconditional love. Now I see that the quality of unconditional love I developed in that lifetime contributed to my being a better mother during my lifetime as Paula.

Irene: So all you knew in *that* lifetime was that you'd given up your little girl so she'd have food and shelter. It wasn't until you were in Spirit that you saw the broader perspective.

Paula: Yes, and although the beings assisting me in this process are wise, no one here in Spirit is considered wiser than anyone else. There are no roles, as in teachers and students; it's an equal sharing. There's great understanding here because I have the experience of having been everyone. I understand what it's like to love unconditionally, because I've done it. I understand what it's like to kill someone, because I've done that, too. There is no judgment here, because even if I haven't personally experienced a particular act, it's easy to connect with someone who has, and I make that experience my own. I am everyone, and every experience is mine.

I'm excited to be where I am! If anyone in my family could feel what I feel now for even one earthly second, they would have no doubt that I'm in a better place. When people on earth use that phrase—*she's in a better place*—they're empty words in comparison to the actual experience. I so want to express what it's like here, yet I feel like I come up short.

Irene: From *my* perspective, you're doing a brilliant job. I can only imagine how challenging it must be to communicate the depth of your non-physical experience to those of us in physical form. Thank you for your strength of heart.

PAULA

CONVERSATION SIX

Irene: I've been reviewing our first few conversations, and I'm deeply moved by your sharing.

Paula: I've learned a great deal as a result of communicating with you, too. Conveying these spiritual perspectives to someone in physical form has required that I deepen my understanding, which has benefited me, as well.

The connection with you isn't tenuous like it is when no one knows I'm present. When you're sitting across from someone over tea, for example, the communication is much clearer than when you're shouting to someone in another room. And when you're not even sure they're *in* the other room, it's even murkier.

Irene: What a great analogy. Aunt Paula, do you ever look forward to events, or are you always fully present *now?*

Paula: There *is* no forward. There is only experience. Once I choose what I want to experience, my only choice is to experience it fully. I choose it, and I experience it. As Physical Paula, I'd often look forward to moments in order to "rev up" my energy and enthusiasm for life, thinking how excited I was because tomorrow I was going to do this or that. People often look for the next moment for their happiness, and that's part of their discontent. We don't have next moments to look forward to. It's always *here,* and it's always *now.*

Irene: (Pause) What advice would you offer someone who is preparing to transition?

Paula: You prepare for transitioning by being present where you are, because where you are holds everything you need for the next step. When you know you're going to transition, time seems to slow. You prioritize what's important. You want to see your family and your friends, and you begin to review your life. Two things stood out for me as I reviewed mine: the moments I'd connected with loved ones and the moments of regret when I had not. Any moment can be the moment you transition, so be fully present. When you're looking to the next moment without noticing the one you're *in,* time seems to pass more quickly—and the dimension of time often accommodates you by hurling you into the next moment.

You have more control over the dimension of time than you think. Take time to fully experience your breath in the moment. You'll have a different experience of eating food if you're present with it and eat slowly instead of thinking of the next bite while you still have one in your mouth. Life is like that, too. Slow it down. Prioritize. Make connecting with another first on your list of things to do. Those who know they're close to transitioning—because they know it intuitively or because they have a terminal illness—can prepare themselves by prioritizing. Those whose physical lives end suddenly may have a more challenging time over here if they've left things unsaid and have a lot of regret. When they attempt to communicate the things that were left unsaid their words often fall on deaf ears.

Irene: My understanding is that regret doesn't linger in the spiritual realm. Is that true in your experience?

Paula: This is true. Regret often signals that love was withheld, and what a spirited being often wants to do is to make up for that moment. They have an opportunity to experience a deeper understanding of themselves and the limitation they had imposed upon themselves. If you say something in the physical realm that you later regret—and if you don't *linger* in the regret—you'll take action to make amends. It's a signal in physical life, just as it is here. The difference is that we don't linger with it, judge it, or justify it. We simply take loving action.

Irene: Did you have many regrets?

Paula: I had many regrets as Physical Paula. I regretted not saying things to my family that I thought I should have said. I regretted withholding love that I thought I could have expressed. I regretted projecting my own shortcomings onto others, judging that I could have and should have done it differently. I regretted those times I reacted in pain instead of from love, thinking I could have and should have done better. The regret was healed when I began experiencing the love, compassion, understanding, and light of the Spirit realm after I transitioned. My love for myself deepened as I began to understand the limitations I'd created for myself during my lifetime as Paula. I was able to see that, given my perceived limitations, there was no other way I could have behaved. I couldn't have done it differently, given the limitations inherent in who I thought I was.

Irene: Yes, absolutely. It's an illusion to think we could have done anything differently. When someone says, "If I were you, I'd have done x, y, and z," I often reply, "No, if you were me, you'd have done it exactly as I did, because you'd have my history, my beliefs, my thoughts, my feelings, my weaknesses, my strengths, and my spiritual agenda."

Paula: Exactly. From a spiritual perspective, I recognize the limitations that prevented me from making other choices. I can relive any given moment and see that, while there clearly were other choices—there are always other choices—given who I was in the moment, I had made the choice that best suited me.

As Physical Paula, all I could do was judge the choice I'd made and regret it, telling myself that I could have and should have done it differently. From this spiritual perspective, however, I see that doing it exactly the way I'd done it had been a necessary step in my learning process. When an infant is first learning to eat solid food, more of it ends up on their face than in their mouth. You wouldn't think of saying, "You should eat properly," because you understand that they're not yet capable of getting the food into their mouth; they haven't developed that skill. It's only by missing their mouth that they learn to feed themselves.

Irene: I understand. It's only by falling that we learn to walk. If we don't judge falling as "bad" or "wrong," there's nothing to regret; it's all part of our learning process.

Paula: That's one of the blessings here: by reliving a moment of my life and deepening my understanding of that moment, I'm able to deepen the love I have for myself.

Irene: I'm inspired. I choose to be openhearted with myself, with others, and with life—and reap the benefits *now.*

PAULA

CONVERSATION SEVEN

Irene: A religious person recently shared a concern with me. He said it's written in the Bible that we should not contact those who've transitioned because it's a distraction from the work you're doing. Do you agree?

Paula: It's impossible *not* to communicate with those we love, for it's the love that draws us together.

Irene: Why would it be written in the Bible?

Paula: These were creeds written to protect followers from being misled by charlatans, that is, people who were taking advantage of those who were grieving.

Irene: But that doesn't answer the question of why it was considered a disturbance to the work spirited beings were perceived to be doing.

Paula: (Laughing) It was based on the misconception that we in Spirit are more powerful or more important than you in physical form. And just as a child hesitates to knock on the office door of an adult for fear of interrupting and being reprimanded, the spiritual leaders were also afraid of interrupting or disturbing beings whom they perceived as more powerful. These fear-filled creeds were created during a time of misunderstanding about the Spirit world. The instructions you referred to reflected the times in which they were written. The broader, more comprehensive message is that we are all equals.

Irene: I appreciate your insight. I heard you say that the instructions reflected the times in which they were written. Can you offer an analogy?

Paula: If you wanted to mail a letter today, and you tried to follow instructions written in the 1800s, you'd be waiting for the Pony Express.

Irene: What a great analogy. Thanks, Aunt Paula.

PAULA

CONVERSATION EIGHT

Paula: I want to reassure anyone who fears death that it's only the body that dies. I feel more alive now than I ever felt in physical form. There are, however, perspectives that can only be experienced in physical form, and I sometimes miss them.

Irene: Like what?

Paula: Touch isn't the same here. It's the sense I miss most, and I realize now that I took it for granted. I experience other things with greater depth. Having access to the bigger picture, for example, provides me with a deeper understanding of physical life.

By contrast, there's a lot to appreciate about the physical realm, and it's with good reason that we return over and over. I'm sharing this with you so you'll appreciate where you are now and not long to leave your body. There's no experience like being immersed in the physical world. (Pause) When there's something happening with my physical family—a party, a celebration, or any emotional event—I can choose to focus on them, or I can just as easily withdraw my focus and participate with those in the Spirit realm.

Irene: How do you participate with your physical family?

Paula: I show up with love regardless of the situation. If it's a happy occasion—a celebration of some sort—I just enjoy being in their joy, adding my love to the mix. If the occasion is filled with turmoil or grief, I assist by adding my loving energy to the situation. I serve as a beacon of light so that my family will see through

313

any confusion. I have never stopped being their mother or doing what mothers do. My capacity to hold love is greater now than when I was in physical form, because I'm no longer affected by their points of view. I can be more objective.

Irene: When you say you *hold* love, can you be specific in terms of how you're being and what you're doing?

Paula: I'm seeing who they are beyond physical form.

Irene: I would call that *seeing the loving essence,* or *seeing the divine being that resides within.*

Paula: Yes, it's maintaining a spiritual reality while interacting with physical form. When you're in the physical play, the script often seems more real than the actuality of Spirit.

Irene: If I set an intention to have the clarity and wisdom about life that's available in the Spirit realm while still in physical form . . .

Paula: Then the part of you that remembers would remind the part of you that forgets. That's a prayer that would serve well.

PAULA

CONVERSATION NINE

Irene: Aunt Paula, I'd like to ask you the same question I asked some of the others. Are people who commit suicide punished in any way?

Paula: No, there's no punishment—for anyone. Would you punish someone for going to a hospital because they're in physical pain? Of course not. Going to the hospital is a strategy for seeking help, and so is committing suicide. People often judge those who commit suicide as cowards. Suicide is an act of desperation, but it is also an act of courage, because the person is putting an end to everything they know and facing the unknown. When fear becomes the dominating force in someone's life, it leads to feelings of powerlessness and desperation. Suicide is an attempt to relinquish those feelings. Fear is a destructive force that erodes your connection to the power of your soul and feeds the illusion that you're separate, that you're a victim, and that life is happening *to* you instead of *through* you. There's nothing to fear. I'd like to whisper *that* in every person's ear. But I know it's not something that can be given. It has to come from within.

Irene: Beautifully spoken. As we bring our conversations to a close, I want to thank you, not just from the bottom of my heart, but from the top, sides, and middle. I'm grateful for your love, your support, and for your contribution to this work.

Paula: The most profound change I've experienced while being in Spirit is my ability to receive love. This shift allows me to hear your words and to receive the sentiment with which they're spoken. As I do, your love not only nourishes me, it becomes a part of me, just as rain nourishes and then becomes part of the plant on which it falls.

Irene: Any final words?

Paula: (Laughing) I'm laughing at the thought that I had to die in order for my words to be important enough that someone would want to write them down.

Each physical lifetime provides an opportunity to expand our capacity to love. I'm eager to experience another physical adventure with all the joys, challenges, and surprises it will provide. I wonder what personality I'll choose and how I'll grow in my capacity to love.

The Power that creates my next physical body and all of my experiences through that physical body is unchanging. It is always with me, and it *is* me, regardless of the form I take. No form could contain such a Power. And so it is with you. You're never without this Power because this Power *is* you. When you're ready for your physical body to fall away and ready to create through a different form, you'll change. But the Power remains, constantly creating form and experience. You change with every physical breath you take. The Power responsible for that change is who you are.

I love each and every one of you. You are all so courageous. Now go and enjoy physical life.

EPILOGUE

Since completing this book, my days are filled with more acceptance, gratitude, and joy than I ever dreamed possible.

I remember the moment I committed to a life of joy. It was when Jerry said that he flows from one joyous experience to the next, guided by wisdom. I was inspired to do in the physical world what Jerry is doing in the spirited world.

I discovered that joy isn't *achieved*; it is *accessed*. Turning joy into a goal made it unattainable. The moment I strived for it, I'd already missed it. We don't achieve joy by adding something. We access joy by subtracting.

Joy is effortlessly ever-present when we remove what we've unwittingly placed in the way of it: (1) misidentification as a separate self (2) attachment to desired outcomes, and (3) judgments that we innocently impose on ourselves, on others, and on life. In the absence of these, access to effortless, ever-present joy is readily available. The inner work is essential, however, and involves releasing the misunderstandings we've naively added to our already joyous Authentic Self.

We've all heard the words *life* and *death* paired so often, we assume they are opposites. But the opposite of death isn't life. The opposite of death is birth. The human experience is finite. It begins at birth and ends with death. Life, however, has no opposite. Life is eternal—and so are we. We are Divine, Eternal Beings enjoying a temporary human experience. This in itself is an extraordinary blessing, yet perhaps an even greater blessing is the freedom to choose our response to life, regardless of circumstance. And, I choose acceptance and gratitude, which naturally lead to joy.

What empowers my choice is commitment. What facilitates my choice is the knowledge that this is a loving and beneficent universe. Trusting life allows me to transform situations I would previously have deemed "predicaments" into opportunities for growth. It allows me to see the glass not just half-full, but refill-able from an inexhaustible well.

Death has become my greatest teacher and most trusted advisor. She reminds me that physical life is finite, and compels me to forgive, release regret, and find peace with the past. Death urges me to question my conditioned thinking and limiting self-concepts. She inspires me to find acceptance for what is, and gratitude for the simplest of pleasures. Death facilitates me in speaking my truth, living in alignment with my values, and prioritizing what truly matters. She empowers me to open my heart, love fully, and live courageously in service to my heartfelt dreams. Death, my closest and most intimate traveling compan-ion, exponentially expands my appreciation for Life, just as it is, here and now.

Jerry says that we plan our life circumstances prior to birth for purposes of spiritual growth. Understanding that the people in my life—regardless of the role they play—are here by mutual agreement and in service to my highest good, helps me take 100 percent responsibility for my experience. For years, I blamed my mother for what wasn't working in my life, which left me believ-ing I was powerless to change. I thought the damage had been done and there was nothing I could do about it.

What I've learned through these conversations is that we choose our parents as much for their *un*consciousness as for their consciousness. One reason we choose our parents is *because* of their wounds. Their wounds, which they hand down to us, are precisely the wounds we need to inherit. This is the material that, on a soul level, we've agreed to heal. Not only are we not victims of our upbringing, our upbringing is by design—*our* design.

When faced with a challenging situation, the questions I ask myself today are different from those I asked in the past. Instead of asking: *Why is God punishing me? What's wrong with me? What's the point?* I now ask: *Why would my soul have agreed to this experience? What did I desire to learn? In what way(s) is this experience serving me?*

In the past, I judged everything and everyone, including myself. Today, I know that I'm not equipped to judge someone if I don't know what they're here to learn or how they will best learn it. How can I judge whether a situation is fair and just without access to all the lifetimes of all the individuals involved? How can I even judge myself? I can't. Judgment cannot co-exist with acceptance, gratitude and joy. By choosing a life of joy, I must relinquish judgment, a source of unnecessary suffering.

I have learned the art of compassionate self-forgiveness. Anytime I judge someone as wrong, I know that what I'm seeing in that person lurks inside of me. I look within for the behavior or attitude that I am judging and I own it. If it's not apparent, I ask myself whether I could conceive of it being a part of my experience under a different set of circumstances. I forgive myself for having made that judgment in the first place, and compassionately embrace that aspect of myself. Compassionate self-forgiveness allows me to release judgment and embrace what is with acceptance. This is what allows me to live moment-by-moment in a state of joy. What's not to love about *that?* Every moment is a new one.

It seems appropriate to end with my favorite Jerry quote. "There is no wrong way to do life."

LIST OF SEQUENTIAL QUESTIONS FROM THE CONVERSATIONS

JERRY
Conversation One

– What did you experience when you released your last breath on earth?
– You kept *breathing*?
– What about contraction?
– What are you breathing *in*?
– Can you give me a minute?
– Jerry, do you remember the actual moment you left your physical body?
– What happened next?
– Were you in a body?
– *Then* what happened?
– Can you describe it further? ("We came together as one . . .")
– What was *that* like? ("The illusion of separation disappeared.")
– What did that feel like? ("We propelled upward and out into a great light with which we became one.")
– There was no individuated you?
– Can you describe the ecstasy of rejoining the whole?
– What happened then?
– How? (i.e., How did you pull yourself back into the same loosely contained light form you'd initially experienced?)
– You mentioned you're in a spirited body now. How would you describe it?
– Given that form follows thought, were you thinking about being a loosely contained energetic light form after leaving your physical body?
– What happened after you pulled yourself back into a form?
– What do spirited beings look like?
– Do spirited beings appearing overweight *feel* overweight?
– What do you mean by *self-created scenes*?
– Is this a *mini* ocean?
– So, back to the people on the beach who had manifested the ocean through thought: if you were to jump in, would you be jumping into their *thought* of the ocean?
– Might you see someone creating a scene that conflicts with someone else's creation?

320

– Why would someone create an ocean scene by the learning center?
– If someone who transitions is unaware of being connected and therefore unaware of their impact on others, do they suddenly get this awareness as a result of transitioning?
– What if their creations are a disturbance to others?
– What happens to their inharmonious creations in the interim?

JERRY
Conversation Two

– What happened after the tour?
– Life Review?
– How did your life review unfold?
– What surprised you most about your life?
– Did you have regrets as you reviewed your life?
– Can you provide a specific example? ("This helped me understand why I had responded the way I had in any given situation.")
– How would you live differently if you were in physical form on earth today?

JERRY
Conversation Three

– When individuals transition, who greets them?
– What did you expect?
– What could we say in written form that would create more trust during transitioning?
– Is the life force the same as the soul?
– Why the "quotes" around *Heaven*?
– What's the difference between how you create heaven in spirited form and how we create heaven in physical form?

JERRY
Conversation Four

– What's it like to *breathe* in a spirited body?
– Can you elaborate? ("As the breath comes in, I feel individualized, and as the breath goes out, my focus expands and becomes unified.")
– We have a spirited body even while still in physical form?
– Why can't I see it? (i.e., the spirited body)
– How does it feel to *breathe* in a spirited body?
– Do you breathe through your nose?
– What recommendations might you have regarding our awareness of breath?
– You mentioned being involved with projects. What kinds of projects?
– Is there an awareness of time where you are?

– I heard you say previously that your fears transitioned with you. Is that accurate?
– Do you have obligations?
– Is there any message you'd like me to give your wife?

JERRY
Conversation Five

– How soon after you transitioned were you able to do this? ("I choose an appearance that matches my objective.")
– What if I manifested something that was simply a fleeting thought and potentially hurtful to someone?
– What if I think a fleeting thought that's hurtful to *me*?
– So if hell only exists if we choose to create it, what happens to suicide bombers who believe they'll be rewarded with seventy-two virgins when they transition?
– I guess my real question is, if the suicide bomber believes his actions are for the good of all, but they're really not, what then?
– Why the "quotes" around *suicide bombers*?
– If we've all agreed to play our parts and fulfill our agreements, and if, therefore, there are no victims, then why, during the life review, do we experience someone else's hurt if it's theirs to own?
– What would you say if I asked, "What if I'm mugged at gunpoint? Have I chosen *that*?"
– Okay, what about an event like 9/11?
– What would be an example of an action that's in alignment with the highest good?

JERRY
Conversation Six

– What suggestions might you have for someone who has an intention to transition with grace and ease?
– What suggestions might you have for someone who's just transitioned?
– Are there consequences for not exercising your spirited body, like, *use it or lose it*?
– But, does your body still require self-care if it's no longer dense?
– What do you learn from changing form?

JERRY
Conversation Seven

– What's the process for returning to physical form?
– Why is draping our shining Selves necessary for our growth and our service?

– Why do we need to strengthen our ability to express the light within?

– When you say that all sentient life forms except humans know who they are, what is it they remember? When a giraffe knows who it is, for example, what does it know?

– Given the importance of remembering who we are while having a human experience, have you decided to refocus into physical form at some point and put what you know into practice?

– And what would you whisper? ("I may choose to be someone's guide or teacher —a consultant, so to say, whispering in the ears of those I love the truth of who they are and the power they command.")

JERRY
Conversation Eight

– I know how challenging it must be to elaborate on a transcendent experience, but would you?

– How did you know? ("It was no longer the world and I. I *was* the world, and I knew it was all good.")

– Can you choose to be in the presence of Jesus now and, if so, how does he appear?

– How do you recognize him (Jesus) if his form is always changing?

– Can anyone choose to be with Jesus?

– Isn't the Spirit world genderless?

– What's it like to be in their presence? (i.e., in the presence of masters)

– How are Jesus, Buddha, Mohammed, and other spiritual masters similar, and how are they different?

– Aren't they also unique in terms of where they chose to appear on earth?

– Haven't some of the words and concepts in sacred books been mistranslated and misinterpreted?

– Jerry, given that you're in touch with your power and we're here, having forgotten some of the things you're talking about regarding our true nature, how might we support each other so that it's mutually beneficial to ourselves, to you, and to the whole?

– Would you elaborate? ("In reality, in truth, it's all here always.")

– Jerry, why go through all of this expressing and experiencing?

JERRY
Conversation Nine

– What are the options in choosing our next physical existence?

– How is your imprint picked up?

– If it's within an even greater mind, is it the *One* Mind?

JERRY
Conversation Ten

– Where does the individuated mind exist?
– If the individuated mind exists both in the physical body and in every particle of light that I am, what happens to the part that belongs to my physical body when it dies?
– Would you elaborate on the One Mind?
– Should *sentient database being* be capitalized?
– If the individuated mind knows how to balance the physical body for optimum health, why aren't we all healthy?

JERRY
Conversation Eleven

– What are the possibilities beyond the earth experience?
– Can you describe what you've experienced? ("I haven't chosen to live in any other paradigm, but I've visited.")
– Does this planetary system have a name?
– What do these beings look like?
– Do they look like us?
– What does their world look like?
– Would it be accurate to say that I previewed my current life during the Preview of My Potential Life you mentioned earlier, and chose it out of all the possibilities?
– If what we're seeing is the optimum outcome available, why aren't we always making optimum choices?

JERRY
Conversation Twelve

– When I look around, I see my desk, a flower, a bottle of water, my hands, my body . . . what do *you* see when you look around?
– You need my permission to see my past lives?
– Do you have five senses as you did when you were in a physical body?
– Would you elaborate? (" . . . it's this 'so much more' that we in Spirit can more easily access.")
– How do you hold someone's hand if there's no physical barrier?
– Does one hand disappear into the other, or do they merge as one hand that's a combination of the two?
– What's your sense of smell like?
– *A* rose or that *specific* rose?
– What about hearing?
– Does this ever become overwhelming?

– Would you elaborate on how you communicate with one another?
– So you communicate with Jana through thoughts, feelings and images?
– Jerry, when I merge with you, how come I don't have access to all of *your* experiences?
– Continuing with our conversation about the senses, do you eat? If so, what's that like?
– If you wanted to pick up something in material form, would you be able to lift it?
– What would that look like to me, the observer?
– Back to eating: knowing what you know now, if you were in physical form today, how would you choose to eat?

JERRY
Conversation Thirteen

– If you were designing a memorial for a loved one, how would it look?
– What special consideration would you give the body?
– What about cremation?
– Are some ways to transition better than others?
– I can hear readers now: "Do you mean to tell me that instead of getting Jesus, I'm getting Jerry?"
– So, if I'm expecting to see my mother, is it actually her?
– Would I still see her if she's already reincarnated and living another life?
– Can you elaborate? ("There's a part of each one of us—our individualized source—that remains in Spirit.")
– Are we all existing in multiple dimensions simultaneously?
– Can we visit these stage sets while we're in physical form?
– Have your beliefs about God changed since you transitioned?

JERRY
Conversation Fourteen

– How have you expanded since our last conversation?
– Are you fully present with the masters as well as with others?
– Really? How? ("Even here, I find ways to distract myself.")
– Would you be willing to share how you're still wounded?
– May I offer a suggestion for your consideration?
– Given that outer experience is a reflection of inner reality, are there ways in which you might be unconscious to what's available?
– Jerry, is it in any way distracting or disturbing when Jana and I contact you?
– Would you clarify? (i.e., What determines whether an experience is optimal?)
– What would I do differently if I was in your presence and I preferred not to reveal anything about myself?

JERRY
Conversation Fifteen

– Don't you have morning where you are?
– Would you elaborate? ("Light arises from the inherent illumination of all things.")
– Darkness doesn't exist where you are?
– So how can it all be *here*?
– What if I didn't choose to have her in my *here*? She'd be *there*, wouldn't she?

JERRY
Conversation Sixteen

– Do you have the ability to assist in orchestrating such unions?
– If the husband, wife, or partner who transitions was controlling or possessive, can they get in the way of their loved one moving on with another partner?
– Jerry, do you have responsibilities?
– What's the next step in your evolution?

JERRY
Conversation Seventeen

– Jerry, on a different note, we don't suddenly evolve as a result of transitioning, do we? In other words, I won't suddenly become wiser when I transition, will I?
– What prevents us from accessing our innate wisdom?
– Jerry, what makes the bigger difference: being in a loving state or doing good deeds motivated by obligation?
– Are you ever on shaky ground in the Spirit world? Are others ever grumpy or not enjoying what they're doing?
– Are you saying that everyone in the Spirit realm is happy and loving?
– But what if two beings come together who share similar wounds?
– Could you be alone with someone if that's what you desired?

JERRY
Conversation Eighteen

– She's not in some sort of perpetual card game, is she? (i.e., Beba, my mother)
– Have you ever noticed that making someone or something *wrong* disrupts inner peace?
– Jerry, do people have themes to their lives?
– So, no matter what circumstances we create, the learning is always about love?
– Can you offer an example? ("Some people create anti-love situations in order to strengthen their love muscles.")
– What about living in areas where genocide is occurring?

Jerry
Conversation Nineteen
- What have you been up to?
- Do you participate in other helping professions?
- Do you ever assist spirited beings in going somewhere other than earth?
- Why do we choose to incarnate on the earth instead of going elsewhere?
- Free will isn't unique to the earth is it? Don't we always have choice, regardless of whether we're on the earth or elsewhere?
- Why would someone choose to have free will withheld?
- What about my consciousness? Will my consciousness continue to evolve and expand?

Jerry
Conversation Twenty
- Does the earth have an intention for her evolution?
- What distinguishes each agenda?
- How can the earth accomplish her evolutionary agenda to express God's essence when so many of her human inhabitants are at war? Why doesn't she shake off what's not in harmony with her, like a dog shakes off fleas?
- How so? ("The violence of war is part of their cleansing process.")
- You said the earth assists us in evolving our own agendas. How?

Jerry
Conversation Twenty-One
- Doesn't one naturally make choices that expand the soul?
- Given that we all have free choice, what if someone chooses not to expand—even by contracting?
- So even choosing *not* to choose leads to expansion?

Jerry
Conversation Twenty-Two
- Can you describe the relationship between the physical body and the spirited body?
- Does the spirited body have an aura that connects it to something else?
- I assume my spiritual body also has an aura that connects *it* to something else?
- What form do these bodies have?
- What does it take to merge with the spiritual body?
- Is the spiritual body also malleable and able to shape-shift?
- Would you like to say something in closing?

JARED
Conversation One

- Jared, what did you experience when you released your last breath on earth?
- Was it painful? ("I was shot out of my body like a bullet out of a gun.")
- Were you aware of having a form or a body?
- How was it stronger? ("It was a body similar to the one I'd left, but pain-free and stronger.")
- Had you lost the ability to hold yourself up straight and stand tall in your physical body?
- What happened next?
- Do you know why her guilt felt like a cramp?
- But, your sister would have had to love you in order to feel guilty about not having done enough for you, wouldn't she? Wasn't her guilt, like your mother's sadness, also the result of her love?
- Who was embracing you?
- Can you elaborate? ("It wasn't a being in a body; that's why I refer to it as a presence.")

JARED AND JERRY
Conversation Two

- Can either of you elaborate on why you were focusing through different forms?
- Jared, did you experience merging with the Light?

JARED
Conversation Three

- You mentioned that you drifted into what you'd call sleep, yet it wasn't. How was it different?
- Am I hearing you say that after years of experiencing pain in your physical body, your *non*-physical body was affected?
- Why would anyone choose to experience illness or disease as part of their spiritual agenda?
- In what other ways do illness and disease serve us?
- So healing takes place in the spiritual body after leaving the physical body?
- When you refer to the energy being released from your physical body, are *you* that energy?
- What were you aware of when this sleep-like state was complete?
- What about being greeted by a loved one? Does everyone experience that?
- You have to be open to the idea of being greeted in order to experience it?
- Do all who transition attend their memorial service?
- Why wouldn't someone attend their own memorial?
- How does the meeting take place for those already in physical form?

– Would it be accurate to say that some people who transition don't have another physical life?
– Could I choose to be a rock or a cloud?

JARED
Conversation Four

– What happened after your memorial service?
– What was your life review like?
– What do you mean, *in a flash*?
– What happens as you have a specific thought?
– If you have the desire to connect with a physical loved one, do you need their permission?
– Do you ever regret having a specific thought?
– Can you elaborate? ("Regret requires a sustained consequence . . . ")
– Jared, what do you enjoy most about the Spirit world?
– Do you ever merge with a spirited being and *not* enjoy it?
– What if you merge with someone who's just transitioned and holds negative, fearful thoughts?

JARED AND JERRY
Conversation Five

– What happened after your life review?
– And what's available? ("I became reacquainted with all that's available.")
– Are you happy, Jared?
– Did you ever experience that kind of acceptance as Physical Jared?
– Is the acceptance you're currently feeling similar to the acceptance you felt as a child, before you began comparing yourself to others?
– Do you have an understanding of why you chose to suffer pain as Physical Jared?
– You lived thirty years as Physical Jared. Did you choose your length of stay?
– How, specifically, do you work with people who are in pain?
– What are dreams?
– Is it true that the soul needs the body to sleep so that it can experience freedom, its true nature?

JARED
Conversation Six

– As Physical Jared, you enjoyed studying with Native American elders. Is that still true for you in Spirit?
– Can you be with them as much as you want?
– Is there anything you miss about being in a physical body?
– What would you suggest to someone who wants to strengthen their connection to a transitioned loved one?
– How do you communicate with them? (i.e., with physical loved ones)

JARED
Conversation Seven

– Do you create the mountain path through memory?
– Can you elaborate? ("Desire is like a magnet . . . ")
– If what's in the physical realm has its origin in the nonphysical realm, why don't you also have litter?
– If the earth is there, litter-free and in all her splendor, why would you choose to come here?

JARED
Conversation Eight

– Jared, knowing what you know, if you were to return to the earth in physical form, what would you do differently?
– Still, given all that, if you could, how would you choose to be, or what would you choose to do differently?
– And, who *are* you? How do you define yourself?
– And what are you learning?
– What are you currently discovering or remembering?
– Do you have a name for where you are, and do others call it by the same name?
– How do you label where you are?
– Do you know where animals go when they transition?

JARED
Conversation Nine

– What specifically have you been working on?
– What else have you discovered?
– Have you ever noticed that making something *wrong* causes internal disturbance?
– Remember when you were a baby and you could do no wrong, or when you were *with* a baby who could do no wrong?
– How would your love for her change? ("When my mother arrives and drops the role of being my mother here in Spirit . . . ")
– Jared, knowing what you know now, how would you love differently if you were here on earth, given the physical constraints of a physical body?
– May I offer something for your consideration?
– Want to give it a whirl from the perspective of Physical Jared?
– Anything else?

JARED
Conversation Ten

– How did suppressing your feelings affect your physical body?
– What advice, if any, would you give someone preparing to transition?

– Is there anything you'd like to say in closing?

BEBA
Conversation One

– Beba, what did you experience when you released your last breath on earth?
– And where were you?
– You said you awoke at your funeral with your transitioned mother telling you what had happened, and as she did, you remembered a scene with family that had taken place the day before?
– You went from being at your funeral to going back in time to an experience that happened *prior* to your funeral?
– Then what happened?
– Where *did* you think next?
– Where did your thoughts take you next?
– Did your thoughts take you to him or bring him to you?
– What happens if you think of *me* right now?
– Am I hearing you say that if you wanted to connect with me as I am in this moment, you'd have an intention to connect and imagine yourself in my current location?
– In other words, you can only visit me when I invite you, *right?*

BEBA
Conversation Two

– You mentioned earlier that you thought of your dad, and there he was. What specifically did you think?
– How does healing in spirited form differ from healing in physical form?
– What did you believe at that point?
– What are some of the similarities between the different personalities through which you've chosen to express?
– Will you choose another constant when this one is complete?
– Beba, given what you know now, how would you choose to live differently if you were in physical form on earth today?

BEBA
Conversation Three

– Where did your thoughts take you when you were no longer thinking about the funeral?
– Who took you?
– What did your new surroundings look like?
– I've been working with an incident that happened when I was eleven. Would you like to hear about it?

BEBA
Conversation Four
– Beba: "Did you do it?" (i.e., Did you take Ireenie to ride the Ferris wheel?)

BEBA AND JERRY
Conversation Five
– You were aware of being in the womb?
– The soul is focused on its developing physical body from *outside* the womb?
– Why doesn't the soul reside within the womb?
– How does the baby's soul participate?

BEBA AND JERRY
Conversation Six
– Can you elaborate on the soul family?
– Is it any wonder there's so much frustration on the part of students, teachers, parents, and administrators?

BEBA AND JERRY
Conversation Seven
– We want so much to be loved, that we adopt the traits of our caregivers as if to say, "See? I'm like you *Now* will you love me?"
– Given that parents love the best they can, and they can only love their children to the degree they love themselves, did I *perceive* that love wasn't present in my relationship with my mom, or was it simply not present?

BEBA
Conversation Eight
– How did you access your life as Physical Beba for the life review?
– Was it challenging?
– What do you mean by, *if they chose to benefit?*
– Were you surprised by the circumstances surrounding your own transition?
– What kinds of hints and message did you receive?

BEBA
Conversation Nine
– What happened after your formal life review?
– If you were to create that living space for yourself now, how would you go about it?
– What does your personal space look like?
– What about the *where* in a larger context—like a neighborhood?

– Where does your energy come from?
– And where's *that*?
– What's the difference between how you and I access energy?

BEBA
Conversation Ten

– What activities do you enjoy?
– Can you help your loved ones on earth?
– What do you whisper?
– How do you see me in my dreams?
– What's your understanding of God?

BEBA
Conversation Eleven

– Any words of advice?
– Was there something specific you read or something someone told you about the afterlife that was untrue?
– Beba, if you were on earth, how would you live differently given what you know?
– What do you love most about the Spirit world?
– What was most surprising to you about shifting your focus from physical life to spirited life?
– What is your priority?

BEBA
Conversation Twelve

– What have you been up to?
– Beba, what do you look like?
– Are there animals where you are?

BILL
Conversation One

– Bill, what did you experience when you released your last breath on earth?
– You could feel the warmth?
– Were you focusing through a form?

Bill and Jerry
Conversation Two

– Was there a penalty for taking your life?
– Why the "quotes" around *natural?*
– Why is there so much condemnation and shame associated with suicide, particularly in religion?
– Jared said he'd planned a short physical life. How can we become more aware of what we've chosen for ourselves?

Bill
Conversation Three
– Bill, what were your thoughts prior to committing suicide?

Bill and Jerry
Conversation Four
– How will Steve's anger affect Shannon's joy and Shannon's joy affect Steve's anger?
– Is it a matter of who's feeling the emotion with greater intensity?
– Will Shannon feel more anger and less joy, or will Steve feel more joy and less anger?

Bill
Conversation Five
– Bill, can you tell me more about this fluid, golden-white light and how it responded to feelings?
– Do you know why?
– So, if I'm feeling said and I think, *it's silly to feel this way,* or *sadness is a sign of weakness,* or *I should be feeling happy*—the flow of energy in my body is slowed?
– Do you know what your agenda was as Physical Bill?
– Did your life in ancient Rome immediately precede your life as Bill?
– How so? ("I created circumstances that challenged my self expression.")

Bill
Conversation Six
– What happened after your experience with the stranger who found your body?
– I was coaching a woman recently who asked, "If that's the case, why bother doing good deeds?"
– Bill, what's the most important thing we can know about ourselves?

334

BILL
Conversation Seven

– What would you say to someone who is in great emotional pain and perhaps contemplating suicide?
– Isn't reincarnation a choice rather than a requirement?
– Why were you so afraid of change?
– If there were one thing you could say to people, what would it be?

BILL
Conversation Eight

– What are some of the false beliefs to which you're referring?
– What are some of the misinterpretations people make about children and power?
– How would you characterize a healthy parent?

BILL
Conversation Nine

– How did your suicide affect your children?
– Have you been challenged by your children's process?
– What about your wife?
– What prompts people to choose one particular method of suicide over another?

BILL AND JERRY
Conversation Ten

– Were you confused when you transitioned?
– What about people who transition who don't have physical loved ones thinking of them or praying for them?
– What would you say to someone who has had a loved one commit suicide and thinks that, if only they had said this or done that, they could have prevented it?
– My friend Archie discovered the body of his friend Judy after she committed suicide. Where's the win in *that*?
– Can you be more specific as to how Archie was of assistance to Judy?

BILL
Conversation Eleven

– What happened then?
– Didn't you mention previously that no one dies too soon or too late?

BILL
Conversation Twelve

– What happened when you met the counselor?
– What was your original intention?
– What was the origin of your self-doubt?

BILL
Conversation Thirteen

– What happened after your life review?
– Did you attend your memorial?

VINCE
Conversation One

– Vince, what did you experience when you released your last breath on earth?
– How would you describe it? ("My spirit or my soul or my life force—I don't know what to call it—was lying right above me.")
– Did you have any thoughts or feelings about it? Was it comforting? Unnerving?
– What was most surprising to you about the process of transitioning?
– Who was it? ("I felt someone's presence.")
– If you could tell people on earth one thing, what would it be?

VINCE
Conversation Two

– What happened after you became aware of your grandmother's presence?
– What happened next?
– What form were you focusing through?
– Why had it been enough to catapult *him* from physical experience and not you?
– Don't we all want to achieve the level of consciousness of a Buddha or a Christ?
– How about Mrs. Peacock?

VINCE
Conversation Three

– What happened next on your tour with Jonifer?
– When you say you had a deep connection with your mother and father through this cell, was this cell *you*?
– Where did this life force exist if it wasn't in the fetal body?
– Is the life force the same as the soul?

– Can you elaborate? ("The soul is the source of the life force.")
– Why might you have changed your mind? ("And it wasn't until I was moments away from birth that I committed to this lifetime.")
– How could you have accomplished helping your parents if you'd chosen to abort your mission?
– Who told you?
– Did you primarily feel empathy and compassion for yourself and others?
– You mentioned that some people had kept you on track. How?
– How so? ("Even something seemingly insignificant—like passing someone on the street—held meaning in my life.")

VINCE
Conversation Four
– When you completed your life review, had you been able to find the loving wisdom in every interaction?
– Is there a point of completion with the puzzles?
– What inherent patterns have you discovered?
– If you could be in physical form right now, how would you choose to live differently?
– How did fear affect your life as Physical Vince?
– What happened when you completed your life review?
– Aren't you always free to do whatever you choose?

VINCE
Conversation Five
– Vince, do you have routines like we have in the physical realm?
– Is there anything else you'd like to add?

ZAYDEH
Conversation One
– Zaydeh, what did you experience when you released your last breath on earth?
– Can you elaborate? ("I looked around the room and noticed how colorful the members of my physical family were.")
– What did you feel as your body released you?
– What kind of form did you find yourself in?
– How did you develop this skill? ("I've had to relearn how to connect with the physical world through a non-physical body.")
– What would you suggest? ("These abilities can be developed while still in physical form.")
– Can you tell me more about thee energetic imprints?

ZAYDEH
Conversation Two

– What was most surprising about your transition?
– Was there anything about the process that was upsetting?
– Were you in physical pain prior to transitioning?

ZAYDEH
Conversation Three

– Zaydeh, what do you look like now?
– Why choose that particular form?
– So you look like you did in your twenties, but your body is less dense?
– What if you meet two people in the Spirit realm that you knew from different times in your physical life?
– Do you experience emotions?
– How is the experience of emotions in non-physical reality similar to or different from the experience in physical reality?
– Under what circumstances might you experience frustration?

ZAYDEH
Conversation Four

– What part did religion play in your physical life?
– With this new perspective, what part would religion play in your spiritual practice if you were on earth today?
– Do you have any suggestions for people who are currently practicing one religion or another?
– Isn't acceptance a way of expressing God?

ZAYDEH
Conversation Five

– Hall of Records?
– What if you just wanted to experience a specific event during a lifetime?
– If love permeates the spiritual realm, and if the physical realm is Spirit made manifest, doesn't love permeate the physical realm as well?
– But, is that true? Could you have done things any differently?
– You can feel the regret and choose to love more now, but the past can't be changed—and wasn't it perfect exactly as it was?
– Why did your life review include more than your physical life as Zaydeh?

ZAYDEH
Conversation Six

– Do you have eyes, and do you see in the way you did on earth?
– What about listening?
– What about touch?
– What about the sense of smell?
– What do you mean by *unconscious limitations*?

ZAYDEH
Conversation Seven

– When you look around, what do you see?
– What if you wanted to see the ocean? Would you imagine it?
– What's your perception/understanding of God, and has this changed from the perception/understanding you held while in a physical body?

ZAYDEH
Conversation Eight

– Zaydeh: "Sometimes we need to be pushed into changing, and when we do, the force behind that push is . . . *what*?"

ZAYDEH
Conversation Nine

– Here on earth, most people have a routine and structure. Is it similar where you are?
– Zaydeh, how would you choose to live if you were here on earth today?

ZAYDEH AND JERRY
Conversation Ten

– When it comes to global warming, though, how are we "warming up" within ourselves?

ZAYDEH
Conversation Eleven

– Do you have any suggestions for someone who is about to transition?
– What suggestions might you have for someone who's afraid?
– How specifically will the body help?
– What about other fears?
– Zaydeh, what might you say to someone who's fearful of being judged when they transition?

– What would you say to someone who's spent a lifetime judging themselves and others and is now projecting that characteristic onto God and fearing God's judgment?

ZAYDEH
Conversation Twelve

– If a person is in physical pain, does the pain stop as soon as they transition into the Spirit realm?
– I've tried a variety of ways to heal the chronic back pain I have. Any suggestions?

ZAYDEH
Conversation Thirteen

– Do you know if there's a penalty for people who take their lives?
– What would assist us in waking up to this panoramic view?
– Zaydeh: "Why would you think it pauses in *your* life?" (i.e., this Intelligence)
– Zaydeh: "Isn't it a miracle that you have access to this Power?"
– Zaydeh: "And isn't it comforting to know that this Power is working on your behalf, under any and all circumstances?"

PAULA
Conversation One

– Aunt Paula, what did you experience when you released your last breath on earth?
– Were you consciously aware of the moment you were released from your physical body?
– Paula: "Have you ever had a lucid dream—aware that you're dreaming while you're dreaming—and you know that you have the freedom to do whatever you want?"
– Did you relinquish your physical body, or did your physical body relinquish *you*?
– Are you saying that you were unaware of being more than your physical body when you were in physical form?
– I heard you say that, as Physical Paula, you were unaware of being more than your physical body. Didn't it follow that the death of your body meant an end to *you*?

PAULA
Conversation Two

– Paula: If they could see me now as a little girl, would they even recognize me?

340

PAULA
Conversation Three

– What surprised you most about the reunion?
– Paula, many people believe they'll face judgment when they transition. Were you judged?
– What happened after your reunion?
– Where did your life review take place?
– What's an example of something you understood with greater depth?
– Paula: "And how do you think I responded to feeling unfulfilled?"
– Paula: "Being in Spirit is like being backstage and seeing everyone without their costumes. And guess what?"

PAULA
Conversation Four

– What's been the most challenging aspect of transitioning?
– What's been the most joyful aspect of transitioning?
– What are you enjoying most about being where you are?
– What's an example of something you've experienced as a result of looking out of any window you choose?
– Paula: "The goal is to allow compassion to flow through your life unimpeded. How do you do this in *your* life, Irene?"

PAULA
Conversation Five

– What are you focusing on in the Spirit world?
– How are your questions answered?
– Can you share an example? ("It's become clear to me that the experiences of one lifetime have affected every other lifetime, as well as everyone in those lifetimes.")

PAULA
Conversation Six

– Aunt Paula, do you ever look forward to events, or are you always fully present now?
– What advice would you offer someone who is preparing to transition?
– My understanding is that regret doesn't linger in the spiritual realm. Is that true in your experience?
– Did you have many regrets?

PAULA
Conversation Seven

– Do you agree? ("A religious person said it's written in the Bible that we should not contact those who've transitioned because it's a distraction from the work you're doing.")
– Why would it be written in the Bible?
– Can you offer an analogy? ("I heard you say that the instructions reflected the times in which they were written.")

PAULA
Conversation Eight

– Like what? ("There are, however, perspectives that can only be experienced in physical form, and I sometimes miss them.")
– How do you participate with your physical family?
– When you say you hold love, can you be specific in terms of how you're being and what you're doing?

PAULA
Conversation Nine

– Are people who commit suicide punished in any way?
– Paula: "Would you punish someone for going to a hospital because they're in physical pain?"
– Any final words?

ABOUT THE AUTHOR

Irene Kendig is an international award-winning author, speaker, and soul-centered coach.

She is one of thirty-seven writers and filmmakers featured in, *What Wags the World: Tales of Conscious Awakening*, a book that recounts the profound, often mystical experiences of its contributors—among them, Larry Dossey, M.D., Anita Moorjani, and Bernie Siegel, M.D.—that have led to extraordinary perceptions of an interconnected and multidimensional universe.

A gifted presenter, Irene has made a positive difference in a variety of settings over the course of four decades. As senior corporate trainer for an international management consulting firm, she has delivered customer satisfaction, team-building, and problem-solving trainings to employees at a wide array of companies, including AAA, Avis, American Express, Lufthansa, Marriott Hotels, Oracle, Trane, and Tumi. Irene was part of a three-person team responsible for training the entire east coast staff of Lufthansa Airlines, and was personally responsible for delivering training programs to over 1,000 Oracle employees with satisfaction ratings consistently over 95%. Irene has also facilitated and empowered middle managers in Corporate America with public speaking skills through in-house Train-the-Trainer programs.

As a certified instructor for Parent Effectiveness Training, (PET) she has led parenting programs in the U.S. and Latin America in both English and Spanish.

A lifelong learner, Irene earned a B.A. cum laude in Psychology from UCLA at the age of forty, and an M.A. in Spiritual Psychology from the University of Santa Monica at the age of fifty-six.

She holds certifications in Alchemical Hypnotherapy and Neuro-Linguistic Programming (NLP), and is a practitioner of Emotional Freedom Therapy (EFT).

Dedicated to living and sharing the gifts of Spiritual Psychology, Irene is part of a team of graduate volunteers from the University of Santa Monica's Masters Program who, for more than a decade, have been bringing the principles and experiential practices of Spiritual Psychology to women inmates at two of the largest maximum-security women's prisons in the world. *Freedom to Choose,* a moving 22-minute documentary that conveys the power of this work, can be seen at: http://freedom-tochoose.net/Film.htm.

Irene is currently connecting with readers in two powerful yet distinct ways. The first is through an online program—*Finding Heaven Within*—designed for readers who would like greater access to the Authentic Self. The second is through *Meet the Author* online presentations for book clubs around the country. For further information about either, kindly send an email to irene@irenekendig.com.

Irene lives in Virginia with her beloved husband Charlie and their dog Scooter. She is the proud mother of two adult sons, David and Josh.

SOUL-CENTERED COACHING

I am in the miracle business. I provide a safe space in which people can see themselves and their world differently. When this happens, people show up differently, allowing them to flourish in ways that looked impossible a moment before. *That* is a miracle. Call me to explore the difference soul-centered coaching could make in *your* life: 571-271-7989.

"Irene was astute, compassionate, pragmatic, efficient, and fearless in her work with me. She utilized her expertise to lead me into a truly empowering and inspiring experience. Without judgment or bias, she went with me, through and under the problematic patterns affecting the concerns I brought to her, and adeptly guided me into a freer perspective directly relevant to my deeper desires. Irene has a marvelous ability to be fully present and hear the smaller voices calling out to be heard, offering them the opportunity to find their place in a solution that does not require sacrifice of either practical or soulful needs. —**Cinda C., MS, MDiv, MFT, Oregon**

"It is rare to find a coach who can move smoothly and intelligently between the roles of guide, mentor, spiritual sister, professional, shaman, mystic and space holder, but Irene seems to do this. Irene is a teacher's teacher, a guide's guide." —**Beverly D., Tennessee**

"The doors of my self-imposed prison are at long last opening, and the illuminating light of truth is replacing the darkness of despair, loneliness and non-acceptance created by my lack of understanding. You, Irene, are an instrument of peace and healing. Thank you for saying 'yes' when you were called to be of service." —**Holly J., West Virginia**

GRATEFUL PRESS

Go beyond the book.

Continue your journey with additional offerings,
including a free process for releasing regret:
www.conversationswithjerry.com

If this book has made a positive difference in your life, your review on
Amazon, Barnes & Noble, iTunes, or Goodreads is greatly
appreciated. Thank you in advance for your time,
consideration, and generosity of spirit.

CPSIA information can be obtained
at www.ICGtesting.com
Printed in the USA
BVHW091544060222
628185BV00009B/240

9 780982 456705